WAYNESBURG COLLEGE LIBRARY
WAYNESBURG, PA.

THE RAPE OF AFRICA

From "Europe in Africa in the Nineteenth Century."

HENRY MORTON STANLEY

LAMAR MIDDLETON

THE
Rape of
Africa

NEGRO UNIVERSITIES PRESS
NEW YORK

Originally published in 1936
by Harrison Smith and Robert Haas

Reprinted 1969 by
Negro Universities Press
A DIVISION OF GREENWOOD PRESS, INC.
NEW YORK

SBN 8371-2720-3

PRINTED IN UNITED STATES OF AMERICA

Foreword

THE title of this volume may be misleading. The writer has given some part of the diplomatic background of the pillage of a continent by Europeans during the last sixty years. Of colonial invasions and military campaigns in Africa, there is parenthetical treatment only: these have been recounted many times in the past and, it may be added, at appalling length.

Apart from disclosing or recalling a few of the major swindles and the horse-trading among the chancelleries of Europe, this informal history is a study of one aspect of the gentle art of acquisitive diplomacy—or, more simply, of hypocrisy. I have sought also to suggest that those contentious economic and political factors which are the genesis of war are fully as threatening in Africa today as they were in Europe less than a generation ago.

By design, this account is not studded with documentation. Where it seems the reader's credulity may be strained, official sources are given. With few exceptions, those sources are either government white-papers, blue-books and legislative reports, or the memoires or other writings of the individuals concerned.

Here are some of the recorded moves and remarks of a small group of statesmen who stole a continent, in the pious conviction that the African races craved the delights of Civilization.

L. M.

Contents

I	SEVEN-PART FUGUE (1877)	13
II	AFRICAN MELON (1877–81)	32
III	CASH, CANNON AND RUM (1882–84)	51
IV	THE HORSETRADERS (1884)	80
V	CONGRESS DANCES (1884–85)	92
VI	THE BRITISH CHISEL (1885–90)	107
VII	—AND OTHER SCALPELS (1885–90)	128
VIII	OPÉRA BOUFFE AT BRUSSELS (1890)	144
IX	"WHY DO YOU PEOPLE KILL ME?" (1890–95)	160
X	AFRICAN CAPORETTO (1896)	179
XI	SUDAN IDYL (1896–98)	201
XII	"LET THE STORM BURST!" (1898–1902)	224
XIII	TURRET DIPLOMACY (1905–12)	243
XIV	"SPECIALIST ASSISTANCE" (1908–30)	267
XV	MARIANNE IN MOROCCO (1912–27)	283
XVI	FIELD-DAY FOR DIPLOMATS (1919)	291
XVII	ROMA REDIVIVA (1934–36)	300
	BIBLIOGRAPHICAL NOTE	309
	INDEX	311

Illustrations

HENRY MORTON STANLEY	*Frontispiece*
GRAPH SHOWING TERRITORIAL ENCROACHMENTS	12
STANLEY ATTACKED BY HOSTILE NATIVES	21
OUTLINE MAP OF AFRICA, 1876	26
CHARLES-LOUIS DE FREYCINET	*Facing* 54
ONE OF PIERRE DE BRAZZA'S FORTS	60
DE BRAZZA NEGOTIATING WITH MAKOKO	67
OUTLINE MAP OF AFRICA, 1885	88
BRITISH OFFICER'S SKETCH OF ELEPHANT	111
THE MAHDI	*Facing* 112
DEATH OF GORDON'S BODY SERVANT AT KHARTUM	114
FALLS OF THE NILE	121
FRENCH AGENTS DESCENDING THE NIGER	176
CECIL RHODES	*Facing* 204
BRITISH FIELD TELEGRAPH, NILE	212
"DR. LIVINGSTONE, I PRESUME?"	218
FLAG OF THE BRITISH SOUTH AFRICA COMPANY	226
DR. LEANDER STARR JAMESON	*Facing* 234
OUTLINE MAP OF AFRICA, 1912	265
OUTLINE MAP OF AFRICA, 1936	301

THE RAPE OF AFRICA

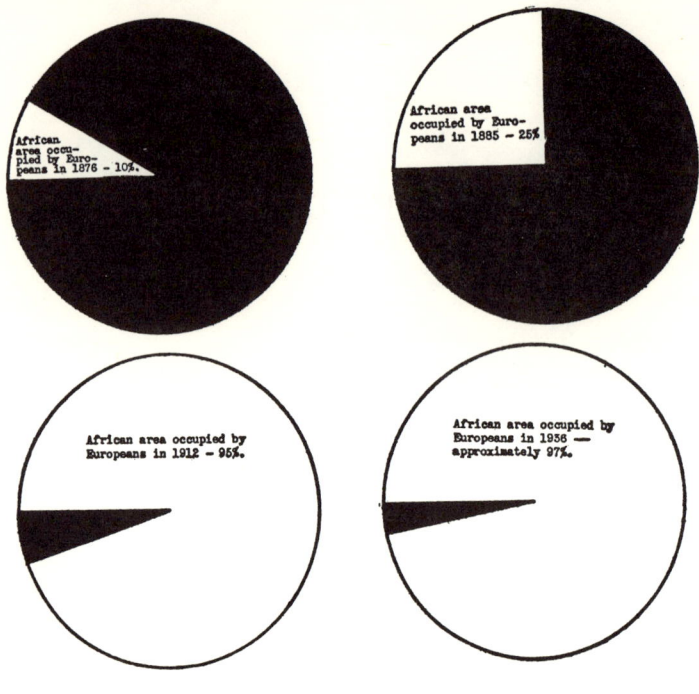

The four circles, representing Africa in 1876, 1885, 1912 and 1936, indicate in percentages the territorial encroachments by Europeans (unshaded area) in sixty years.

I

Seven-Part Fugue
[1877]

THE *grandes-dames* of the Faubourg-St. Germain who still held to the tradition of penning salon-memoires early in the Third Republic, long after de Sévigné and de Staël were dust, agreed that the summer of 1877 in Paris was atrociously hot, a fact they doubtless attributed to the hated republicanism. Those who had not fled the capital had strength to write of little else save the insufferable heat; even the newspapers were dull, reflecting the mood of their prostrated readers. The liveliest article in the *Figaro* of that August is an envious dissertation on new divorce laws in Sweden, permitting domestic cleavage on grounds of "bilious temperament."

But it was not heat alone which depressed the usually volatile spirits of the city. France herself was suffering from "bilious temperament,"—the after-effects of the disastrous war with Germany. Under the heavy taxation necessitated by Bismarck's demand for five billion francs' ransom, life for rich and poor alike had become insupportable. The Duc de Broglie, the distrusted premier and Bonapartist leader, was nervous, the Commune painfully fresh in his memory. With Gallic precaution the Senate had voted the dissolution of Parliament—its firebrands now were forced to scuttle back to the provinces. And with more than a little defeat in his tone, President Marshal MacMahon pleaded at a pathetic military review at blistering Longchamps:

"I appeal to the army to defend the dearest interests of the country."

Dog-days for the early years of the Third Republic, meteorologically and politically. Frenchmen that summer felt shut in by the steaming streets, by the premonition that the future was insecure, by their shrunken frontier on the east. There was no promising horizon, no beckoning land of opportunity. The less said of pestilential Algeria, the better. . . . Yet to regain what the Prussian war had cost in wealth and prestige, France must look beyond her frontiers.

But where?

Thus the Parisian argued with his customary vehemence over his triple-taxed aperitif, that depressing summer of 1877.

ii

I have arrived at this place [Nsanda] *from Zanzibar with 115 souls, men, women and children. We are now in a state of imminent starvation. We can buy nothing from the natives, for they laugh at our kinds of cloth, beads and wires. What is wanted is immediate relief.*—Henry M. Stanley, Aug. 4, 1877, on the lower Congo.

iii

London is nearly three degrees farther north in latitude, but the nerve center of the British Empire was not less sultry, for all that. The Trafalgar lions, now ten years old, lost bluster in the pitiless glare. Victoria, niece of Leopold I of the Belgians, snored faintly at Sandringham, dreaming of her coronation at Delhi, the past January, as Empress of India. Lord Salisbury, then Foreign Secretary, and the Earl of Carnarvon, Colonial Secretary, were unworried if not apathetic over the state of their world: for now the sun never set on the Empire, while the benevolent offices of its colonial administrators were uplifting the benighted savage in Africa—and disseminating Anglo-Saxon culture by dressing for dinner in the jungle. In the eleven-year-old mind of Master Rudyard Kipling were gestating those rhythms which were later to make of modern imperialism a whimsical adventure for the people of the British Isles.

For imperial Britain, the year was a breathing-spell. To be sure, British might had been threatened in the Transvaal in attempts to persuade the Boers that annexation was desirable, but otherwise the year abroad was uneventful for Downing Street. Bordering the five seas, Britain had colonies and markets in abundance. The astute "Dizzy" two years before had purchased from Khedive Ismail, Pasha of Egypt, 44 percent. of Suez-Canal shares, given the latter by the French Government. The occupation of Egypt was a comfortable five years in the future.

In the blanketing sun of that August, *The Times* of London, thermometer of British emotions, was exercised primarily over the "unseemly augmentation of the temperature," and in Mr. Gladstone's remarkable feat of "cutting down a large tree in the presence of an enthusiastic body of spectators."

There was speculation, although infrequent, over the progress of Stanley, five thousand miles distant. The British at home had wearied of reading that the burly Welsh-American had navigated another stream of outlandish name, or penetrated through miles of "totally worthless territory." Even in the northern latitudes of the British Isles, it was too hot to think comfortably of that explorer, sweltering through cannibal-infested jungles only a few degrees beneath the Equator.

iv

Resolved to cling to the river we dragged our canoes by land past the rapids, lowered them again into the river, paddled down a few miles, with great rock-precipices on either side. We encountered another rapid, and again we drew our canoes overland. It grew to be a protracted and fatal task—at Kalabu Falls six of my men were drowned. . . . The whirlpool sucked all down to the soundless depths.—Stanley, Aug. 6, 1877, descending the lower Congo.

v

In that year, the fever for colonial expansion had begun to spread throughout the breadth of the new German Empire. Victor in the war with France, Bismarck saw that increasing prosperity demanded German markets overseas, and that in time the Empire must find room for its surplus population—the old argument employed by Alexander the Great twenty-two centuries before, to be used later by an ex-Socialist, Benito Mussolini. But strangely, Bismarck did nothing to seize new outlets.

Not that year. "No colonies," he wrote. "They require too large a navy."

Added to these economic and social factors was the undoubted genius of the Teutonic people for painstaking exploration. Alexander, Baron von Humboldt, dead eighteen years before, was one of a long line of German scientist-explorers of the nineteenth century. He did not lack successors.

In Berlin, interest was lively. Stanley's travels, regarded by his countrymen more as a sporting venture than the preliminary to the confiscation of new lands for the Empire, were discussed exhaustively at scientific meetings in Berlin, Dresden, Munich and Hamburg, and found prolix treatment in newspapers and magazines. The colonial cause was first espoused realistically in 1873 by the German Society for the Scientific Exploration of Equatorial Africa, and again in 1876 by the German African Society of Berlin. These were the forerunners of the predatory German East Africa Company—precisely as there were elsewhere in Europe British, Italian and French Africa "companies" subsidized by their several governments.

It had become evident to the mass of the young Empire that the German star was clearly in the ascendant, and that accordingly the moment had arrived to employ the Teutonic genius at exploration for tangible objectives. Wilhelm Roscher, founder of the "historical school of political economy," stated the new doctrine in terms more precise than circumspect when he wrote:

"The fruits of colonization are usually reaped only in the second generation, and such long waiting is not to the mind of our time. Yet Germany must lose no time if the last suitable territories are not to be seized by other and more resolute nations."

The "colonial cause," as it became known in the Germany of 1877, could have been expressed with greater diplomacy, but not with more realism.

The interest of Crown Prince Wilhelm, then studying political economy at Bonn, in the colonial future of the Reich was incessant, and at the junior college at Kassel his major concern had been political history—the next Kaiser contracted early the virus of the empire-builder. Bismarck, outwardly indifferent to the cry for colonies in Africa, was inwardly dismayed, however, to learn that year of the formation of the British African Exploration Committee, and the start of the expedition of Joseph Thomson to Lake Tanganyika. The Iron Chancellor was attacked on many sides for his "short-sighted refusal to acquire colonies . . .

when pearls of great price were to be had for the picking up." But he had deemed it more expedient tacitly to encourage Britain in Egypt, and France and Italy in Tunisia, provided those three powers kept their clutches off Alsace-Lorraine.

Bismarck's relative indifference to the colonial picture was unquestionably one of the reasons for the later enmity and break between him and Wilhelm II. It will be seen that instantly upon mounting the throne, eleven years later, the Kaiser sought to "extend our civilizing influence" to East Africa.

vi

. . . My eyes rested on the river. Ah, the hateful, murderous river, now so broad and proud and majestically calm. As though it had not bereft me of a friend, and of many faithful souls, and as though we had never heard it rage and whiten with fury, and mock the thunder. What a hypocritical river! . . . How civilization was advancing upon me!—Stanley, Aug. 9, 1877, at Boma.

vii

In the symmetrical palace at Brussels, the forty-two-year-old Leopold cast a far-sighted eye that summer over an enormous map of central Africa. It covered an entire wall and, more significantly, dominated the king's mind. The tall ruler of a diminutive nation dreamed of vast expansion. In Europe there were few men, certainly no kings or ministers, better acquainted with that teeming region of the Dark Continent which came to be known preposterously as the Congo "Free State," a land, under that monarch's rule, of merciless slavery and exploitation of the natives. Unable to extend his rule in Europe, Leopold's imagination far outstripped the frontiers of his little kingdom.

Delusions of grandeur, his advisers concluded, not knowing their man.

For Belgium and the Belgians, the summer of 1877 was pregnant with expansionist possibilities surpassing even the visions of their "unloved king." In the northeast corner of the Palais du roi, in a rococo suite overlooking the formal gardens, Leopold reconsidered the map. Awkwardly for him, France, Britain and Portugal were already entrenched in the most accessible areas.

Yet—and he wrote that political aphorism himself—"over-populated, my country requires an opportunity for her subjects, her industry, and her wealth." Again, the time-worn pretext. But he was a realist, and his speeches to the Senate revealed him in the light of a merchant, the single-track businessman interested in commercial statistics, exports, new markets.

If other nations were to move into Africa, if not already there, why not Belgium—the traditional battlefield of Europe—whose future was less secure than any country? Indicative of his dominant interest in Africa, and his mounting excitement in the possibilities of a Belgian empire, the preceding year Leopold had staged at Brussels the International African Conference, at which his inaugurating address was a masterpiece of indirection and under-statement. Its burden, of course, was that familiar necessity of "improving the state of the African."

It was hot, too, in Brussels that summer, but the torrid blanket that stifled Europe did not enervate the King of the Belgians. Momentarily France could not look beyond Algeria, because of the imperative need to concentrate on preservation of her internal regime; British official policy for further penetration of that continent was in abeyance; in Berlin, the chancellor was occupied with cementing the new Empire. Was not today a propitious moment for a Belgian expedition to west-central Africa, say, under the guise of "disinterested science" or of "civilizing the savage"?

The question was politically reasonable, whatever its morality. Leopold must act cautiously, however, lest he arouse the Powers. A major problem was the selection of a leader for such an ambitious expedition. The incorruptible Livingstone was dead. And doubtless Stanley, who had disappeared into the jungle from Zanzibar three years before, had long since been dished up to cannibals in that barbarous land between the two oceans.

viii

At noon, after a last little banquet and songs, hearty cheers, innumerable toasts and fervid clasping of friendly hands, we embarked. . . . The color of the water, the numerous islands, and the enormous breadth recalled those days when we had sought the liquid wilderness to avoid incessant conflict with the human beasts of prey in the midst of Primitive Africa, and at the sight my eyes filled with tears at the thought that I could not recall my lost friends.— Stanley, Aug. 11, 1877, leaving Boma.

ix

Portugal had pretensions to vast areas in Africa, but in 1877 they were not accorded unqualified respect by the other governments of western and central Europe. True, the Portuguese colonial tradition was older by centuries than any other of the nations of modern Europe: with not a little confidence and authority, King Emmanuel in 1500 had assumed the title "Lord of the Conquest, Navigation and Commerce of India, Ethiopia, Arabia and Persia," and Pope Alexander VI had given his endorsement to that grandiloquent claim.

King Luiz, glumly pacing the marble halls of the Palacio

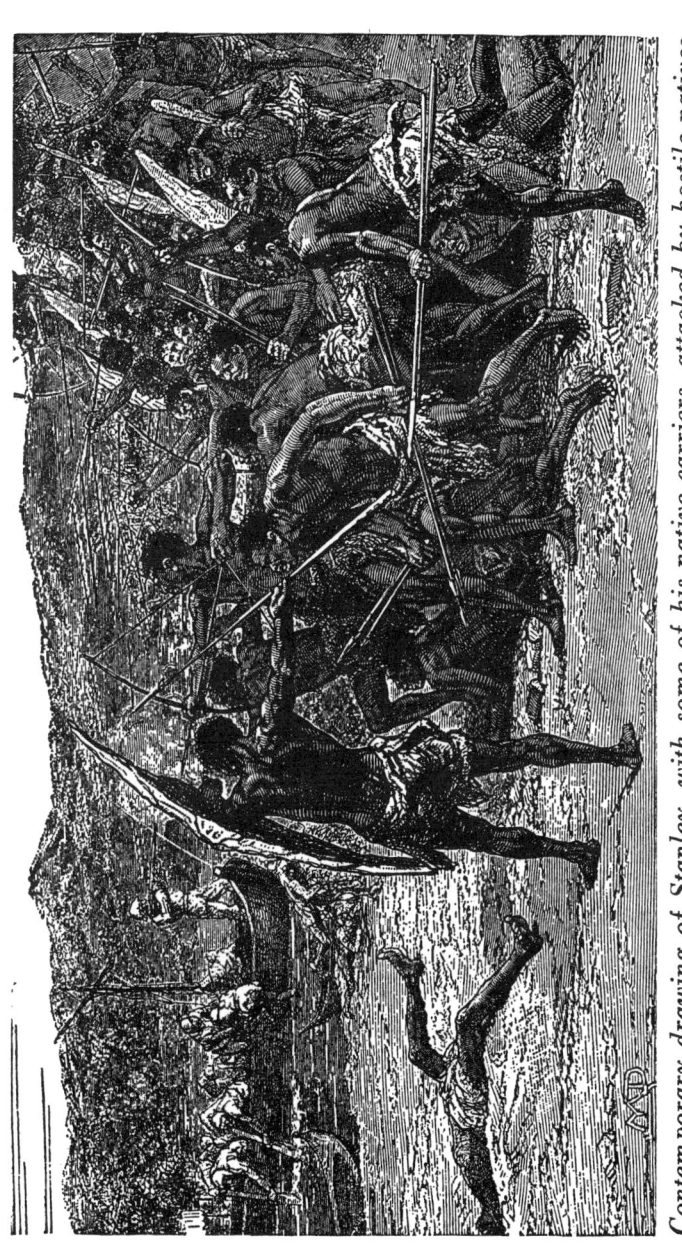

Contemporary drawing of Stanley, with some of his native carriers, attacked by hostile natives along the Upper Congo.

das Necessidades in Lisbon, was at this juncture, in 1877, more concerned with replenishing the royal coffers—the banks had failed the year before—than with a search for more dependencies. That summer, moreover, the old Liberal parties were shattered by the Progressives, and on one occasion Luiz had fled the palace in terror. Portugal was fortunate to hold the territories she had in Africa—Guinea, on the coast of Senegambia, Angola (Portuguese West Africa), and Mozambique (Portuguese East Africa), wild trackless lands, for the most part, none of whose limits was definitely affixed by international accords; nor were they to be for another decade. Luiz' hands were tied at home, and no Portuguese monarch had much stomach for imperial adventure since the humiliating loss of Brazil half a century before. By right of priority in Africa, by virtue of the first circumnavigation of that continent, she had a more valid claim than either France or Britain, but the Lisbon government in 1877 was in no position to assert its pretensions forcibly. On the eve of the progressive seizure of Africa, Luiz was seeking a felicitous rendering in Portuguese of "To be, or not to be"—he was translating "Hamlet" as an antidote to politics. But it is noteworthy that before undertaking these and other dilettante labors, he thought he had abolished slavery in the Portuguese colonies.

At Madrid there was at this moment a similar aversion to any elaborate colonial undertaking—a nation which had been occupied by Arabs and Berbers for more than seven centuries shrank from arousing an old enemy. With difficulty Alfonso XII had suppressed the Second Carlist War, and was now quarreling with his ministers over the new constitution.

Of the nations which had already established settlements in Africa, and were by degrees wresting more territory from the natives, Spain had the smallest "zone of influence" (a "zone" eventually becomes a colony in the history of the partition of Africa). Madrid controlled a strip on the Moroccan coast, Ifni on the northwest coast, the Canaries and other scattered islands. On the mainland the orange-and-red flag flew over less than 1,000 square miles, most of it worthless to the mother country because there were no port facilities. But together with her neighbors, Spain was later to increase her African holdings at a rate controlled only by the unscrupulousness of her government, the courage of her army, and the state of the Treasury. It may be noted that the 1,000 square miles held by Spain in 1877 had swelled to nearly 80,000 in 1900. (The enormous rate of increase was typical of all the powers later in Africa.) But for the present Spain had not even a minor Cortez or De Soto, as had Britain, France, Belgium, Germany and even Portugal.

x

The view inland is dreary, bleak and unpromising. But fresh from the hungry wilderness, from the storm and stress of the Cataracts, the solemn rock defiles and the bleak tablelands, I heeded it not. The glowing warm life of Civilization, the hospitable civilities which the merchants of Boma showered on myself and people, were as dews of Paradise, grateful, soothing and refreshing.—Stanley, Aug. 11, 1877, nearing the Atlantic.

xi

The Italy of 1877 had none of the imperial expanse of the Roman Empire. Nothing of those vast African provinces, extending from the Atlantic to Egypt, were left to modern Italy. The kingdom was merely the Peninsula. But that is not to say that Rome was disinterested in colonies. A new and ardent spirit was abroad. The unification of 1870 had loosed an eager nationalism from the Alps to Sicily.

The rule of Victor Emmanuel II was alert to the restiveness in Germany, France and Belgium. The Government had not yet the strength to steal colonies openly, but covertly it encouraged discussion of the necessity for territory abroad, and in fact subsidized exploration. Premier Depretis was worried that soon the French, in adjacent Algeria, would manifest a possessive interest as well in Tunisia, whose involved finances had been controlled since 1869 by Paris, Rome and London. That foreboding was to be amply justified four years later when the international scramble for territory was well underway, and Italy herself had likewise begun to grab colonies.

The experiences the year before of an expedition to Africa, sponsored by the Italian Geographical Society, are illustrative. This "scientific expedition" (there were soon to be scores of British, Belgian, German, French and Portuguese equivalents elsewhere in Africa) traveled by the Suez Canal to the Somali coast and made a suspiciously long stay at Zeila. The ambitious Ismail Pasha, that same khedive who sold his shares in the canal to Britain, had determined then to extend his "zone of tribute" southward along the entire Somali coast. The Italian party was attacked by natives —the wily Ismail apologized, expressed innocence and profound sorrow. In itself trivial, the incident gave united Italy, nevertheless, a foretaste of the potential perils of imperialism, even when it functions in the guise of disinterested science; but of stronger historical accent was the warning, served by Italy upon Europe, that she too had a covetous eye on eastern Africa.

None of the chancelleries doubted who supported this abortive venture of the Italian society. The Somali contretemps told Bismarck, Leopold, Salisbury, Luiz, de Broglie and others in plain words that Italy must be reckoned with in the imminent partition of Africa.

SEVEN-PART FUGUE

xii

... *A few hours later and we were gliding through the broad portal into the Atlantic, the blue domain of civilization. Turning to take a farewell glance at the mighty river on whose brown bosom we had endured so greatly, I saw it approach, awed and humbled, the threshold of the watery immensity, to whose immeasurable volume and illimitable expanse, awful as had been its power, and terrible as had been its fury, its flood was but a drop. . . . I felt my heart suffused with purest gratitude to Him whose hand had protected us, and who had enabled us to pierce the Dark Continent from east to west, and to trace its mightiest river to its bourne.*—Stanley, Aug. 12, 1877, at the mouth of the Congo.

xiii

The political map of Africa toward the close of 1877 showed one-tenth only of the vast Continent under white domination—but that fraction, even in an area roughly of 11,500,000 square miles, constituted a sharp spear. Within the next twenty-three years, nearly all of Africa was to be divided up in the European capitals, by men thousands of miles from the desert, the jungle and tablelands. There were conferences at Berlin, Brussels, Paris, at which pious lip service was paid to the natives' pressing need of the benefits of civilization.

A few figures are illuminating—and incredible. In 1877 the African area under control of Europeans was approximately as follows:

BRITAIN	250,000 sq. mi.
FRANCE	170,000 " "
PORTUGAL	40,000 " "

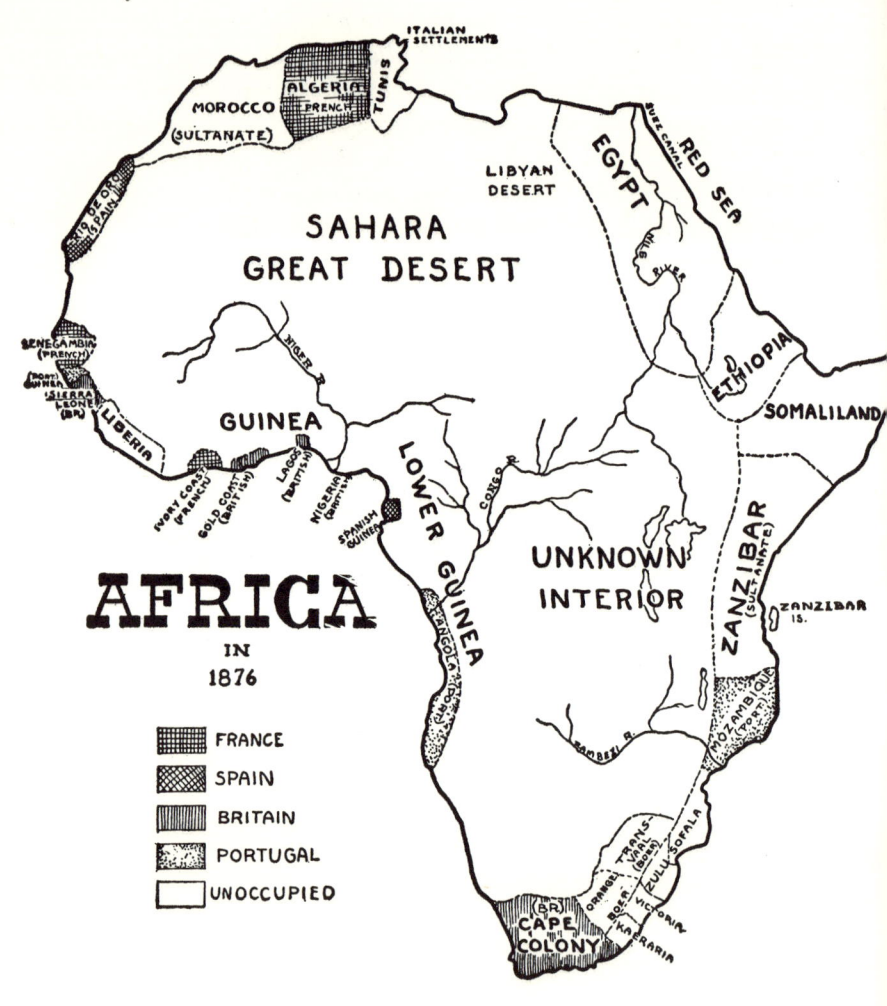

SPAIN	1,000 " "	
TURKEY (EGYPT AND SCATTERED)	809,000 " "	
TOTAL	.1,270,000 sq. mi.	
INDEPENDENT AFRICA	10,230,000 " "	
TOTAL AFRICA		11,500,000 sq. mi.

The political map twenty-three years later, in 1900:

FRANCE	3,866,950 sq. mi.	
BRITAIN	2,101,411 " "	
EGYPT (NOMINALLY BRITISH)	1,600,000 " "	
GERMANY	910,000 " "	
BELGIUM	900,000 " "	
PORTUGAL	787,000 " "	
TURKEY	400,000 " "	
ITALY	200,000 " "	
SPAIN	79,800 " "	
TOTAL		10,845,161 sq. mi.
INDEPENDENT AFRICA		613,000 " "
TOTAL AFRICA		11,458,161 sq. mi.*

By 1925, independent Africa had been further reduced, losing half of its 1900 area, mainly by French and Spanish inroads. It consisted then only of Ethiopia and Liberia, totaling 390,000 square miles. Parenthetically, many of the 1,500,000–2,000,000 blacks of Liberia are free only so far as they comply with the forced labor demanded by their Government, a "shocking" situation, to employ the adjective of U. S. Secretary of State Henry L. Stimson at the time (1930) of the League of Nations' investigation.

* The discrepancy between the totals is due to variation in the surveys of the two dates. The exact area of Africa still remains undetermined.

There remained therefore only Ethiopia as the last of free Africa.

Greed in mankind is no cause for surprise, but one of the several astonishing aspects of this history of theft is that never did these elder statesmen of Europe consider retribution from the multiple African races—in a continental uprising, for example, regarded now as a probability of imminent menace; nor had these ministers the sagacity to foresee that, could they delay annihilation of the white man and his settlements, a conflict in Europe among the partitioners of Africa was inevitable.

Recently both of these ominous prospects have been recognized as more than subjects for exclusive treatment by that press which battens on jingoism. The first danger provoked a warning at the regular League Assembly meeting in September 1935, when Charles T. TeWater, delegate of the Union of South Africa, defined the "new partition of Africa" in these words:

"[It is] the beginning of a yet undefined movement by Europe toward capitalization of the still thinly overlaid war-mindedness of the savage and the warlike instincts of Black Africa—the training of the teeming black races of Africa for war.

"If that crime is to be committed, and Africa to be conscripted by Europe for its own purposes and designs, armed Africa will in due time arise, as it has done before in its long dark history, and revert to black barbarism. . . . The long memory of the black of Africa never forgets, never forgives an injury or an injustice."

To which that rhetorical delegate might have added pertinently that Italy has been inciting those very "warlike instincts" of her tribesmen in Libya, and that Ethiopia's clamor for munitions and arms is equally prophetic. Seemingly, Leopold, Bismarck, Granville, Rhodes *et al* shut their myopic eyes to the fact that in time the white man could have no monopoly on his weapons of murder.

That second threat—of a European war over the spoils of Africa—is yet so real that it needs no emphasis. (As the South African delegate was uttering his warning at Geneva, Britain and Italy were massing warships in the Mediterranean and the former was closing the south approach to Gibraltar and considering also closing the approach to Suez.)

xiv

The electrifying news of Stanley's feat was not to reach Europe for several weeks, and its significance was still known only to the explorer and to a handful of European traders. There was no way by which he could file cables to the London *Daily Telegraph* and the *New York Herald,* for whom three years before he had contracted to tell his experiences—if he lived. His eventual dispatches (rich in hosannas), brought to London by a homebound Englishman, at once created excitement in the foreign offices of at least six of the seven capitals—official London was still asleep to their portent. But across the Channel the import of Stanley's discovery of a navigable waterway from the African interior to the Atlantic was recognized immediately.

In effect, it was a Mississippi system into the heart of another continent.

On the day that Stanley viewed the Atlantic from the mouth (seven miles wide) of the Congo, France, though eager for colonies, was forced to devote her energies to solving the series of domestic crises. The embittered President MacMahon, with no bowels for statecraft, smarting from the humiliation at Sedan and his internment at Wiesbaden, yearned to leave Paris politics: he would have been content leading an expedition into Africa where he had seen long service in the Algerian campaigns and served briefly as Governor-General. The meaning of Stanley's navigation of the Congo was not to be lost on that veteran colonial. "But," he confided sadly to intimates, "I cannot abandon a post in which the Constitution has placed me."

Leopold in Brussels was, of all the chief actors in the African partition between 1877 and the turn of the century, most alive to day-by-day developments, and the most wily and ruthless of the entire *dramatis personæ*, not excepting Bismarck. For one thing, he had known Africa at first hand when, as the inquisitive Duc de Brabant, he visited Algeria, Tunisia and Egypt, the last on two occasions. Now, in the palace gardens, he was telling Emile Banning, his military adviser, that "privately, I can assure you of my conviction that nations which renounce ambition are nations without a future. A people which is content with its homeland, and which dreads even the shadow of a conflict, lacks the characteristics of a superior race." The cynical, Napoleonic observation perfectly reveals the man and his mood that torrid summer. He had said the precise opposite in the Senate.

Disraeli's concern over the outbreak of war between Russia and Turkey gave him little time or interest to think in practical vein of new conquests in Africa. Two of his utterances that summer may be recalled as prime evidence that "Dizzy" was preoccupied. One was his sardonic observation, apropos of empire, that "all diplomacy is fiddle-faddle," and the other his manifest slip, in the House of Commons, that "there are, of course, millions who are bound to us by military sway." At this historic instant in the modern progression of empire, there was singularly little disposition in Downing Street to distrust Paris, Brussels, Rome or Berlin, so far as Africa was concerned.

But in Berlin, Stanley's famed dispatch to London and New York was certain to provoke excitement. For despite the policy of Bismarck to play Britain, France and Italy one against the other in north Africa, while Germany grew stronger at home, the weight of public opinion was increasingly disposed toward obtaining colonies overseas. The Sahara and Sudan travels of Gustav Nachtigal, if less spectacular than the travels of Stanley farther south, had done much to create expansionist sentiment in the Empire. Crown Prince Wilhelm, then eighteen, that August remarked to his French tutor in history on the "intrigues of ambitious ministers, who will do anything to keep in power." It was a juvenile but pointed criticism of Bismarck.

Italy, it has been seen, that summer nearly matched the colonial fervor of Belgium and Germany.

xv

In the London *Daily Telegraph* of Oct. 9, 1877, there appeared the following dispatch from Stanley:

Kabinda, West Coast of Africa, near the mouth of the Congo, Aug. 13, 1877— With a feeling of intense gratitude to Divine Providence, who has so miraculously saved me and my people from the terrors of slavery, from the pangs of cruel death at the hands of cannibals, after five months of daily toil through fifty-seven cataracts, falls and rapids, I inform you that the work of the Anglo-American Expedition, which you commissioned me to perform, has been performed to the very letter. We have discovered that the great highway of commerce to broad Africa is the Congo. . . .

The race was on. Leopold sped two top-hatted envoys to Marseilles to lure Stanley to Brussels.

II

African Melon
[1877-81]

IT MAY have been loyalty to England, or a real illness, as he claimed, that moved Stanley to decline the invitation of Leopold's emissaries. Fresh from three years in the jungle, the explorer's suspicions may have been aroused by the silk-toppers and the mannered suavities of their owners at the railroad station in Marseilles.

The date—January 1878. The Congo navigator, flattered, hurried on to London; the Brussels envoys, rebuffed but still hopeful, deflated their toppers and returned to Brussels. They were a Baron Greindl and General H. S. Sanford,* of Florida, erstwhile United States minister to Belgium.

"The two commissioners made me aware," said Stanley, "that King Leopold intended to do something substantial for Africa." The irony of the phrase was lost to the Civil-War veteran. He told the envoys that "six months hence, perhaps,

---

* In explanation of Gen. Sanford's selection by Leopold as one of the envoys, the late Ludwig Bauer in *Leopold the Unloved* comments that ". . . he [Sanford] could serve as an example to Stanley, the Anglo-American, that a man of Anglo-Saxon origin need not hesitate to enter the service of a foreign ruler." Incidentally, Sanford obtained the military title when Minnesota enrolled him as a major-general in the militia during the Civil War, in recognition of his gift of a pair of field-pieces to the First Minnesota Volunteers.

I shall view things differently, but at present I cannot think of anything more than a long rest and sleep."

Stanley was probably sincere in wanting the Congo to become British. He had a decided sense of empire, and foresaw British cotton-spinners clothing hundreds of thousands of naked blacks. In one of his early dispatches to the *Daily Telegraph*, the explorer had written:

"If it were not that I fear to damp any interest you may have in Africa, or in this magnificent stream [the Congo], I could show you very strong reasons why it would be a politic deed to settle this momentous question immediately. This river is and will be the grand highway of commerce to West Central Africa. The power possessing the Congo, despite the Cataracts, would absorb to itself the trade of the whole of the enormous basin behind."

He returned to London a conquering hero. There were lectures, banquets, toasts. The adjectives spilled in the London and the provincial British press somehow recall the tone of American newspapers upon Colonel Lindbergh's return in 1927. But the emphasis he put on his hardships, and on the dangers of central Africa, had repercussive effects. His listeners were discouraged; and he and his friends overdid lobbying among both politicians and industrialists. Downing Street and Whitehall, now beginning to see trouble threatening in Egypt and South Africa, were indifferent to the prospects he painted. Stanley significantly passes over the official indifference at London in his own account of the Congo steal.

"A friend finally suggested Switzerland," he wrote, "and I took the hint." Consciously or otherwise, Stanley had in mind accepting the invitation to discuss his map of the Congo with Leopold—if he were asked again.

He had not long to wait. Leopold had kept a watchful eye on the explorer. Once again the hireling Sanford met him, at Paris in August. In November Stanley was at Brussels—the king in a royal lather of excitement and impatience. On the 25th Stanley met in the Palace "various persons of more or less note in the commercial and monetary world, from England, Germany, France, Belgium and Holland." These commercial and monetary figures, he adds naïvely, "were well known for their benevolence." Immediately a Comité d'Études du Haut Congo was organized, consisting of two Englishmen, two Dutchmen and fourteen Belgians; a million francs were proposed for first expenses, and "every subscriber bound to answer each call when further funds were necessary."

Incidentally, less than three-quarters of the sum was raised, the Dutchmen investing 130,000 francs only as insurance to protect their trading-stations on the coast, and the Belgians most of the remainder. M. Lambert, a banker and Leopold's "gilt man of straw," was persuaded to disgorge 250,000 francs on the King's insistence.

In Stanley's words, the object of the Comité was "to consider the best way of promoting the very modest enterprise of studying what might be made of the Congo River and its Basin." (How immeasurably this fell short of Leopold's intention!) To this end, an expedition was organized with Stanley at its head. At this stage the explorer was either unbelievably gullible or had tongue in cheek when he wrote that "the charitable and philanthropic character of the [Comité's] resolutions clearly showed whose hand and mind had formed them, even if I had not had the honor of learning the sentiments of the Royal Founder [of the later Free State] from his own lips at private audiences." It will be recalled that only a year before the Royal Founder had told Banning, privately, that ". . . a people which is content with its homeland . . . lacks the characteristics of a superior race."

Stanley signed a contract. From the King's list he received £1,000 yearly. The Comité d'Études in addition undertook "to pay him £1,000 for three years, and for a further term of two years, if the Committee desired to extend their operations." The latter sum was independent of any understanding between Leopold and Stanley. Thus for approximately $10,000 yearly the King and the Comité obtained the services of an explorer who was eventually to make an overseas empire for Belgium of nearly 1,000,000 square miles in area. In justice to Stanley, it should be said that before signing the contract he made one final effort to interest the British Government. Leopold waited, content, sure of his man. The contract stipulated that the explorer was to "lease or purchase ground" on which stations might be established along the Congo. It is illuminating that as currency with which to negotiate some 450 treaties with native chiefs, Stanley took quantities of cloth, whiskey, beads and copper wire. On January 23, 1879, with a party of officers consisting of one American, two British, five Belgians and one Frenchman, he sailed for Zanzibar, his old headquarters, to obtain the native personnel for three "modest expeditions": two westwardly from the east coast, and the third, led by himself, to push east from the mouth of the Congo inland.

In this vast project, which was to occupy Stanley five years, he was more the titular than the actual leader. The real head of the expedition was the tall bearded man with the mocking big eyes in the Palais du roi at Brussels, relaying orders through Colonel M. Strauch, the Belgian army engineer. The King, scheming and planning far into the night, had need in addition to plan for the domestic future, for he saw that disputes with the other powers of Europe over Africa were inevitable.

Give Leopold credit for a prescient nose.

ii

The Comité d'Études du Haut Congo, under whose benign auspices Stanley had set out, was merely the "front" which hid Leopold's greed for territory. Seen in historical perspective, its origin in the International African Association of 1876, and its evolution into the Association International du Congo of 1882, reveal the canniness of the Belgian monarch and his genius for political and commercial intrigue, qualities that made him a match any day for even a Bismarck—the Prince once complained that "apparently no one leaves Leopold with a whole shirt."

In August 1876, a full year before Stanley reached the Atlantic by way of the Congo, Leopold's colonial fever had reached a point where action was imperative. No longer would he remain head of a country the size of a handkerchief. Leopold had convoked his skeptical cabinet and informed its members he was sending invitations to the governments of Britain, France, Germany, Austria-Hungary, Italy and Russia to an "unofficial geographical congress." Its sublime ideal, the embossed cards read, was "to deliberate on the best methods to be adopted for the civilization of Africa." The Congress opened at Brussels September 12. The explorer-delegates, their expenses to and at the capital defrayed by the King, numbered such contemporary bigwigs as Gustav Nachtigal, Georg Schweinfurth and Frederich Rohlfs of Germany, Lieutenant A. E. Lux of Austria, Commander Verney Cameron, Colonel James A. Grant, and Sir Henry Rawlinson of Great Britain, Commander Christoforo Negri of Italy, leader of that abortive expedition to Somali, and Henri Duveyrier, Admiral (Baron) Clément de La Roncière, and the Marquis Louis de Compèigne of France.

Inevitably Leopold was elected President—the first time

a king presided at other than a political congress. He took the chair, stroked his patriarchal beard (which he affected even at forty-one), and made one of three great speeches of his life.

"Do I need to assure you gentlemen that when I invited you to Brussels, I had no selfish aims?" he pleaded in the royal auditorium. "The subject which brings us together concerns all the friends of humanity. To pierce the shadows which envelop Africa, to end the slave traffic, are, I venture to say, a crusade worthy of this century of progress."

His hearers were impressed with his tone of "pure idealism"—stressed so redundantly the next day by the Brussels newspapers that what journalists characterize as "inspired opinion" is self-evident. The liberal press in Paris, on the other hand, was suspicious and one organ defined the royal address as "proof of a profound Machiavelisme." In the light of the King's squeeze-play three years later, and the fate of natives in his Congo Free State, that definition was a marvel of prophetic vision.

After the explorer-delegates had been decorated with the Leopold Cross—of which the elder Leopold had distributed a paltry 18,000—the King at last brought himself to speak of money.

"What abundant funds we shall procure if all those to whom a franc is little or nothing will contribute one to the fund for the suppression of the slave trade." Fortunately for his own ambitions, the King was to learn that the number of people to whom a "franc is nothing" is exceedingly small.

Before adjourning the delegates voted the establishment of the International African Association. This society made way three years later for the Comité d'Études du Haut Congo. Thus the first body whose objectives were officially benevolent was supplanted by a committee of private investors whose aims were mercantile, however much ambushed in references to philanthropy; and this in turn was to be suppressed for a third organization, the Association International du Congo which was the King's own promotion.

The Comité d'Études, then, was an international but private business enterprise, the creation largely of Leopold and one in which he eventually risked his own fortune, and that alone.

iii

Later the same year, 1879, after Stanley had reached Zanzibar, the King of the Belgians pulled off a coup in the best tradition of Wall Street. The two Hollanders dissociated themselves from the Comité d'Études, one by means of a self-inflicted bullet through the temple in a moment of morbidity over financial peccadilloes, and the other by absconding with public funds. Under the charter of the Comité d'Études, this withdrawal made dissolution almost obligatory, since it withdrew one of the pledged financial contributors. Wasting no time in ethical scruples, Leopold appointed a Belgian liquidator who, in turn, ruled against payment of further subscriptions into the Comité treasury. A second meeting of the Comité d'Études was summoned at Brussels, and the delegates told bluntly that the Dutch withdrawal meant (a), the Comité must be dissolved or (b), the funds already subscribed must be returned.

It was a case of heads the King wins, tails the investors lose.

Leopold's duplicity is self-evident—he had had a large part in the drafting of the articles of association, as Stanley remarked in his glowing tribute to the King. For the subscribers there was no alternative, save to ask their money back and to forget what now appeared, at best, a risky investment. But even Leopold sensed that the affair stank of sharp practice. Through an intermediary, who laid stress on the King's "well-known generosity," it was disclosed that he was willing to reimburse the capital subscribers in full, together with *five per cent interest.*

The stockholders rubbed their hands, delighted. They saw no further than their pocketbooks.

Thus, for slightly more than 1,000,000 francs, then $200,000, Leopold obtained one-man control of the Comité —now ostensibly dissolved. But he kept a skeleton organization, its members sworn to secrecy; most important of all, Stanley was in Africa and there was none to give him orders —save the King himself.

iv

In the first five years following upon Stanley's navigation of the Congo, Britain had other fish to fry in Africa. Downing Street, with its forty per cent ownership of the Suez, felt that Ismail Pasha must be deposed. The British Government's concern over this eventuality, as well as the Empire's greed for the Sudan, combined to give the Belgian king a free hand in west and east central Africa.

But there was still another reason why Britain, traditionally the most rapacious of empire-builders, gave Leopold all the rope he wanted. In this instance it was private greed, rather than governmental gluttony. Many British missionaries at or near the Congo mouths stood on their supposed rights to act both as evangelists and traders.* Should the British Government elect to colonize in the Congo jointly with Belgium, the missionary societies feared—justifiably —that their profitable trade with the tribes would be taken

* The charge is elaborated by John de Courcy MacDonnell, among others, in *Belgium, Her Kings, Kingdom and People.*

from them; they would be left empty-handed, save for their Bible tracts. At home the societies lobbied frantically to keep Britain officially out of the region. The appeals to MP's, the emphasis laid by interested bodies on the dangers to life in the Congo, were fully as effective as any political consideration which had finally led England to withdraw from Leopold's International African Association. The pretext for this move was that the laws of the Royal Geographical Society forbade the nation "from [joining] an enterprise which was not one purely of exploration."

In truth, the withdrawal and the official indifference were due to concern over the imminent "necessity" of intervention in Egypt, the Transvaal and the Sudan, combined in some degree with the jealous wailing of those English missionaries who had long had commercial as well as spiritual dealings with the blacks.

v

In the modern history of the British Empire, little is more malodorous than its record in South Africa. The apologist argument is that Lord Carnarvon, colonial secretary in 1878 and the sponsor a decade before in Parliament of the Dominion of Canada Act, believed that the four independent communities would prosper under one government.

The historical background of the British steal of South Africa, up to the time of Stanley's arrival at the Atlantic, may be told briefly—despite the appalling mass of conflicting records and narratives. The Cape was seized from the Dutch in 1795, the Empire needing a coaling-station on the route to India. Eight years later, when Britain was flirting for Dutch support in the Napoleonic wars, the Cape was returned to Holland. But its strategic value to England, and the growing suspicion that the Boers possessed a natural wealth far beyond their own knowledge, provoked the Admiralty and War Department, in 1806, to send out a second raiding party. The Boers capitulated, and a military governor ruled until 1814 when the British obtained the Dutch colonies of the Cape and Guiana for a "tribute" of £6,000,000.

Conscience money.

To consolidate the occupation, Parliament appropriated £50,000 to "assist and induce" immigrants to go to Cape Colony whose population was, of course, predominantly black. The Boers were relatively few in number. Similarly, but without marked success, Mussolini has urged emigration of his countrymen to Libya. The provincial Dutch officials were booted from their posts and all representative government abolished. Abuses of the British administrators multiplied with the result, beginning in 1835, of a nineteenth century equivalent of the exodus of the children of Israel. One of the Boer leaders in the Great Trek north, Pieter Retief, wrote that "we all went off in the full assurance that the English government will allow us to govern ourselves without its interference."

This the Government by no means proposed to do, on superficial grounds that once a British subject, always a British subject. But the Great Trek * nevertheless began toward the Orange territory, Natal and the Transvaal to the northeast, the colonists strangely optimistic.

In Natal the Boers found the Zulus adamant against what might be called a peaceful invasion. Retief succeeded at length in establishing a republic. The British trader-missionaries at Port Natal grew nervous, Downing Street was informed of a "Boer menace" to the west, and the inevitable took place in 1845: British troops annexed all Natal as a

* The expulsion by the British of thousands of French colonists from Nova Scotia, beginning in 1755, and the ensuing "trek" to Louisiana and elsewhere northward, was a historical precedent.

Crown possession, and the weary, disillusioned Dutch farmers retreated westward to a region north of the Orange River. (The conventional British extenuation for the Natal seizure is that the Boers were not strong enough to keep order among the Bantus within the new Republic.)

For a brief interval, the Boers were left alone. In 1852 two British commissioners were sent north of the Orange River, and negotiated a convention extending "freedom to govern their own affairs" to the Boers in what was now the Transvaal. Two years later similar "rights" to independence were extended by the British to the Boers in the Orange Free State, lying south of the Transvaal. London was momentarily jittery over the Dutch problem, now blowing hot, now cold. But the Cape administrators did not vacillate. They added approximately 18,000 square miles to the colony by extending their rule east and north to Kaffraria, and in 1865 baldly annexed the territory to the Cape. Three years later the Colonial Office authorized the theft of the land of the Basutos, west of Natal and south of the Orange Free State.

The stolidest Boer could foresee the end.

In 1867 a black child, belonging to a tribe along the Orange River, gave a trader a pretty pebble she had found on the banks of the stream. The trader took it to Grahamstown, Cape Colony, where a Dr. W. G. Atherstone pronounced it a diamond.* British imperial policy, as it affected both Boers and blacks, changed overnight, simultaneously a horde of prospectors sailed for Capetown.

Both the Transvaal and the Free State laid claim to most of the area reputed to be diamondiferous. The former's claims were arbitrated by R. W. Keate, the lieutenant-

* The stone sold for £500 and was placed on view at the Paris Exhibition of 1867. Two years later another diamond, weighing $83\frac{1}{2}$ carats, was found near the same stream. It became known as the famous "Star of Africa" and was purchased by the Earl of Dudley for £25,000.

governor of Natal. Inevitably he rejected the Transvaal's claims, while a native chief named Waterboer and the Dutch diggers similarly dismissed the well-authenticated pretensions of the Orange Free State.

In 1871 the conflict was resolved—to the eminent satisfaction of Britain—when Lord Kimberley, then Colonial Secretary, authorized seizure of the diamond-fields by the Cape governor. In this instance the pretext was that "the Empire alone was competent to enforce order among the miners."

Two years later the governor, Sir Henry Barkly, renamed the region of the De Beers and Colesberg Kopje mines "Kimberley" in honor of the Liberal statesman who had made the extraordinary decision in the Orange Free State controversy.

The unmitigated illegality of the confiscation was not lessened when Downing Street refused the reasonable demand of Jan Henrik Brand, Free State president, for arbitration by a disinterested power, i. e., some nation other than Britain or the Netherlands. A Liberal and an attorney, Brand was quick to point out that during the period 1854–70 British colonial secretaries had repeatedly admitted that the Crown had no territorial title north of the Orange River.

But there had been then no question of diamonds.

In 1876 Lord Carnarvon, Kimberley's successor, succumbed to the moral weight of the Boer argument and considered some "compensation" to the Orange Free State for the grab. This took the form of the payment of £90,000 for the oblong strip which, while relatively small, was and is still worth unknown hundreds of millions. The most artless apologist for the confiscation which this writer has found is Sir Henry Hamilton Johnston, the late African explorer and colonial administrator who wrote that "if the British had transgressed their rightful [Cape] borderland to some slight degree, they atoned for it by paying the Orange State an indemnity of £90,000. . . ." As an illustration of the weird functioning of the imperialist mentality, this can scarcely be matched—even by Leopold.

Although under the 1852 convention Britain had recognized the right of the Transvaal Boers to govern themselves, after kicking them from the Cape Colony, in 1877 the Colonial Office had another change of heart, and determined upon annexation. Here the juridical pretext—if any were required—lay in the complaints of both Cape and Natal administrators that Transvaal finances were hopelessly muddled and, moreover, in the familiar complaint that the Boers could not control the natives. In justice to British colonial policy of that day, it should be said that a few Boers themselves petitioned for annexation, hoping in this transfer for a solution of their economic problems. President Burgers of the Transvaal parliament warned delegates that unless they accepted confederation with the British colonies, even a modicum of independence could not be guaranteed—an utterance which lacked nothing in realism. But there is no good record, of course, that the natives desired annexation or, for that matter, even a substantial portion of the Dutch farmers.

"Provided he was satisfied that a sufficient number of the [Transvaal] citizens desired to become British subjects, and that in his judgment it was necessary," Sir Theophilus Shepstone, then Secretary for Native Affairs in Natal, was authorized to seize the territory by the Colonial Office, which ordered him to Pretoria as a special British agent. Shepstone did not wait for Transvaal sanction and over Burgers' perfunctory protest he declared April 12 that annexation was in effect.

But Lord Carnarvon in Whitehall had overreached himself in this larceny, as events were to prove 5,000 miles from

London. The Colonial Secretary, though pining for a South African Union (to be deferred to 1910), failed to give the Transvaal the autonomous institutions which Shepstone glibly promised. Meanwhile, Cape Colony officials showed distrust of a new governor sent out from London. British prestige, such as it was then, lost ground rapidly in South Africa. The defeat of a British force in the Zulu War of 1879 (casualties, 806 Europeans and 471 natives) * led Transvaal Boers to conclude that their new masters, although courageous, were not the best of soldiers against blacks—an inference not destroyed when by "unpardonable bungling" the life of Louis Napoleon, Imperial Prince of France, who had accompanied a British punitive expedition, was killed with a reconnoitering party.

vi

As evidence of the Boer discontent with the British regime, the Transvaal burghers refused to align themselves against the Zulus. Their temper was not improved when Sir Garnet Wolseley, the new High Commissioner for Southeast Africa, told them at Pretoria that "the sun would forget to shine and the Vaal River flow backwards sooner than the British flag would cease to fly over the Transvaal"—a threat not, it must be said, typical of British diplomacy. In December 1880 the Transvaal re-proclaimed itself a Republic, and with notable energy took the initiative of invading Natal. The Boers destroyed several British detachments; among the killed was Sir George Colby, successor to the highblown Wolseley. London newspapers screamed for "retrieval of British honor."

A disgraced Colonial Office hurriedly instructed its Cape

* The War Department embarked 10,000 troops for Capetown when it learned February 11 of the Zulu victory at Isandhlwana.

administrators to negotiate with the Transvaal, an order tantamount to admission of defeat. In the final Pretoria Convention of August 3, the Transvaal was "granted" internal self-government; there was face-saving for the home government, however, in a clause "formally preserving British suzerainty." No further attempt to annex this Dutch hornet's nest was made until the opening of the Boer War, in 1899, and then at huge cost of men and money. Unfortunately for the Transvaal, gold deposits had by this time been found in many regions; and Britain could resist its allure no more than she had resisted the diamond-mines of the Orange Free State, eighteen years before.

vii

Before examining the second British occupation of Egypt and the theft of the Sudan, it may be well to note briefly here the Empire's other possessions in Africa at the beginning of 1879—when Stanley was enroute to Zanzibar in Leopold's hire.

They comprised Lagos, the Gold Coast, and Sierra Leone, all on the west central coast. Lagos, now capital of Nigeria (seven times the size of England), had been wrested from the French by the privately-owned British United African Company. The Gold Coast seized from the Fanti and Ashanti tribes in 1844, on hypocritical grounds that the natives must cease human sacrifice, became a Crown colony in 1874; and by purchasing the old Dutch forts and annexing more Ashanti lands the British by 1879 had gained a valuable possession of nearly 55,000 square miles. It is worth noting that in the seventeenth and eighteenth centuries both the English and Dutch found this coast a profitable source of victims for the slave-trade.

Sierra Leone, directly northeast of Liberia, originally

AFRICAN MELON

discovered by the Portuguese, was in part obtained by "purchase" from a Timni chief who, in 1788, relinquished a strip of territory to British settlers for "goods worth thirty pounds, including English clothing, jewelry, firearms, tobacco, cloth, spirits and a telescope." * In return for this munificent outlay the British obtained eventually an area of nearly 31,000 miles.

viii

The British conquest of Egypt and the invasion of the Sudan has scant parallel in method with the subjugation of South Africa. It is one thing to invade a region populated by hapless blacks and a few Dutch farmers; it is something more formidable to attempt the conquest of a nation which in modern times had been successively the vassal of France and Turkey—and of Britain a half century before—and in whose fate Italy had a political concern, and Germany and Austria a financial one.

The ostensible reason for the European intervention, which began once again in 1879, lay in the "Oriental idiosyncracies" of Ismail Pasha, first Khedive, whose uncle had given Comte Ferdinand de Lesseps permission to undertake the Suez Canal (chiefly because of an old friendship born, it appears, of eating spaghetti together in Paris). Long denounced as a "spendthrift, a voluptuary and a thief," Ismail was given the imperial boot, after a constructive reign of

---

* The Timni chief, the celebrated Nembana or Naimbana, appeared soon thereafter among the British settlers "dressed in a purple embroidered coat, white satin waistcoat and breeches, thread stockings, and his left side emblazoned with a flaming star; his legs, to be sure, were harlequined by a number of holes in his stockings through which his black skin appeared . . . [Falconbridge] prefaced his arguments with a final donation of rum, wine, cheese and a gold-laced hat . . ."—From *Letters* by Anna Maria Falconbridge, London 1794.

sixteen years, when Britain and France complained to Turkey that the Khedive had returned to his autocratic methods of governing—the bill of complaints against Ismail was long, its charges mainly of a financial and constitutional nature. A defense of this modern exotic is not required here, particularly since in recent years Pierre Crabitès and others have shown he was grossly maligned. But after the Turkish Sultan abruptly removed him from office, at the instigation of London and Paris, that discharge provoked Judge E. E. Farman, United States consul at Cairo, to report to the State Department (June 27, 1879):

"There will be very different opinions not only as to the merits and demerits of the reign of Ismail Pasha, but also as to the arbitrary acts of the Powers in procuring his deposition or abdication without any request of his own people and against the wish of all the leading personages of the State, civil, religious and military." And in his *Egypt and Its Betrayal*, the consul added that "Ismail Pasha's real crime consisted of putting himself into the hands of the Shylocks of London and Paris. These Shylocks, who were mostly Jewish bankers [the Rothschilds, Oppenheims *et al*], had sufficient power to control the governments of England and France and to induce them to establish a new precedent relative to official aid in the collection of contractual debts, even those not resting upon any moral obligation."

The British and French stake in the Suez was unquestionably a vital one; the Bank of Egypt was British-owned as was the Alexandria-Cairo railroad, and the Suez harborworks, the Alexandria breakwater, the telegraph and lighthouses had been built by European contractors, to whom money was owing; finally, the British, French, German and Austrian bankers, who had urged loans at ruinous interest upon Ismail in the sixties and seventies, were now clamoring for unpaid interest and capital. Official bluebooks show

AFRICAN MELON

that by 1880 a debt of £90,000,000 had been imposed on Egypt by European speculators, in consideration of which only some £45,000,000 were received.*

Besides this, for twenty years the suzerainty of the Sublime Porte over Egypt had been growing weaker. Thus the Sultan was delighted to remove Ismail, so long as Britain and France supported his dirty work. He was only human.

Ismail's son, Tewfik Pasha, was appointed successor by the Sultan, and the new Khedive took office in June 1879, the tool of Britain and France. Diplomatic representatives were advised of the change in regime and invited to pay their respects to Tewfik at the Palace where they smoked chibuk, sipped coffee, and wondered if he would tolerate increased taxation—to swell the pockets of bondholders back home. They found the Khedive a spineless and amiable youth who obviously would not, even if he could, oppose the British habit of "persistent encroachment on, and truculence towards, the native governments." †

The immediate consequence of this puppet's accession was the establishment of dual control by Britain and France, although Tewfik had a constitutional cabinet. The representatives of the two nations were Major Evelyn Baring (afterward the Tory Lord Cromer) and M. de Blignières, both of whom had been foisted on the ousted Ismail when he had formed his last cabinet in 1878. They served as watch-dogs respectively of income and expenditures when the British, French and German bondholders began screaming for more interest and the two governments had obligingly supported the collection of private claims. (In a few months, British naval shells were fired as moral inducement to pay up.)

* J. Seymour Keay, *Spoiling the Egyptians: A Tale of Shame*, London, 1882.
† Ibid.

As might be expected, Messrs. Baring and de Blignières were immensely unpopular. Their two-year management in open support of the international bankers proved so harsh to all classes that it accelerated the spread of a quasi-nationalist movement. This had as its primary objective the expulsion of all Europeans. Cairo was weary of mixed tribunals, inquiry commissions, and other meddlesome European bodies, which exist to this day, and the fellah faced a lifetime of bondage to pay the taxes. The ground was ripe for revolt, and the party of unrest found an eloquent and fanatical leader in Arabi Pasha, minister of a non-existent army. Overnight he became the symbol of Egypt's passion to rid itself of the bondholders' rule.

Both London and Paris smelled the incipient uprising. But Arabi could not be summarily removed.

III

Cash, Cannon and Rum
[1882-84]

A RUSTLE of expectancy swept over the Commons benches one January afternoon of 1882 when Gladstone arose ponderously to read a report from Sir Edward Malet, British agent and consul-general in Egypt. That official laconically informed Her Majesty's Government that "armed intervention [in Egypt] will become a necessity. . . . The united Powers will be listened to, but not England and France alone because they [the population] think we are actuated by selfish motives, and that the other Powers will not allow us to deal with the Egyptian question alone."

As usual, in Egyptian and colonial affairs, Sir Edward was wrong.

The sense of this report was that Sir Edward Malet believed Britain had need of the other Powers to pull her chestnuts out of the fire in northeast Africa. On the other hand, Lord Salisbury, Conservative leader in the house, felt that the Empire had better act alone in Egypt. To Count Karolyi, the Austro-Hungarian envoy to London, he made unwittingly the perfect definition of the British imperialist attitude as it affected Egypt (but it was equally applicable to the Government's viewpoint toward South Africa or Afghanistan). To that ambassador, Salisbury explained with refreshing candor that:—

"The action of England [the eventual occupation],

though her interests are largely commercial, is dictated in the main by political considerations. Egypt has, in that point of view, an importance for England which it has for no other country in the world, and we are unable to forego our own claims to influence in that country or to accede to an arrangement of which confusion would be the necessary result. An international government of Egypt is, I think, quite impossible."

ii

If one substitutes Ethiopia for Egypt in this *apologia*, and Italy for England, the result is the specious argument which Mussolini repeatedly shouted during the autumn of 1935. When the Council of the League of Nations in September proposed an international mandate over Ethiopia, as a final compromise to avert the slaughter of natives, the Duce, like Salisbury, judged it "quite impossible." France has argued similarly in North Africa. There is no military back-talk to warships.

iii

By 1882 the Egyptian situation was so packed with dynamite for Britain that Lord Granville, the Foreign Secretary, opened negotiations with Gambetta, the French premier. For whatever Salisbury's view, an ostensibly Liberal cabinet member needed to give the imminent occupation the appearance, at least, of a move of international benevolence.

Gambetta was disposed to "joint material intervention," he informed the French ambassador to London. The reasoning of the French premier, then also minister of foreign affairs, is transparent: the Sultan of Turkey had reportedly appealed to Bismarck for aid against the British in Egypt, and French diplomacy insisted "that under no

CASH, CANNON AND RUM 53

circumstances should the idea of Turkish intervention be entertained";* moreover, the Quai d'Orsay had learned that while Bismarck might be useful to England in checking the desire of Russia and Austria to meddle in Egypt, he was annoyed that "Great Britain had thought it necessary to share her interest in Egypt too exclusively with France." In view of this disclosure, combined with its interest in the Suez, the Paris government reacted favorably to Granville's overtures. Prussian diplomacy has rarely been brilliant.

iv

It is worth noting here that in the early eighties the partition of Africa first became an affair of bargaining among the European chancelleries. The claiming of land by exploration continued, but the proverbial writing on the wall was clear—Africa was Europe's concern, not the affair of Europeans in Africa, and by no means the affair of the Africans themselves.

v

Gambetta, inclined to join intervention with Britain, was voted down by the Chamber of Deputies on January 26. Charles-Louis de Freycinet, his successor, had cold feet toward an Egyptian adventure. That timorous statesman suffered from the mental infirmity common to his race today— a profound dread of Germany.† He feared that should France confer with Britain over what to do in Egypt, Bismarck might be provoked to support an immediate Turkish occupation, and that this in turn would obtain the moral

* *Life of Lord Granville*, Lord Edmond Fitzmaurice.
† De Freycinet had reason to fear Germany. As chief of the military cabinet in 1870–71, he raised 600,000 men for Napoleon III, and was the author of the elaborate Coulmiers battleplan—all to no avail.

endorsement of Austria, Italy and Russia. In October 1935 Pierre Laval showed the same hesitancy to support Britain against Italy in the Mediterranean, fearing Germany.

Accordingly the French withdrew. Later when de Freycinet decided that the Alexandria rioting justified or necessitated the landing of French marines on the Isthmus of Suez—and begged Parliament for the requisite credits—he and his cabinet were howled out of office. It was too late. By then, any part of the spoils of Egypt were lost to Marianne.

Lord Salisbury had reason to rejoice.

Granville continued fearful, however, that armed intervention by Britain alone would excite jealousy and suspicion on the Continent. As the anti-foreign agitation mounted in Cairo and Alexandria, the Foreign Secretary made another effort to obtain international sanction for any eventual British occupation. He invited the powers to a conference at Constantinople to consider the "instruments of coercion" which the European nations would permit Turkey to employ in Egypt.

In May, the British and French at last agreed upon a "precautionary move." An Anglo-French fleet of twelve ships, six of each flag, was dispatched to patrol the harbor of Alexandria. The word "patrol" is found in both the British and French records of the negotiations, and it has a high and moral connotation. In reality the fleet was to serve as a back-stop for the Sultan of Turkey, should he send an armed force to Egypt, as well as a warning to the Porte not to go too far. On May 25 the young Khedive, Tewfik Pasha, more intimidated by the British and French agents than by the rising nationalism, dismissed the militant Arabi Pasha and the rest of the ministry. Immediately Arabi bounced back into the next cabinet, and his followers —now an impressive body numerically, if not militarily—

From "Europe in Africa in the Nineteenth Century."

CHARLES-LOUIS DE FREYCINET

were delirious with joy, and filled with new threats against foreigners.

The immediate *provocateurs* of the Arab uproar, Messrs. Baring and de Blignières of the Dual Control in Cairo, were thoroughly frightened. Sir Edward Malet had returned to England, not feeling very well. And with good reason were other foreigners nervous both at the capital and at Alexandria. The merest spark could lead to slaughter. Fortunately for Downing Street, it was provided by a street-brawl in Alexandria between a Maltese Greek (a British subject) and an Arab, on June 11.* The eleventh was a Sunday, and the streets and cafés were packed. Foreign warships in the harbor had electrified the air. Greeks began firing on Arabs from housetops, and the latter swarmed into the European quarter, clubbing every European found on the streets. In all, fifty-six foreigners were killed.

vi

Less than three weeks before the Alexandria riot, on May 7, Sir Edward Malet, at Cairo, wrote Lord Granville the following report:

"I believe that some complication of an acute character must supervene before any satisfactory solution of the Egyptian question can be attained, and that it would be *wiser to hasten it than retard it.*" †

vii

The gendarmerie suppressed the rioting without the aid of British or French marines on the men-o'-war. But

* American, British, French and German critics, some of them Alexandria residents at the time, charge the riot was premeditated and financed by Britain. The evidence is not conclusive.

† Parliamentary Papers, 3249, of 1882, p. 107.

eleven days later, on the 22nd, Granville let the cat out of the bag, so far as Britain's real intentions were concerned. From Downing Street he wrote Lord Spencer, President of the Council, that "I own to dreadful alarm at occupying Egypt militarily and politically with the French."

The Constantinople conference opened the next day. After the fashion of most international conferences, there had been no preliminary spade-work. The Turkish genius for intrigue and indirection, combined with Bismarck's refusal to commit the Reich, made a Continental joke of the deliberations.*

The British fleet off Alexandria, originally six ships, had by now been increased to eight iron-clads and five gunboats under command of Vice Admiral Sir Beauchamp Seymour. The six French vessels in the harbor were commanded by Admiral Charles Conrad. There were, in addition, gunboats, cruisers and other naval types from the United States, Italy, Austria, Russia, Spain, Turkey—the United States was represented by Admiral James W. Nicholson, aboard the flagship *Lancaster;* there were also the *Galena* and the *Quinnebaug*. The neutral ships stood by to protect their nationals, to see how far Britain would go.

The Khedive Tewfik—the bondholders' tool—had fled to Cairo. Arabi Pasha, now virtual dictator, began throwing up earthworks below the harbor forts to command the entrance: he foresaw that bombardment was inevitable. Seymour delivered an ultimatum to Arabi on July 6 demanding the Egyptians cease protecting themselves—or he would open fire. Like every other naval expert of the day, he was professionally curious to ascertain what damage five-ton steel shells might do against masonry: up to that

---

* An Italian newspaper cartoon showed the diplomats in the guise of five crocodiles, attempting to play the music of Handel's "Moses in Egypt" in concert on a grand piano.

CASH, CANNON AND RUM

time, they had not been tested in actual warfare against helpless civilians.

The consuls of the foreign Powers in Alexandria pleaded with the admiral to withdraw the ultimatum. Toubla Pasha, commander of the harbor garrison, appealed with quaint confidence to the "well-known humanity" of the British commander. (Although the harbor defenses were deserted by day, the burden of evidence bears out Seymour's charge that preparations were continued by night, as apparently revealed by naval searchlights.)

Foreigners who could, fled the city. The American consul and his staff arrived from Cairo on the afternoon train of July 10 and boarded the *Lancaster*. Meanwhile, Admiral Conrad received orders from Paris not to join in "material naval action." He steamed off for Port Said, "*et emportant avec son pavillon notre prestige en Egypt*"—thus most of the Paris newspapers. Nicholson withdrew seaward of the British. At 7 A. M. on the 11th, the British fleet of thirteen ships opened fire on the old stone forts, and shells rained upon the city behind. . . .

The Arabs stood bravely by their cannon against a bombardment the like of which was then without parallel. The forts proved to be slaughter-houses, affording no protection against the most formidable fleet assembled for battle, up to that time. After two days marines were landed. They found the city in flames, a blood-stained ruin.*

Two thousand Europeans, chiefly Levantines, were killed. Arabi's losses were unknown, but the marines found only

---

* Admiral Nicholson landed 175 U. S. Marines on the 14th of July to reëstablish the razed consulate, help extinguish the fires and bury the piles of dead. For this he received the thanks of Great Britain, a gold medal from the King of Sweden, and was promoted the following year to Rear-Admiral. For his leading rôle in the massacre, Admiral Seymour fared somewhat better: later that year he was raised to the peerage.

pieces of flesh and bone in the forts. Five British were killed. Since then few English historians or statesmen, save the individuals immediately incriminated, have sought to justify the bombardment of Alexandria, or put any construction on it other than the palpable criminal one.

The day following, July 12, Granville apparently realized the enormity of the massacre, and feared complications with France. He instructed his ambassador at Paris, Lord Lyons, to convey to M. de Freycinet that "the bombardment was considered a legitimate act of defense, and that there was no hidden purpose (arrière-pensée) on the part of the British Government." Sharp criticism in England was met with the laconic explanation that Seymour's fire was legitimate in view of Intelligence reports to him that Arabi planned to seize the Canal, and also because of Arabi Pasha's persistence in protecting rebels against British authority.

Occupation was complete by the close of the year. Parliament approved an expedition of 25,000 men to Egypt under General Sir Garnet Wolseley. He invested Cairo, slaughtered 2,200 of Arabi's forces in the battle of Tel-el-Kabir, northeast of the capital. British casualties totaled fifty-eight. (For his victory in this "battle," Victoria promptly elevated Wolseley to the peerage.) Arabi, the national idol, was banished to Ceylon, the authority of the bondholders' Khedive restored, and a puppet ministry formed under Sherif Pasha. The Egyptian exchequer, the army, administration of justice and communications were placed securely under British control. Lord Dufferin, ambassador at Constantinople, was sent to Cairo as High Commissioner.

The rape of Egypt was accomplished. Forty-one years later, in 1923, the British Government was to grant the

CASH, CANNON AND RUM 59

nation "independence," a word that looked decorative in the new constitution but in practical fact signified no more than it had to the Transvaal Boers.

viii

Although the French Government in 1877 was preoccupied with internal crises, Stanley's discovery did not pass unnoticed by the Quai d'Orsay. And the explorer's retention by Leopold for a "modest scientific expedition" to the Congo was interpreted correctly by the government as nothing less than a major-scale African adventure by the Belgian monarch. Other nations including Britain might be deluded by Leopold, but not the realistic French.

Not only were the Waddington and, later, the de Freycinet ministries eager for expansion, once the domestic crisis subsided, but a group of Paris and provincial newspapers had whipped up civilian interest in adventure abroad—provided, in the cautious French mentality, such adventure did not entail war with a superior power. It is more than a plausible supposition that the newspaper campaign of 1879, the exhortations of editors for national glory abroad, were nourished by the secret funds at the disposal of the Ministry of Foreign Affairs. In the history of the Third Republic that portfolio has usually been held by men of more than common astuteness and sense of political realities.

Citizens of the new Republic were reminded over their *croissants* and *café-au-lait* that France was in a humiliating position among the colonial powers. In Asia she had a paltry 22,000 square miles; in Oceania, 8,100; in the Americas, 48,000. Apart from Algeria, her principal colony (258,217 square miles), in Africa she had Senegambia—and Gabun on the west coast.

One of Pierre de Brazza's forts in the French Congo.

Gabun, a rude settlement immediately north of the equator, was established by the French in 1849, and in the seventies was no prize; eventually it grew into French Equatorial Africa (982,000 square miles), a possession four times the size of France. Senegambia was the name of a strip of coastal territory between the Senegal and Gambia rivers, along the western extremity of the continent; it was the nucleus of French West Africa (4,665,000 square miles), with an area one-half that of Europe.

Anxious to divert the electorate from political dissensions within itself, the Government drew public attention to the necessity of increasing French markets abroad. To judge by the Paris newspapers of the fall of 1879, almost overnight Pierre de Brazza became a hero, the Gallic equivalent of a Stanley.

De Brazza's travels marked the beginning of the French scramble for colonies, and he was fully as important a figure to that nation as Stanley was to Belgium.

The man who was to establish the French Congo, nucleus of French Equatorial Africa, was born an Italian, becoming a naturalized Frenchman at twenty-one. (The fruits of the labors of two of the greatest African explorers, Stanley and de Brazza, did not go to the lands of their birth.) Aboard a French warship, on which he was serving, he arrived in 1874 at Libreville, capital of the Gabun colony. Here the youth's imagination was fired by the tales of the Marquis de Compiègne and Alfred Marche, who had just returned from exploring the lower Ogowé river district.

The Ogowé is a stream approximately 500 miles north of the Congo, emptying into the Atlantic just south of the Equator. De Brazza, then a French naval officer, obtained permission to ascend the river, which he thought might be the lower course of the Lualaba (which Stanley had realized was one of the headstreams of the Congo). He left the Ogowé basin, discovered the Alima and Likona streams, and returned to the coast. When de Brazza arrived back in Paris, he realized that the two rivers must be Congo tributaries.

"In France," wrote General de Chambrun in a volume on de Brazza, "it is frequently the gloating of the neighbors which reveals to us the value of our own possessions." Here was a reference to the London and Brussels newspapers in which Stanley was dished-up matutinally as a world hero.

De Brazza's journeys had required nearly three years. He was scarcely more than a skeleton on his return to the capital, his clothes in rags. Admiral Pierre de Montaignac, minister of the marine, hurried the scarecrow to the Bon

Marché, whose director outfitted him from head to foot and, refusing payment, declared "the store is happy to manifest in this manner its homage to a young explorer upon his return from a superb expedition." The Parisian has a profound sense of economy: it is no libel to say that if he gives something away, he is deeply moved, if not slightly insane. . . . The incident is barometrical of the excitement of the French over de Brazza's travels and the possibilities therein of new colonies in Africa. Figuratively, the French now felt they could thumb their collective noses at Stanley and Leopold.

But Leopold was indefatigable. Just as he had trailed Stanley, so he determined to win over de Brazza. Once again General Sanford, the Florida millionaire in the service of the Belgian king, donned his silk-hat and sought out the young naval ensign at Paris.

De Brazza accepted the King's invitation to the Palace at Brussels. He arrived there early in 1879, shortly after Stanley had sailed for Zanzibar. Leopold instructed servants the interview was not to be interrupted by dinner.

"Your real place," the King said, "is on my side."

"But, Sire, I am a French officer. If you desire something from me, your Majesty must address yourself to my Government."

Leopold glanced slightingly at the naval insignia on de Brazza's sleeve.

"Is it possible that flimsy braid is an obstacle to the great career which I open to you? What marvelous things we could do together!"

De Brazza was silent. He returned posthaste to Paris.

The account of the Leopold-de Brazza interview is by General de Chambrun, brother-in-law of the late Nicholas Longworth.

Leopold, forty-four at the time of his audience to de

Brazza, believed he could entice the young explorer—he was only twenty-seven—away from France. The King might have succeeded but for de Brazza's conviction that France should have part of the Congo—apparently a stronger emotion than Stanley's feeling that the Congo was rightfully Britain's. And at Paris, de Brazza did not meet official indifference, as Stanley had in London, but found two influential supporters. They were Gambetta, President of the Chamber of Deputies, and Jules Ferry, Minister of Education, both of whom subsequently became premiers.

To them de Brazza explained that the territories adjacent to the Alima and Likona rivers which he had ascended were French by virtue of exploration; and earnestly he warned the MM. Gambetta and Ferry of the secret intention of the Belgian king.

"Leopold has sent off Stanley on a so-called scientific expedition—with an impressive party and unlimited resources.

"Now, France has more right to the Congo basin than any other nation, because of its Gabun colony and the official explorations of one of its naval officers. France cannot abstain in the peaceful struggle for the Congo. We must plant the tricolor above the Falls before Belgium gets there."

The two ministers concurred. Nor was de Brazza's plan impractical. Stanley, his party organized, had left Zanzibar, and sailed around the Cape to the Congo mouth, from which point he would work inland, along the south bank, negotiating native treaties with whiskey,* wire, artificial pearls and cloth. It was conceivable that de Brazza, given adequate support by his Government, could get to the

* Many explorers paid their black porters with gin. The fatal effect on the natives of European spirits is treated at length by Francis Mury in *Le Correspondant*, April 10, 1905, Paris.

district above the Falls, at Stanley Pool, before the British explorer worked his way past the Cataracts to the Rapids, a distance of 325 miles. But speed was essential.

The project was kept secret—so far as it is possible for a cabinet of fifteen men to keep their counsel. Somehow a leak occurred, and a hint of the proposed expedition came to Léopold's ears. He instructed Colonel Strauch to speed word to Stanley to "extend the action of our representative as far as Loango," on the coast north of the Congo mouths, to cut off de Brazza's easiest means of access.

Doubtless the Paris government learned of Leopold's move. De Freycinet, who had trembled over French participation in the occupation of Egypt, now feared that de Brazza's plan would lead to complications with Belgium. Accordingly officials proposed instead that de Brazza explore the Niger basin, and eventually he obtained the promise of 100,000 francs, to be raised by the ministries of foreign affairs, education, the navy, and the French Geographical Society. In contrast to this fund, Stanley had millions.

De Brazza set forth for Lisbon in December 1879, dismayed that Paris officials would not let him undertake a Congo expedition. It was not altogether timidity, however—fear of differences with Leopold—that turned the Government's eye to the Niger. The Colonial Ministry had learned that summer of the London promotion of the United African Company, the private combine headed by Sir George Goldie. The Niger territory, well north of the Congo, was then somewhat of a No-Man's Land, and reputedly a rich one. France had as much right to plant flags in the Niger Basin as Britain. And an added advantage was that no vast colonization project was underway there, such as Stanley had launched from the mouth of the Congo.

What then happened in Paris is without documentary

explanation. The Colonial Office telegraphed de Brazza at Lisbon, ordering him to proceed to the Middle Congo, in accordance with the original plan. The project of deepening the French Niger frontier was given to Captain Joseph Gallieni of the French Marines, whose task was to consolidate the position of the thirty French trading stations on the lower Niger, and *embêter* the British United African Company. (The move was admittedly political, calculated to distract British attention from the French push into Senegal interior, north of British Sierra Leone. In 1884 the French interests, subsidized by the Government, sold out to the United African Company.)

The Government's reversal in Paris, whatever the motive, vitally affected the political fate of Africa. That decision in the French chancellery did not, on the other hand, alter in the slightest degree the lot of the natives. Had the energetic de Brazza gone to the Niger, the British would possess today much less of Nigeria, while Belgium would doubtless have obtained rule over the entire Congo Basin.

De Brazza was elated. He wrote to a Paris friend that "I am happier than had I received millions from an American uncle."

The explorer reached Gabun early in 1880, outwitting Leopold who hoped to bar him north of the Congo by annexing Loango. He hurried up the Ogowé, establishing Franceville near its headwaters, and pushed southeast overland toward Stanley Pool. His main station there, on the north bank, was subsequently named Brazzaville; and territory was also claimed south of the Congo. Flags were formally planted at both Franceville and the Congo Station.*

* Stanley scoffed at the importance de Brazza placed upon the planting of the tricolor. "All that the natives see in a flag," he wrote, "is a gay rag with which to make a belly-band or a tur-

There was as yet no sign of the perspiring Stanley, far down the Congo. Leopold had failed to head off the French. De Brazza wasted no time. He was courageous, and he had an ingratiating and disarming manner of dealing with the most truculent of native chiefs. He found Makoko, "king" of the Bateke tribes, with whom he signed treaties placing the vast region north and east of the Congo, as far as the Alima, under French protection.

Makoko knew of the depredations of Stanley along the Congo two years before, the seizure of hostages and the murderous weapons with which Stanley fought. De Brazza was unarmed, mild-mannered, sincere. Makoko went to his witch-doctor, who advised him to accept the protection of the "peaceful" French as against the alternative of attack and occupation by Leopold's agents.

De Brazza did not give a *sou*, a case of gin or a bolt of cloth in exchange for the Makoko concession granting a French protectorate. He negotiated two treaties, ratified by the French Parliament in 1882.

The French-Italian explorer then started down the Congo, and on November 7, 1880, encountered Stanley at Isangila, approximately midway between Stanley Pool and the Congo mouth.

ix

The relations between Stanley and de Brazza, rivals in the Congo, may not belong rightfully in an account of the political rape of Africa, but they may be mentioned briefly for their comic value.

There seems to have been much punctilio between Euro-

---

ban." To which de Brazza replied, "On the contrary, Stanley should know that the black kings recognize in the emblem of France a guarantee that no other nation would set foot on their territory, and none would dare fire upon them." The disagreement seems slightly academic, in view of subsequent raids by the European Powers.

CASH, CANNON AND RUM

pean explorers meeting on the Dark Continent. Stanley's celebrated greeting, "Dr. Livingstone, I presume?" was perhaps the first. De Brazza sent ahead to Stanley, by a native porter, an engraved card which read "Le Comte Savorgnan de Brazza, *Enseigne de Vaisseau*." Stanley notes that "an hour later the French gentleman appears, dressed in helmet, naval blue-coat, and feet encased in a brown leather bandage. . . . I speak French abominably, and his English is not of the best, but between us we contrive to understand one another." The tone is stiff—there was professional jealousy and distrust on both sides, later to become acute. Stanley smiled deprecatingly at the naval

De Brazza negotiating with Makoko, after the conception of an English illustrator. Note the liquid "currency" in the French explorer's right hand.

ensign's account of concessions from Makoko, and scoffed to his engineers of "that poor barefoot, about whom there's nothing remarkable save his tattered uniform and his battered hat. His so-called 'concessions' are worthless scraps of paper."

De Brazza's riposte to this was the claim that "I have never had the habit of traveling in Africa after the belligerent fashion of M. Stanley, who is accompanied invariably by a legion of armed men. . . . Stanley can make himself respected only by use of fire-arms."

In 1884, when both explorers were in Paris the same month, they met on the Boulevards. General de Chambrun relates that Stanley stopped de Brazza in his tracks and hissed, "Count, I am going to kill you tonight!"

It was the eve of an American banquet in honor of Stanley, who had just returned from Africa to report to Leopold. The inoffensive de Brazza could not believe his ears. He hurried to the French Geographical Society which procured him the immediate collaboration of a young American "ghost." At de Brazza's home on the Boulevard des Italiens the pair wrote a short speech in English which the count memorized. "He wanted to be sure not only of memorizing the address perfectly, but certain that despite his accent the Anglo-Saxon audience would understand him"—thus Chambrun.

De Brazza arrived late, and the American ambassador, Levi Parson Morton, former Vice-President, motioned him to a seat of honor at the ambassadorial right. Stanley, on Morton's left, was finishing a harangue against de Brazza. It was so bitter toward de Brazza, and so unfriendly to France, that Thomas Tisdel, an Embassy attaché, reported to Thomas Bayard, Secretary of State, that "only alcoholic abuse could explain or excuse the violence of Stanley's language."

In the speech that was to "kill" de Brazza, and which seems to have been inspired by rage that the French officer was victor in the race to Stanley Pool, the Anglo-American explorer told his audience:

"May there be a curse upon him who, animated by a senseless jealousy and a malevolent spirit, will force us to burn our settlements, to destroy the work begun so auspiciously, and to abandon Africa to its misery and its primitive barbarism. When I met M. de Brazza on the Congo in 1880, about forty miles from our lower station, I was the last person to consider myself in the presence of a man who would very soon exercise a powerful influence upon us. A man without shoes, whose costume consisted of an old military tunic and a misshapen felt hat. . . . We discerned in him the happy combination of diplomatic genius with the philosophy of a Florentine. I am no longer a journalist but I still have enough of the newspaperman's instinct to assure you that had I recognized in M. de Brazza a great explorer, a great liberator endowed with all the virtues to which he pretends, I should have hastened to cable the *New York Herald* and the press of the world."

De Brazza did not understand this singular address, and after Stanley sat down, he cordially shook hands with the speaker. When a moment later he was informed of Stanley's venom, he turned to him and said:

"I have just learned, my dear colleague, that a moment ago you attacked me violently. Before I am told the exact terms you employed, let me once again offer you my hand."

Ambassador Morton thanked de Brazza "for having, by your conciliatory attitude and the tact of a man of the world, prevented a distressing incident." Thereupon the American diplomat tactfully declared the banquet at an end. Stanley never mentions the snub.

X

What may be legitimately described as the first major theft by France in Africa, was Algeria, as distinct from the vast Saharan areas now known as the Southern Territories. In 1877 North Algeria had an area of 258,217 square miles; in 1835, due to administration and jurisdictional revisions, Algeria proper had an area of 343,500 square miles, or nearly the extent of France, Italy and Scotland combined. The total area, i. e., with the Southern Territories, is 847,552 square miles, or slightly less than twice the size of Panama and slightly less than either French or Belgian Congo.

The invasion of that part of northwestern Africa, after the collapse of the Roman Empire, began again at the hands of the Arabs in the twelfth century. In the sixteenth century both Spain and Portugal extended their influence along a considerable part of the coast, until the Turkish conquest. For the ensuing three centuries, Algeria was the haven of pirates, whose activities were scarcely hampered by punitive expeditions sent from Europe.

In the history of imperialism there is almost invariably an "incident" to serve as the convenient pretext for occupation. In the case of Algeria, the grounds for French hostilities were at once so slender and ludicrous that they merit inclusion here as more or less typical.

In April 1827 Dey-Hussein, of the Turkish Directory, contested the payment by him of over-due amounts for French wheat imports supplied by two Jews of Algiers, subjects of France. The latter invoked the intervention of the French consul, M. Deval, who lost his temper. Dey-Hussein unfeelingly kicked him from his office.

In revenge for this "slur," France established a blockade which endured for three years. Thereupon the Paris govern-

CASH, CANNON AND RUM 71

ment dispatched 103 naval vessels to the coast, carrying 37,000 troops under General Louis Bourmont—a fly-whisk launching a hundred ships. Sidi Ferruch was occupied; Algiers capitulated: the incident had been avenged.

The Turks were expelled, and the long work began of subduing the native Berber and Arab population. Railroad construction began in the fifties. In the next decade a governor-generalship was established, but Napoleon III was not kindly disposed to colonization efforts, holding that most of Algeria was Arab. In 1871 the native chiefs revolted, the uprising serving as pretext for French imposition of enormous reparations and the confiscation of lands of the rebel leaders.

Although its conquest of Algeria over a half-century had cost the French considerable in men, money and prestige, by 1881 there were at least 370,000 Europeans seeking their fortunes within the colony. Thenceforth the work of assimilation proceeded rapidly. The most intransigent chiefs fled west into Morocco, whose conquest the French began in 1904, after a deal with Britain by which the latter was given a free hand in the Egyptian steal.

xi

The remaining four nations among the group which later divided up Africa—Italy, Portugal, Germany and Spain—did not steal on any vast scale at the beginning of the eighties, mainly for domestic political reasons already reviewed. But all had explorers in Africa.

In 1879 the Lisbon government sent an expedition to south central Africa (led by Major Serpa Pinto),* but the nation's

* In 1890 Pinto nearly precipitated war with Britain. The explorer, then in the Shiré (Zambezi) highlands, now part of Rhodesia, scoffed at British claims that the territory belonged to her "zone of influence"; Salisbury on January 11 delivered an ulti-

claims were not delimited for nearly a decade, long after the Berlin Conference.

Since 1862 Italy, it has been noted, had had a covetous eye upon Tunisia. In 1880, when Rome had a finger in the administration of the bankrupt country's finances, together with Britain and France, Italy purchased the British-owned railroad running from Tunis, the capital, to Goletta, eleven miles in length.

The Cairoli government in Italy had no suspicion that Britain and France had made a private deal over the eventual disposition of Tunisia. The deal had the secret approval of Bismarck and was negotiated while the German chancellor served as president of the Berlin Congress of 1878 (summoned to settle problems arising from the Russo-Turkish war of the year before). At this meeting Salisbury, the British representative, had agreed with W. H. Waddington, the French foreign minister, that France should seize Tunisia whenever feasible, in return for which the Paris government would condone the British "lease" of Cyprus.

In 1881 France thought the moment propitious to extend its rule eastwardly from Algeria. A French force crossed the frontier, ostensibly in pursuit of some Kroumir tribes, marched on the capital and forced the Bey, representative of the Sultan, to acquiesce to a protectorate. In 1883 the French, following the precedent established in Algeria, sent out a governor-general.

The wrath south of the Alps was pronounced, and one of the effects of the French steal of Tunisia was to send Italy, now fearing isolation, into the entente which became subsequently the Triple Alliance (with Germany and

---

matum ordering the Portuguese, military and civil, to leave, and Her Majesty's warships were sent to seize Portugal's islands off southeast Africa. Of necessity, the Lisbon cabinet backed down, then resigned when the incident provoked a republican uprising.

Austria-Hungary). Italian alarm, however dubious the morality of her claim to Tunisia, may be readily understood, nevertheless, for her economic and political interests there were greater than those of any other nation of Europe; and there were, moreover, far more Italians in the country than French. The dispute of Italy with France over African colonies, and the distrust in which Rome holds Paris today, may be said to date from the grab of Tunisia in 1881.

As meager compensation for the loss of Tunisia, Italy in 1882 declared Assab, Eritrean port on the shore of the Red Sea, an Italian colony. The district, the first territory acquired by the kingdom in Africa, was purchased from Sultan Berehan of Raheita for £1,880, for use as a coaling depot by the Italian Rubattino Steamship Company. Three years later, when the Egyptian hold on the Sudan was slipping, Italy began extending her influence along the western coast of the Red Sea, and seized the principal port of Massawa (where the majority of the present Italian expeditionary force to east Africa was disembarked). . . . Properly speaking, Italy's invasion of northeast Africa dates from the pronouncement of Assab as a colony in 1882, an act robbing Ethiopia of an outlet, just as the French obtained another (Djibouti, French Somaliland) six years later in a concession from Britain.

xii

In the decade under discussion, of the seven powers of Europe which eventually carved up Africa, only Spain made little appreciable progress.

But in 1883 "Colonies for Germany!" was a national slogan within the Reich. Bismarck might assure the British ambassador—

". . . no colonies! Colonies could only be defended by powerful fleets, and Germany's geographical position did not necessitate her development into a first-class maritime power. . . ."

—but the Crown Prince and the public at large would not long be ignored. The eighties saw the genesis of the Pan-Germanic sentiment of *Deutschland über Alles*. Germany eventually intervened in Africa, and supported such intervention with warships, because her prosperous export-trade in intoxicants and other items to the southwest coast was threatened by a treaty Britain negotiated with Portugal during the period 1882–84. The treaty, subsequently abandoned because of Belgian, German and French protests, would have recognized Portuguese sovereignty on the Congo up to Noki, and given both parties exclusive trade and tariff advantages.

As early as 1842, German missionaries had been sent to Africa by various evangelical societies of Leipzig, Berlin and other large cities. For the greater part they had established themselves along the Atlantic coast territory north of Cape Colony (subsequently German Southwest Africa), and along the southeast coast (later to become German East Africa). Britain, preoccupied both in South Africa and in Egypt, hesitated to declare a protectorate northwest of Cape Colony.

German chambers of commerce saw a magnificent opportunity, and brought pressure to bear upon Bismarck. Berlin and Hamburg newspapers of the early eighties made much of the fact, for example, that the Woermann Steamship Line had a profitable monthly service to the Congo; and that from January 1883 to March 1884 the company had sold there 4,452 tons of liquor (mostly cheap gin), 1,029,-904 pounds of gunpowder, and 555 tons of weapons and rice. The significant increase in the Africans' consumption of German liquor alone is shown by the fact that in January 1883 the Woermann carriers took 76 tons in various liquors to the Congo, for coastal and interior sale, while fourteen months later, in March 1884, the monthly consignment was 502 tons, an increase of 560 per cent.*

The civilian spearhead of this move for African colonies and trade overseas was Herr Franz Lüderitz, a Bremen merchant, who proposed establishing a tobacco factory on the west African coast. In the absence of a statement from Granville as to whether or not Britain would respect the ostensible rights of such a project, the German government informed Lüderitz's agent that "if he was successful in acquiring territory not claimed by any other Power, he [Lüderitz] would receive protection."

Bismarck was still cautious. But soon his hand was forced. The Lüderitz expedition arrived at the Bay of Angra Pequena, 150 miles north of the Cape frontier, marched inland, and with the persuasive effect of cloth and beads, negotiated a treaty with a native chief, John Frederic, in May 1883. By the instrument the Bremen manufacturer obtained 215 square miles, to include Angra Pequena, with an Atlantic frontage of ten miles. The German imperial flag was raised immediately.

Thus the nucleus of a colony of 835,100 square kilometers.

The success of the German raids on the west coast lay in their speed. They remain in modern colonial history one of the rare instances where the Wilhelmstrasse out-bluffed or out-maneuvered Downing Street. For Britain had had no intention of permitting German colonies anywhere near Cape Colony or within its "zone of influence." In November 1883, six months after Lüderitz had landed in Africa, Granville instructed his ambassador at Berlin, Lord Ampthill, to inform Bismarck that—

"Although Her Majesty's Government had not pro-

* *Europe and Africa,* Norman D. Harris, Houghton Mifflin, 1927.

claimed the Queen's sovereignty along the whole country [above Cape Colony] but only at certain points, such as Walfisch Bay [north of Angra Pequena] and the islands of Angra Pequena, they considered that any claim to sovereignty or jurisidiction by a foreign Power between the southern point of Portuguese jurisidiction at a latitude 18° S. and the frontier of the Cape Colony would infringe their legitimate rights."

This was a belated threat and a weak one. Bismarçk was not intimidated. A German war-vessel, the *Carola*, steamed into Angra Pequena, to support Lüderitz's colony, and served notice upon a British gunboat, the *Boadicea*, that the latter was in German territorial waters.

The Cape Colony government informed the German consul at Capetown, in 1884, after lengthy correspondence between Berlin and London, that its intention was to seize Angra Pequena. Bismarck now realized that Britain was attempting the unwritten promulgation of a Monroe Doctrine for herself in Africa. Without mincing words he had conveyed to Granville that "the German Government could not maintain a friendly attitude on Egyptian matters if Great Britain maintained an unfriendly attitude on colonial matters." *

The German threat was effective. In value, the arid coastal districts north of the Orange River mouth could not be compared with the political importance of a complacent German attitude toward British occupation of Egypt. On June 22, 1884, Granville summoned the German ambassador and announced that the British Government "conceded" German sovereignty at Angra Pequena.

Thereupon the British perforce abandoned the territorial and trade treaty with Portugal. Berlin sent another gunboat to Angra Pequena, lest the Cape Colony attempt

* *Life of Lord Granville*, vol. II.

CASH, CANNON AND RUM 77

to seize the Lüderitz settlement, unaided by London. In August 1884 the coast from latitude 26° S, excepting Walfisch Bay, was declared German territory.

At home, Germans slapped one another vigorously on the back, and raised steins to the forthcoming empire overseas. There might have been less jubilation had they foreseen the eventual costs of the German colonial empire, in money as well as prestige abroad. In two decades the criticism of Germany for cruelties exercised upon the natives were matched in vehemence only by the attacks upon Leopold's atrocities in the Congo.*

xiii

One other German colony, the Cameroons, lying between Nigeria and the territory de Brazza had claimed (French Congo or French Equatorial Africa) was acquired—again largely at British expense—before the Berlin Conference of 1884–85.

In 1860 the Woermann interests had built a factory in the Cameroons estuary, immediately south of the "big bend" on the West Coast. There were a relatively large number of British missionaries, chiefly Baptist, in the territory which a tribal king twenty-five years before had given the British—an extensive concession. The Colonial Office had not, however, exploited it. In view of the apparent indifference of Britain, the German Foreign Office in April 1884 informed Granville that it was sending Dr. Gustav Nachtigal, the explorer, "to visit the west coast of Africa . . . to complete the information now in the pos-

* Prussian administrators employed forced labor, forbade beards, used the lash, and were unquestionably guilty in several instances of murder. There is a considerable literature on the subject; see *The Germans in Africa*, Evans Lewin, London 1915, and *The Prussian Lash in Africa*, "Africus," London 1918.

session of the Foreign Office at Berlin on the state of German commerce on that coast. . . ."

The Foreign Secretary was given a verbal guarantee that Dr. Nachtigal's interests were only scientific, where they exceeded his commercial mission, and accordingly Granville consented that British authorities in the territory be instructed to give the German explorer whatever perfunctory assistance he needed.

Dr. Nachtigal's real interests, in accordance with his instructions at Berlin, were not "scientific" but purely colonial, a fact which Bismarck took great pains to keep secret. The warship *Möwe* brought Nachtigal to the Cameroons estuary. He proceeded inland and on July 15, 1884, his advance agents negotiated a treaty with Kings Beel and Acqua who "conceded" a territory of roughly sixty square miles.

The native kings received £1,000 each, and the minor chiefs along the Cameroon River "unlimited and plentiful supplies of rum." * The British protested vigorously, but Granville had only his own procrastination to blame.

An exchange of curt communications is revealing. In January 1885, the smarting Granville wrote that "had Her Majesty's Government supposed that Dr. Nachtigal was authorized to annex territories in which they took a special interest, and over which they had then decided to proclaim the Queen's Protectorate, then they would have exchanged explanations with the German Government, which must have prevented the present state of things."

In response to which the realistic Bismarck wrote that "English officers would have prevented German acquisition if it had been known beforehand at what points it was intended to make them."

The British consul-general on the Gold Coast, E. H.

* *The Germans in Africa*, Evans Lewin.

Hewett, arrived in the Cameroons five days after the German explorer, "empowered" to annex the country. Nachtigal had signed the treaty July 15 (1884). Hewett arrived July 20, and on July 26 a French gunboat also appeared off the Cameroon estuary on a belated mission of annexation. The scramble for any African territory was underway in earnest.

Dr. Nachtigal, after raising the German flag and planting frontier poles, proceeded to Togoland, much of which he claimed on the pretext that Bremen and Hamburg traders feared a native uprising "of British machination." The German flag was raised at Bagida, Loma and Porto Seguro. Another march had been stolen on Britain.* The trade war between London and Berlin for overseas markets was now well launched: it was to prove one of the cardinal factors that catapulted the nations into war in 1914.

* British protection had been asked by the Cameroon chiefs in August 1879, and the request ignored. "Dear Madam," King Acqua wrote to Victoria, "We your servants have join together and thoughts its better to write you a nice loving letter which will tell you about all our wishes. We wish to have your laws in our towns. Plenty wars here in our country." It was apparently beneath the dignity of either Victoria or her Foreign Office to acknowledge the communication. Similarly, Victoria ignored an offer of marriage made her by a Sudan chief, shortly after the Prince Consort's death in 1861.

IV

The Horsetraders
[1884]

HENCEFORTH the political history of Africa is shaped almost entirely by events in Europe, by diplomatic horse-trading, chicanery, threats, bribes and—behind the official acts of the various ministers, ambassadors and special agents—by the constant pressure exerted on these actors from private industrial and trade interests.

The fears of Bismarck, the "honest broker," that Germany could not undertake the acquisition of colonies, because the Empire was not geographically situated to maintain a powerful navy, had been somewhat quieted after negotiation of the Triple Alliance. The past, to which Italy adhered in May 1882, chiefly because of resentment over the French grab in Tunisia, was in Bismarck's devious mind calculated to guarantee to German (1) the aid of Italy against Britain or France in the Mediterranean should war be provoked over the African conquest or another cause, and (2) the aid of Austria-Hungary against Russia. Like all pacts designed to maintain a balance of power, the textual burden of the Triple Alliance was upon peace, but explicit stipulations provided for armed intervention by the three powers should Russia or France, in particular, seek to change the *status-quo*.

The alliance negotiated, then, Germany was in a better position to engage in African adventure. But now that the

THE HORSETRADERS 81

international scramble had fairly started, there was in 1884 evident anxiety in all the chancelleries that the seven interested nations might find themselves at war over the despoliation of Africa.

Leopold, near insanity with anger over the French steal north of the Congo, had good reason to fear that Germany and Portugal would also encroach upon the empire that Stanley was carrying for the King. Early in the year, however, Leopold had one signal diplomatic victory as regarded the Congo. Foreseeing that his African project would, as it already had in informed quarters, aroused suspicion, envy and criticism, he determined to hoodwink the United States into formal recognition of the "philanthropic and unselfish character" of his Congo promotion (from which, it will be recalled, he had squeezed all foreign participants).

Accordingly the services of the pliant Sanford were again enlisted. At Washington the Florida "general" exploited to the fullest that section of official opinion which was sympathetic to anti-slavery and, more especially, to the suppression of the slave-trade. This was, of course, Leopold's favorite—and emptiest—cliché.

But it proved effective in the United States. To Senator John T. Morgan of Alabama, who was somewhat suspicious, Sanford wrote in disarming vein that "the only practical difficulty in this wonderful progress by Leopold in the Congo proves to be an unrecognized flag, which is liable to be misunderstood or abused, and the people under it subjected to impediments in the *philanthropic work* on the part of those engaged in the slave trade or for other selfish ends."

General Sanford, recently made a grand officer of the Legion of Leopold, on April 22, 1884, succeeded in obtaining the signature of the Secretary of State to a remarkable document, placing Leopold's Congo venture within the scope of international law—and thus giving the vague State benefit of sovereignty under international law. It had been necessary, of course, to obtain the Senate's approval. The preamble to this extraordinary instrument, which immeasurably strengthened the position of the Belgian monarch vis-à-vis the Congo, read as follows:

"The Association Internationale du Congo [actually Leopold's African International Association] declares by these presents that, in pursuance of treaties concluded with the legitimate sovereigns in the Basins of the Congo and the Niadi-Kivillu, and in the adjacent territories on the Atlantic, it has been granted a territory *for the use and to the profit of free States already established or being established,* under the protection and supervision of the said Association in the said Basins and adjacent territories, and that the *said free States* benefit of right from this cession."

The italicized references to free States was unadulterated eyewash. Leopold had no intention of conceding any rights to any nation unless forced to do so—as indeed he was within a few months. The reference to "adjacent territories on the Atlantic" was an oblique attempt to obtain the recognition of the United States to the regions immediately north and south of the Congo mouth, which de Brazza and Pinto had claimed for France and Spain respectively. In this respect, Leopold's greed was to defeat him at the momentous Berlin Conference later in the year.

The liberal tone of the document, and its stress on the King's intention to abolish slavery, impressed Secretary Frederick T. Frelinghuysen, who placed his signature below the statement that "the Government of the United States proclaims the sympathy inspired in it by the *humanitarian and generous purpose* of the International Association of the Congo, managing the interests of the free States established in this region, and commands the officers of the United States on land and sea to recognize the flag of the

'Association Internationale' equally with that of a friendly government." *

ii

Such recognition by a major Power of Congo sovereignty had an immediate effect upon the interested chancelleries in Europe. So far as the writer knows, this part that the United States played, more or less unwittingly, in the partition of Africa has never been seen in its full importance.

Confronted with this *coup de main,* France moved quickly to get into Leopold's good graces, recognizing that the bearded gentleman in Brussels had obtained via Washington a quasi-acceptance of his Congo claims as valid in international law. But the French would not extend recognition to the blue flag (with a resplendent gold star to connote the astral objectives of the swindle) unless such affirmation brought a tangible return. Fortunately for their ambitions, Colonel M. Strauch, Leopold's chief-of-staff and then president of the African International Association, was momentarily in a dither over Britain—chiefly because Granville in a letter to Lord Aberdare the preceeding February had expressed skepticism over how long the King would desire to maintain the character of the "great philanthropic enterprise . . . and also [Granville] believed that he [Leopold] had fomented the agitation both at home and abroad against the Anglo-Portuguese treaty." †

All of which was excessively true and pertinent, but not a diplomatic confession on the part of a Foreign Secretary.

In any event, Strauch wrote to the French foreign min-

* The moralistic tone of this memorable document remains in somewhat ironic contrast to the official and unofficial attacks subsequently directed at Leopold from the United States, the first nation to recognize the sovereignty of the Congo State.
† *Life of Lord Granville,* vol. II.

ister, Jules Favre, that should Belgium find it expedient to sell or abandon any of the Association's holdings in the Congo, France would be given the right of preëmption— in return for immediate recognition of the legal validity of Leopold's holdings. The French lost no time in signing an agreement: it seemed at once to hold out promise of future colonies, should Leopold's project fail in part, and to prevent incursions of the other nations into the Congo domain of the King.

The Franco-Belgian agreement was explicit. Its first article stipulated that "the Belgian Government recognizes that France has a right of preëmption over its possessions in case of their alienation by sale or exchange in whole or in part." The document was signed at Brussels the day after Frelinghuysen had affixed the seal of our Department of State to the instrument handed him by Sanford at Washington.

Germany followed suit, suspecting from the text of the Franco-Belgian agreement that Leopold was discouraged by the enormity of the Congo project, and was prepared to make concessions to stronger and richer powers. Bismarck recognized the flag of Leopold's Association as that of a "friendly State" and intimated Germany's "readiness to recognize the frontier of a new [Congo] State."

Distrust of England was another reason for Bismarck's acquiescence to Leopold's solicitations. In his private correspondence of that year, in the months immediately preceeding the Berlin Conference, he refers repeatedly to "the Gladstone prophecy." This was a curiously intuitive remark, made in August 1877 (before news of Stanley's discovery reached the outside world), that "our first site in Egypt, *be it by larceny or be it by emption,* will be the almost certain egg of a north African empire that will grow and grow . . . till we finally join hands across the Equator with Natal and Cape Colony."

Recognition of Leopold's sovereignty in the Congo came from the other Powers after the Berlin Conference was underway.* Leopold had held out the bait of colonies to twelve European nations, all of whom greedily snapped. North of the Alps the popular (and newspaper) sentiment was Africa for Europeans.

iii

The Berlin Conference was significant not only because of its political decisions, which gave the map of Africa more or less definite frontiers and color sub-divisions (see page 88), but also for the attitude and point of view of most of its delegates.

That attitude escapes precise definition, for the degree of rapaciousness of all the delegates was not the same. Germany's greed far exceeded that of Austria-Hungary, for example, which necessarily had no territorial ambitions in Africa. The United States, which also sent delegates, was present in its traditional rôle—at European conferences—of the innocent bystander or, if you like, the impotent observer: official Washington may be absolved from taint of the brush which tarred most of the other nations at the Berlin parley.

The common attitude of the forty-odd men who attended was a mixture of greed, cold-blooded indifference to the fate of the races to be subjugated, and fear of treachery from neighbors; to this might be added the same lip-service to "civilizing the Africans" and suppressing the slave-trade that was heard at the Brussels geographical congress in 1876.

* The dates may be noted here—Britain, December 16 (1884), Italy, December 19, Austria-Hungary, December 24, Holland, December 27, Spain, January 7 (1885), Russia, February 5, Sweden and Norway, February 10, Portugal, February 14, Denmark and Belgium (the latter as distinct from Leopold), February 23.

Possibly these are the components of what may be called the imperialistic attitude of the last third of the nineteenth century.

The Conference indeed was born in fear and distrust. The original proposal came from the Lisbon Government, embittered by the British abandonment of the Anglo-Portuguese treaty which would have extended recognition to Portugal's ancient and shadowy claims to the Congo mouth, and to a part of the immediate interior claimed by Leopold and Stanley. Portugal was, moreover, annoyed with Britain, as has been seen already. Bismarck preferred a weak power (Belgium) in the Congo to a power of Britain's magnitude. In Downing Street there was mistrust of all the Continental nations involved, particularly of Germany after the Cameroons seizure, but Lord Granville hoped a Conference might clear the air. Spain meanwhile was hungry for any crumbs that might fall, while Italy hoped for an opportunity to repay France for the invasion of Tunisia. That invasion, parenthetically, had delighted Bismarck who saw immediately that France would be required to send additional troops to North Africa, thus reducing danger of a French attempt to recapture Alsace-Lorraine.

Such a mass of conflicting interests and opposed rivalries was the peculiar joy of the German chancellor. Better than any of his contemporaries he knew thoroughly the profit available in the game of playing one nation against the other. His ability in this field was the root of his diplomatic genius. And in the convocation of the Berlin Conference, the leading rôle of Bismarck—acting behind the scenes through Portugal—is clear to whoever reads history between the lines.

The proposal, then, came from Portugal, and was addressed to Bismarck (who had almost certainly written the original draft suggesting a conference). Germany obtained the approval of France to a Congo and African congress. On October 8, the two nations in concert issued invitations to the leading maritime nations to attend a conference at Berlin to discuss:

1. Freedom of commerce in the Basin and mouths of the Congo;

2. The application of the Congo and the Niger of the principles adopted by the Congress of Vienna (1814), "with a view to preserving freedom of navigation on certain international rivers";

3. A definition of the formalities necessary to be observed so that new occupation on the African coast should be deemed effective.

iv

The personalities of a few of the cultivated brigands, known in their day as diplomatists, who assembled at Berlin, November 15, 1884, to sit in at political poker—with Africa the stake—may bring into focus the predatory objectives of the Conference, or the aforementioned prevailing attitude of the delegates.

Secretary of State Frelinghuysen nominated General Sanford. That ubiquitous gentleman, off and on hireling of Leopold, was delighted to go to Berlin, and his pleasure was matched by that of the Belgian monarch. Sanford was still a member of the African International Association. To add dignity and authority to the American delegation Frelinghuysen also nominated John A. Kasson, the United States ambassador at Berlin.

In the appointment of a third member to represent the United States, there is the refreshing presence of simonpure farce, not a common element in the history of diplomacy. It was Henry Morton Stanley, the Anglo-American explorer in Belgian employ.

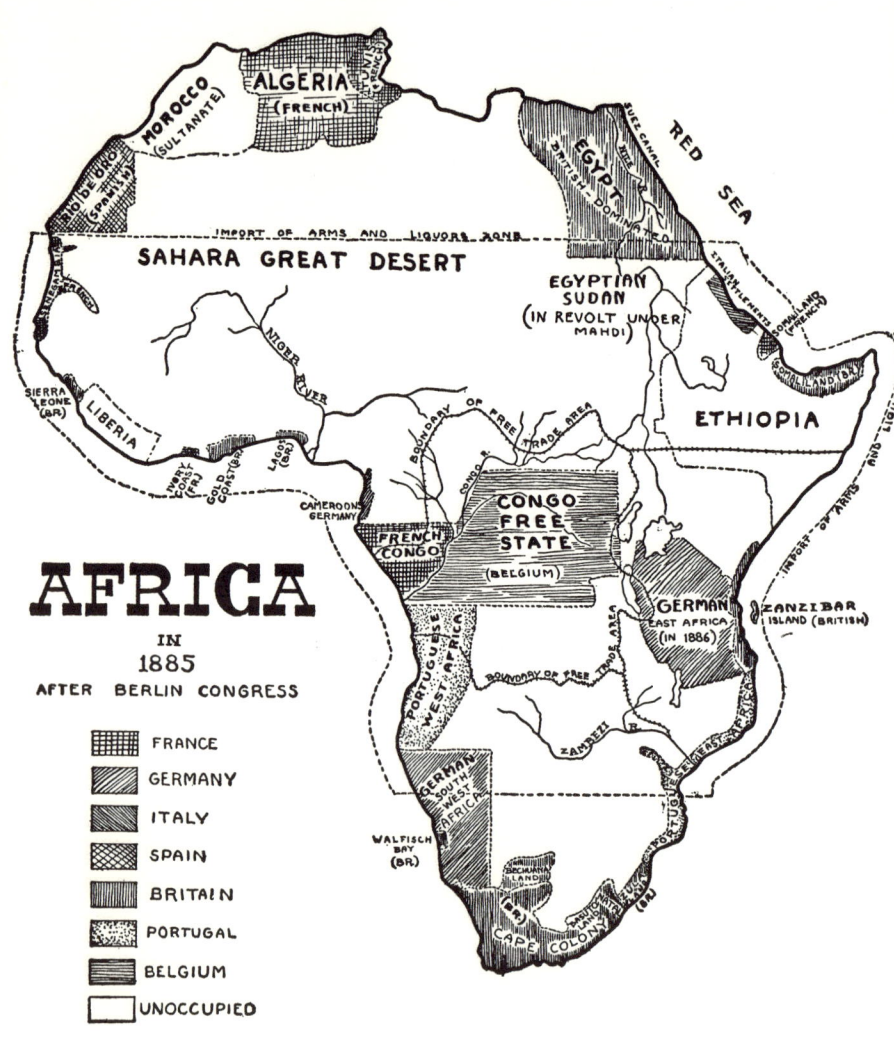

Leopold had hurriedly recalled Stanley when, in the summer of 1884, the chancelleries of Europe buzzed with reports that a Congo conference—to check Leopold—was an autumn probability. It was enroute to Brussels that Stanley, changing trains at Paris, threatened de Brazza's life and ridiculed the naval officer before an audience of Americans.

Stanley was in a highly anomalous position. By virtue of his service in the Confederate Army (ironically for him, in defense of slavery!) and subsequently in the United States Navy, he had lost his British nationality (restored to him in 1892) and become a subject of the United States. It was as an American, incidentally, that he had failed to interest the British Government in the Congo, although his acquired nationality was not, of course, the reason. He returned to Africa in 1879 in the employ of the Belgian king and while there remained under the sovereignty of that monarch.

Sanford realized that Leopold's avowed philanthropy might appear considerably less than genuine if the forthright and pugnacious Stanley went to Berlin openly on behalf of Belgium. The explorer accordingly joined the United States delegation as the "technical adviser." His real function was to watch out for the interests of his employer at Brussels.

Granville distrusted the entire idea of the Conference, but accepted the German and French invitation after the agenda had been enlarged beyond discussion of the Congo, to include the "formalities necessary to be observed" in new occupations along the Coast. For there was no longer the slightest doubt that what territories remained unoccupied after the Conference—if any—would be seized just as rapidly as the interested nations could get their nationals on the ground, with adequate supplies of gin, cloth, beads and wire.

A formidable crew of horsetraders was sent by Downing Street to the German capital. The British delegation was led by Sir Edward Malet, the agent-provocateur of the Alexandria riot of 1882, which, we have seen, resulted in occupation. Because Granville realized that the Germans particularly might be expected to display marked skill where the Conference's labors touched upon geographical knowledge and scientific experience, as well as new problems of international law, he sought to bolster his delegation by the inclusion of Percy Anderson, chief of the African Department of the Foreign Office, and Sir Edward Hertslet, the official archivist. Robert Meade, Under-Secretary of the Colonial Office, and one-time private secretary to Granville, was entrusted with the post of second-in-command. Others in the group, charged with protecting British interests against those of six Continental nations, were Sir Travers Twiss, a well-known jurist and once Victoria's advocate-general—his repute was such that Leopold asked him later to draft the constitution of the Congo Free State; J. Bolton, a geographer, and Sir Eyre Evans Crowe of the Consular service.

When the party arrived at Berlin, critics of British policy in Africa predicted confidently that Sir Edward Malet was leading what would prove a humiliating "pilgrimage to Canossa"—a reference to that German emperor's submission in Italy to Pope Gregory, who before seeing the German forced him to stand barefooted in a courtyard for three days and nights. . . . The remark is indicative of the hostile atmosphere in which the Conference began. But so far as its value is concerned as a diplomatic prediction, it stands as another example of the myopic German tendency to disparage the British cleverness at negotiation.

Leopold's delegates were Colonel Strauch, Émile Banning, the military expert, Theodore Pirmez, and Baron

August Lambermont, who were to prove an effective quartet against the French and Portuguese. The French mission was led by Baron Alphonse de Courcet, the French ambassador at Berlin. Representing Germany, besides Bismarck were Paul, Count Hatzfeldt, the Foreign Secretary, and also Herr Adolphe Woermann, of the aforementioned shipping line. The others were represented by their respective ambassadors or ministers to Berlin, or by lesser fry.

V

So much for the horsetraders in the foreground of the Berlin Conference. Three of the more powerful of the actors remained discreetly in the background—Bismarck who, although President of the assembly, did not attend the often acrimonious sessions; Granville in London, and Leopold in Brussels. Royal dignity perhaps would not permit of the presence of the Belgian king at Berlin, but he was to make the weight of his influence felt in very real terms, despite the 450 miles which separate the two capitals. Every day from the Palace at Brussels Leopold dispatched lordly telegrams and letters instructing Banning, Strauch *et al* what to demand, and the precise strategy to employ at each session.

In this, the head of one of the smallest and most defenseless States of Europe made a series of Gargantuan bluffs, directed primarily at France and Portugal—and incredibly emerged chief victor.

V

Congress Dances
[1884-85]

THE epochal Conference opened November 15, 1884, in the Chancellor's palace in the Wilhemstrasse, incidentally the present abode of Adolf Hitler. Inspired oratory was loosed to impress the assembled journalists, and hence the world at large, that the aims of the fourteen nations toward Africa were benevolent and disinterested. The peculiar direction that that benevolence took is best indicated at this point by a glance at the map of Africa before the Conference (see page 26) and the map 104 days later, February 26, 1885, when the "legal partition" was an accomplished fact (see page 88).

As at nearly all international conferences where there is a nigger in the woodpile, most of the bargaining was done at embassies and in hotel rooms and not in the compromising foreground of open meetings. Early in the deliberations the British made a shrewd but illfated attempt to win over Germany, recalling Bismarck's blunt warning the year before that "the German Government could not maintain a friendly attitude on Egyptian matters if Great Britain maintained an unfriendly attitude on colonial questions," meaning the west coast of Africa.

Behind the scenes the British cultivation of the Germans was assiduous, to put it mildly. Meade had an interview at Berlin with Dr. Moritz Busch, Bismarck's chief publicist who had to be courted by anyone wanting the Chancellor's ear, or his favor. Previous to the opening of the Congress, Dr. Busch had written a number of "inspired" articles for newspaper publication at the direction of the Wilhelmstrasse. "On the 16th of November, the day after the opening of the Berlin Conference," wrote Dr. Busch, "Bucher [Bismarck's private secretary] again sent me material for an attack upon England. . . ." And early the next year, Busch refers with undisguised joy to "England's misfortunes in the Sudan, and I expressed a hope to Bucher that Wolseley's head would soon arrive in Cairo, nicely pickled and packed." *

Meade made little headway with the wily Busch, although the latter let the Englishman believe he had won over Bismarck to joint action in Africa, or at least to an effective degree of non-interference. The Under-Secretary told the German publicist repeatedly "how baseless was the idea that the action of the [British] Colonial Office [in the Cameroons grab] had been animated by feelings of hostility to Germany . . . that the Colonial Office had suggested that Germany would do well to annex the mouths of the remaining rivers [in the Cameroons], the Lunyassi, the Kwa-Kwa, and others . . . *and that the Colonial Office had informed the [British] Foreign Office that it preferred Germany as a neighbor to France.*" †

Meade went even further, proposing as an added inducement for German collaboration at the Conference concessions in New Guinea, in the Pacific. Dr. Busch listened, hinted Bismarck was favorably impressed with this token of sincerity from the British. Thereupon, almost overnight, the Reich acquired the suggested concessions by the simple

---

* *Bismarck, Some Secret Pages of His History*, Dr. Moritz Busch, London 1898.
† *Life of Lord Granville*, vol. II.

process of annexation. It was dog eat dog. The discomfited Meade reported to Granville that "the German Government have behaved very shabbily by you . . . Dr. Busch has behaved equally ill by me."

The sessions were protracted by similar instances of diplomatic double-crossing. Besides courting Germany on the one hand, Sir Edward Malet and his aides for a time evidenced sympathy for Portugal, although Downing Street had denounced the Anglo-Portuguese treaty when the other nations protested vigorously (together with British chambers of commerce which feared for their Congo trade). But Britain's game, so far as Portugal was concerned, was to uphold the old claim of the Lisbon Government to the mouths of the Congo and the river itself as far upstream as Noki, to checkmate Leopold; or failing that, to use threat of such support to intimidate Brussels into agreement upon free navigation of the Congo.

His fortune invested in the African project, Leopold had had no intention of giving the nations unrestricted access to the Basin, via the great waterway, at least not without a struggle to obtain material concessions in return. But when Baron Lambermont and his delegates, complying with the King's instructions, refused to consider any diminution in territory, the other Powers began discussion in open of partitioning the Lower Congo amongst themselves. Airily they dismissed the fact that most of them only recently had explicitly recognized the sovereignty of Leopold's Association.

Leopold nearly had a stroke when he learned of this move from his alarmed delegates at Berlin. Lambermont was frightened. The King telegraphed him that if the Powers did not recognize his claim to the Congo outlet to the sea, "he would abandon his African project and take measures that no one else should ever profit by his past troubles and sacrifices"—thus Count Louis de Lichtervelde. This unmistakable threat of sabotage of his own investments meant unmistakably destruction of Stanley's infant railroad along the south bank, of trading station, hospitalization facilities, docks and piers—and the menace of antagonization of the blacks against all Europeans.

A heroic bluff—but effective. France foresaw the potential danger in a vindictive Leopold. Baron de Courcel retreated slightly. Meanwhile the Belgian delegates reminded the Conference that seven months before France had been granted by Leopold (more correctly, by the Association Internationale du Congo) the right of preëmption—a threat which to some degree checked the colonial appetite of Germany and Britain.

But somewhere along the line Leopold had to yield. He made concessions in the field of free trade as well as in territory. In favor of the French he surrendered the Niari-Kuilu stream, north of the Congo (which de Brazza had claimed by reason of the treaties with King Makoko); while de Courcel in return relinquished the French pretensions to territory on the south bank of the Congo, opposite Brazzaville, and agreed in secret to aid the Belgians in discouraging the Portuguese. Eventually Portugal, abandoned by both France and Britain, yielded many of her claims, some of which were certainly as legitimate as Leopold's in the Congo: Lisbon had indisputable evidence, for example, that Diogo Cam, a Portuguese, had discovered the mouths of the Congo in 1482—nearly four centuries before Stanley navigated its length. But she gained the south bank as far upstream as Noki; and in exchange she withdrew all claims to the north bank except for an awkward *enclave* at Kabinda, cherished particularly as the origin of an old and royal title.

Stanley, the Anglo-Belgian expert in American guise, was

disgusted with the concessions made by his employer. But it was not in his temperament to understand the exigencies of political skullduggery. Disgruntled with Lambermont, Banning and Strauch, none of whom, in his opinion, understood the geographical picture or the extent of the wealth in central Africa, he told them bluntly in Berlin that by his reckoning Leopold's Association had "yielded to France 60,366 square miles, and to Portugal 45,400 square miles." * For his part, he could not appreciate that in return Leopold had obtained the good-will of France and Portugal, and in addition had won nearly 600 miles of territory on the north bank of the Congo, between the Atlantic and Boma, to which the Association had no valid claim.

It may be noted in passing that Stanley's judgment of politicians and their motives was invariably ingenious. On November 24 he was invited to dine with Bismarck, who reacted on the explorer in much the same way that he had been affected six years before by Leopold.

"This evening I dined with Prince Bismarck. I am glad to have seen the grand man, but I am still more rejoiced to discover that the grandeur to which he has attained is due solely to his honesty, resolution and clear-eyed commonsense, unalloyed by any one grain of cant or false sentiment." † . . . It never occurred to him that Bismarck had his own reasons to prefer a weak power in central Africa.

Apart from the trade concessions and the regulations laid down for future occupation of Africa, which in great or less degree benefited all the nations attending the Conference, who were the chief victors? If Stanley had no political acumen, he did have geographical perception, and on February 23, 1885, three days before the close of the Congress, he noted in his diary:

* *The Belgian Congo and the Berlin Act*, A. B. Keith.
† *The Congo*, Henry M. Stanley, vol. II, London 1885.

"Two European Powers emerge out of the elaborate discussions protracted for such a long time, principally through the adroitness of Baron de Courcel and the concurrence of Prince Bismarck, with enormously increased colonial possessions.

"France is now mistress of a West African territory, noble in its dimensions, equal to the best tropic lands for its vegetable productions, rich in mineral resources most promising for its future commercial importance.

"In area it covers a superficies of 257,000 square miles, equal to that of France and England combined, with access on the eastern side to 5,200 miles of river navigation; on the west is a coastline nearly 800 miles long, washed by the Atlantic Ocean. . . . Portugal issues out of the Conference with a coastline 995 English miles in length, 35,500 square statute miles in extent, a territory larger than the combined areas of France, Belgium, Holland and Great Britain."

Characteristically Stanley neglects to mention the swag of his employer at Brussels.

However much envy and disgruntlement may be read into Stanley's account of what was won by France and Portugal, a considerably different view was held by Leopold when the Conference ended. He had risked much, and had bluffed unconscionably. "With what contraction of the heart," noted Count Lichtervelde, "he abandoned to his rivals the territory which today forms French Congo!" But to Baron Lambermont the King wrote gleefully, when the negotiations had ended, that:—

"Here we are in port. . . . Certainly we do not get all we would have wished, but at least the destiny of the new State is assured, and it has the wherewithal to live and prosper."

A precise conclusion. The Association had twenty-one

miles of coast north of the Congo, the "co-sovereignty" of the river's mouths (with Portugal), and the necessary space along the south bank to build a railroad to Stanley Pool. Altogether, Leopold's Congo covered 900,000 square miles —the lion's share.

ii

The cardinal achievement of the Berlin Conference was the settlement—in part at least—of a problem sufficient then, as now, to provoke a world war. Since 1885 the problem has become far more acute, with the increase of European populations, European nationalism, the frantic race for markets, and the continued abuse and exploitation of the African native by Europeans. Finally the modern-day problem has been made graver by the Allied confiscation at Versailles of the German colonies.

The Berlin Conference of a half century ago, in any event, led to the ratification of the so-called "General Act" which set forth:

1. Freedom of trade to all nations on the Congo and its watershed, defined as extending to the Niari, Ogowé, Shari and the Nile on the north, the eastern watershed line of the Tanganyika affluents on the west, and those of the Zambezi and the Loge on the south;
2. Differential duties on the Congo Basin were forbidden and "only such taxes to be levied on imports as represented fair compensation for expenditures in the interests of trade";
3. Monopoly grants were forbidden;
4. Equal rights guaranteed to all nations;
5. A Congo navigation treaty, with reference to pilot, lighthouse, beacon and buoy dues, to be collected and funds administered by an international commission;
6. Essentially the foregoing conditions were to apply to the

CONGRESS DANCES 99

Niger, but the regulations and their enforcement was entrusted to Britain and France instead of to international commission;

7. The territorial revisions forementioned, dealing principally with France, Belgium and Portugal;

8. An agreement that "occupation on the coast of Africa in order to be valid must be effective, and any new occupation on the coast must be formally notified to the signatory Powers for the purpose of enabling them, if need be, to make good any claim of their own." (Here for the first time in an international treaty appears that salient phrase "zones of influence," destined to become a notorious pretext for further robbery from the natives: northern and southern Ethiopia, for example, in the current Italian argument belong incontrovertibly to that European nation's "zone of influence.")

iii

The Berlin Act has thirty-eight articles. It is significant that all but two dealt with trade, navigation or questions of international law. Before the Conference adjourned it occurred at last to someone that there might reasonably be a place in such an Act—-apportioning Africa to the Europeans —for incidental mention of the Africans.

Accordingly in this "General Act of the Berlin Conference," a document nearly 60,000 words in length, a full 200 words were expended by the delegates upon the natives, and the undesirability of slavery and the slave-trade. The pertinent sentences in these two articles (VI and IX) read:

"All the Powers exercising sovereign rights, or having influence in the said territories, undertake to watch over the *preservation of the native races, and the amelioration of the moral and material conditions of their existence,* and to coöperate in the suppression of slavery, and above all of the slave trade; they will protect and encourage, without distinction of nationality or creed, all institutions and enterprises . . . tending to *educate the natives, and lead them to understand and appreciate the advantages of civilization.* . . . Liberty of conscience and religious toleration are expressly guaranteed to the natives.

"The Powers which exercise or will exercise rights of sovereignty or influence in the territories forming the Basin of the Congo declare that these territories should serve neither for the place of sale nor the way of transit for the traffic in slaves of any race whatsoever. Each of the Powers undertakes to employ every means that it can to put an end to this trade and to punish those who engage in it."

In the complete vacuity of these stipulations there could be no effective guarantees that the African would be protected against abuse and exploitation by the European nations, and it is evident that none was intended in 1885. The history of Africa since those pompous phrases were drafted has demonstrated that exploitation of the blacks was essential if Europeans were to make rapid headway in developing markets in Africa in which to dump surpluses.

As the delegates gathered finally to sign the Berlin Act, Bismarck foresaw one of the inevitable abuses from which the natives would suffer and die by the thousands—the conscription of Africans into Europe's colonial armies or constabularies. But the Chancellor affected to believe that the delegates had happily removed all danger of any such fate befalling the blacks.

"The particular conditions under which are placed the vast regions you have just opened up to commercial enterprise have seemed to require special guarantees for the preservation of peace and public order," he declared. "In fact, the scourge of war would become particularly disastrous if the *natives were led to take sides in the dispute between the civilized Powers.*"

Subsequently all the European nations in Africa recruited native forces, and tribes were pitted against tribes as annexation, occupation and "pacification" went forward.

The embarrassing question of the growing liquor traffic, which was in ample measure the backbone of enforced labor, i. e., the slavery imposed on the blacks by the European purveyors of civilization, was studiously avoided in the Act; it was not even to gain informal recognition as a major evil until the Brussels Conference of 1890, by which time much of the damage was done. For one thing, Germany would not have permitted tampering with a profitable trade in stimulants for the Africans.

Yet Stanley—the explorer who six years before had displayed so great an enthusiasm for the "charitable and philanthropic character" of Leopold's project—could have described in specific detail the increasing exploitation of the natives by way of the bottle. More than five years before, in March 1880, he had written Colonel Strauch from the Congo as follows;

"Many of the coast people take their pay largely in gin to retain when home at a profit. Bottles of gin or rum are marketable and serve as currency. . . . Though we may regret that gin is considered as currency, we cannot help it. We require native produce for food daily; without an assortment of currency we should be put to great shifts frequently.

"The gin and rum are also largely consumed as grog by our native workmen. We dilute both largely, and so reduce its spirit, but we are compelled to serve it out morning and evening. A stoppage of this would be followed by a cessation of work. It is 'custom,' custom is despotic, and we are too weak and too new in the country to rebel against custom. . . . It would be madness to try to stop a team of frightened horses by standing directly in the way. One must run alongside, if possible, and restrain the natives gradually." *

The inanity of the two brief articles dealing with slavery in the Berlin Act is finally manifest in the absence of any provisions for an international tribunal to rule in cases where natives complained of forced labor. That omission adduces more evidence that none doubted at Berlin that the bondage of the tribes was essential if "civilization" was to be brought to the jungle; and in the realistic view of the Conference, it mattered intrinsically very little whether this necessary bondage was attained by means of rum and gin, or by way of Tyrolese hats and jack-in-the-boxes.

iv

All the Powers except the United States and Turkey ratified the Berlin Act. Ambassador Kasson signed the document but it was never presented to the Senate where, the Cleveland Administration felt, members would certainly not vote adherence of the United States to a document primarily of concern only to Europe. Evidently Secretary Frelinghuysen felt, with good reason, that he had been duped by General Sanford, and been made a tool of Leopold's. For there was nothing in the Berlin Act which remotely suggested that Sanford had fought energetically in the German capital for "certain destruction of the slave-trade," which

* Mention has been made in preceeding pages of such European "currency" as cloth, wire, beads and spirits. Also of persuasive value in obtaining concessions from the natives, according to Stanley, were jack-in-the-boxes, Tyrolese hats, umbrellas, lackey-coats, cast-off military uniforms, red knitted-caps, straw-hats with gay ribbons, fezzes, dog-collars, fancy paper-boxes, mirrors, mugs, bottles and spectacles.

he had pledged to Secretary Frelinghuysen and to Senator Morgan. But although the United States would not ratify the Act, it is curious that the State Department on December 3, 1885, while the agreement was in gestation, sent William P. Tisdel to the Congo "to report upon the advantages to American trade." This was the gentleman, incidentally, who had reported Stanley as inebriated to Secretary Frelinghuysen. Under the terms of his appointment as special agent to the States of the Congo Association, Tisdel was "to investigate the conditions and to introduce and extend the commerce of the United States." *

If in the United States there were well-grounded suspicions that all the Berlin Conference signified was a division of the immediate and future profits in Africa, in the German capital there was glowing emphasis on the nobility of Leopold, the General Act, the aims of the Association Internationale du Congo, and the virtues of the horsetraders themselves. On the closing day of the Conference, each representative made a Rotarian address, tongue more or less in cheek. As President of the Conference, Bismarck referred to "the noble efforts of His Majesty the King of Belgians, founder of a work which has gained the recognition of almost all the powers, and which as it grows will render valuable service to the cause of humanity." (Not many years were to pass before the attacks upon Leopold as a slaveowner grew vitriolic.) Count de Launy of Italy continued the back-scratching in magnificent, rolling strophes.

"Prince Bismarck," he said, "has been prevented much against his inclination from presiding in person at all our sittings, but his mighty mind has hovered over the assembly. . . . Whatever may be reserved for our work in the future —it remains subject to the vicissitudes of all things human

* His dispatches may be found in U. S. Foreign Relations, 1885, pp. 282–315.

—we can at present, at least, bear witness that we have neglected nothing that was at all possible to open up into the interior of the African Continent a broad road for the moral and material progress of its native races."

The French delegate, Baron de Courcel, was not less rhapsodical and, as it was to develop, an equally poor prophet. The neighbors of the new State, he predicted, "will be the first to profit by the development of the prosperity in the Congo State, and by all the guarantees of order, security and good administration with which it undertakes to endow the center of Africa. . . . The State has been consecrated from its cradle to the practice of all liberties."

Sir Edward Malet, in the name of that nation which had lost some 900,000 square miles in Africa because it distrusted, or was skeptical of Stanley's claims, remarked with understandable irony that Queen Victoria's Government "salutes with the greatest cordiality the new-born State, and expresses a sincere desire to see it flourish under his [Leopold's] shield."

And there were other tributes in similar vein. . . .

v

The major sequel to the Berlin Conference was the emergence of Leopold's vaguely defined Congo holding as a constitutional State. Just before the close of the meeting, the King at Brussels asked a reluctant Parliament to permit him to "accept" the post of sovereign of the territories of the Association Internationale du Congo. The legislature voted the permission; it is one of the peculiarities of the Belgian Constitution that it makes provision for the accession of sovereignty by its king over other lands. There was far from unanimous support, however, since political leaders, and several of the King's personal advisers, believed this move susceptible of jeopardizing the prized neutrality of Belgium

—the danger of conflicts with the other powers in Africa was clearly foreseen. But the distinction was made by Leopold's supporters in Parliament that it was the King himself, and not Belgium, who was responsible in the event of war. (Not for twenty-three years did Belgium annex the Congo and then, in 1908, only with the consent of the European Powers.)

The authority voted, Leopold lost no time in scrapping the several titular "fronts" for his holding—the Comité d'Études, Association Internationale du Congo, *et cetera:* there was no further need for flowery *décor* after the Berlin Conference. In the German capital Colonel Strauch, president of the Association, and Leopold's minister plenipotentiary as well, made the gesture of renouncing the sovereignty of the Association in favor of the King. The successor to the Association was the État indépendant du Congo, misleadingly translated into English as the Congo Free State.*

On August 1, 1885, Leopold deemed it propitious to notify the Powers of the creation of the new State, delimited by the treaties of 1884–85 with Germany, France, Portugal and the United States. To this notification was added a proclamation that it was a neutral State under the Berlin Act—thus in some measure quieting fears at home of ultimate entanglement in war. Thus by a series of diplomatic and political coups, beginning with the Brussels Geographical Congress of 1876, the King became absolute monarch over 900,000 square miles in Africa, containing then unknown millions of inhabitants.† He was, noted A. B. Keith of the British Colonial Office, now "subject only to the re-

* Leopold's advisers dissuaded him from naming the State the Kingdom of Boma and of the Upper Congo, which had an autocratic complexion more to his liking.

† Estimated native Bantu population, 1934, 8,500,000; Europeans, 10,000, more than half of them Belgians.

straints imposed by his own conscience, public opinion and the positive but vague prescriptions of the Berlin Act." Be that as it may, it will be seen that the royal conscience was singularly dormant in later years when Leopold learned that rubber could be cultivated most profitably by inhuman exploitation of the natives.

In recent years the King's defenders have argued that Leopold was justified in asking—and requiring—a return upon his huge investment. It is true that the strain on the royal purse had been stupendous. From his own resources he had paid the costs of development, amounting by 1885 to more than ten million francs, and since 1883 he had expended more than two million francs yearly to establish the sovereignty of the Association (or more correctly, his own) over a population which, save for an infinitesimal group, had never heard of him, the Association, or much less the Berlin Act. If this typical investor's argument has weight, it is fair to examine it in the light of the King's declaration at the Geographical Congress when he loftily observed that "the subject of the Congo which brings us together concerns all the friends of humanity."

But however much the chameleon, Leopold had an unconscious gift for the farcical. If he was inhuman in the Congo, he was human enough in petty affairs of the purse. Because of the cost of Stanley's enterprise, he now deemed it necessary to reduce his outlays on Court functions. The monarch who could promote an immense empire—which he never saw—who dealt and thought in millions, marched into the kitchens of the Palace at Brussels where, by his own confession, "I suppressed the number of dishes at Our dinners." The savings on banished omelets and truffles went into the purchase of more gin and jack-in-the-boxes for the blackmen of the Free State.

VI

The British Chisel
[1885-90]

THE fact that the major Powers had agreed substantially to policies profiting them all in the Congo and Niger basins had averted immediate risks of war. But in addition to its geographical, juridical and economic results, the Berlin Conference had psychological results which can scarcely be over-emphasized. The partition of Africa, in other words, could now proceed under the tranquil conviction in London, Paris, Berlin and elsewhere that it was both a legal and a moral undertaking—if not a duty.

If there had been before 1885 the occasional sting of conscience among the European governments over the seizure of the natives' territories, or over corruption of the tribes by means of gin and gun-powder, any such compunctions were now dissipated. Had not the Powers at the German capital expressly agreed that the rights of the natives were to be respected and the slave-trade suppressed? Henceforth, until the exposure of the Congo scandals early the next century, the raids by the Powers at the expense of Africa were regarded by most European civilians in the light of humanitarian projects. They were organized to expose the unlettered African to the advantages of European civilization, to lead him from his state of moral darkness to the spiritual levels of Europe. In the public mind generally, each new encroachment was felt to be something of a missionary enterprise. . . . And if there were any trade benefits accruing incidentally to the several Governments concerned, or to private individuals and companies, they were certainly inconsequential compared to the advantages brought to Africa by the British, French, Germans, Belgians, Italians, Spaniards, Portuguese and, after 1925, by the Americans. (Yet in less than five years, by 1890, the abuse of the natives, and their degradation due to the liquor traffic were to reach such depths that the governments themselves were constrained to summon another conference to restrict a degree of exploitation that, it was feared, would lead to the expulsion by the blacks of all the Europeans.)

The Powers, then, were ready in 1885 to begin in earnest the confiscation of such territory as remained unoccupied in Africa, or which they could wrest from one another, and wherever possible to extend their respective "zones of influence." In the subsequent five-year period, the international scramble in Africa grew frenzied. There was no need for concern over the native's fate, for the morality of Europe's conduct in Africa had been explicitly recognized at the Berlin Conference. More to the point, and apart from such casuistry, the two paragraphs in the Berlin Act relating to the natives had no teeth. Nor need attention be paid to the stipulation that "occupation . . . in order to be valid must be effective"—a loose clause which could be left to individual interpretation.

It was devil-take-the-hindmost. The primary concern among the chancelleries was to extort subsidies or appropriations sufficient to underwrite the expedition to Africa of parties adequately large and well-armed. For the black man, given the taste of gin and occasionally the feel of a rifle (the use of fire-arms for "currency" had inevitably increased), was proving himself an utterly fearless antagonist, even when armed only with a spear.

THE BRITISH CHISEL 109

In Africa the five-year period saw the British expelled from the Sudan and their seizure of Bechuanaland and north Somaliland; the Italians invaded east Somaliland over which they proclaimed a protectorate, and extended their "zone of influence" into Ethiopia; Germany moved into east central Africa; France launched raids in the upper Niger; Belgium began the practical exploitation of the upper Congo; Portugal sought to extend her colony in east central Africa; and Spain sent warships at last to Rio de Oro, on the northwest coast, which she placed under her protection.

So much in summary of the physical changes in the map of Africa during the five years here considered. Let us now turn to Europe, for the province of this work lies in the main in the diplomatic and political aspects of the rape of Africa.

ii

By 1884 the British occupation of Egypt was complete. The next year the Salisbury Government became aware that the position of Britain in Egypt was not only anomalous, but militarily dangerous. The uneasiness in London resulted, on the initiative of Lord Randolph Churchill, in overtures to the Sultan for some arrangement whereby Turkey would assume the responsibility of maintaining order in Egypt, provided that if tranquillity and *revenue* were not maintained, a British army of occupation might return unopposed.

The proposal fell through because the French, distrusting Britain in matters pertaining to Egypt, intervened energetically at Constantinople and induced the Sultan to refuse to sign the agreement. There is good reason for believing the Russians supported the French. Nevertheless, the move had been shrewdly calculated in London: it had seemed certain to attract the Sultan, whose cherished authority over Egypt was even slighter than in the days of Ismail Pasha, while it would relieve the British of the expensive and dangerous task of maintaining an army in Egypt. But the French Government, bitter over its lost rôle of co-administrator in Egypt with the British, were determined to block a project that would have made Britain's position easier. Ironically, the French opposition in 1885 to British evacuation led ultimately to London's acquisition of the enormously rich Sudan.

Since 1882 the precarious situation of the British forces in Egypt had grown increasingly evident to army officers, to whose pleas for more troops London was indifferent and then hesitant. At home it was believed alike by Downing Street and the public, if not altogether by the conservative newspapers, that the costs of the Egyptian occupation in money and prestige had reached an excessive figure. Soon the Gladstone Government learned it would have to reckon also in human lives.

The reasons for the military and political nervousness of the British in Egypt are obvious. Early in 1883 Colonel William Hicks, of the Bombay army, went to Cairo, following the bombardment of Alexandria and the occupation of the country. To bolster the forces of the pliant Tewfik Pasha, the British officer was appointed chief-of-staff of the Sudan, over which Egypt had exercised an intermittent sovereignty since 1820. Nominally, Hicks had no army affiliations when he entered the employ of the Khedive, but his enlistment was patently suggested by the British commissioners. Under the threat of the Empire's forces in Cairo, and of her Majesty's warships lying off Alexandria, an army of between five and eight thousand fellahin were sent in chains to Omdurman, a camp on the Nile opposite Khartum; for the most part the conscripts were drawn from the forces which had followed Arabi Pasha in resisting the British the year before. Hicks was ordered, ostensibly by the timid Tewfik, to destroy the authority of one Mohamed Ahmed, a Dongolese who had proclaimed himself the long-awaited Mahdi, or guide, of Islam, who promised to deliver the country from the despised "Turks": to the Sudanese all Europeans were invidiously identified as "Turks." The British-dominated Cairo ministry minimized the strength of the Mahdi, then

British officer's sketch of elephant on Nile banks.

encamped at El Obeid, 200 miles southwest of Khartum, and scoffed at Hicks' report that his army of chained, unhappy slaves was the weakest force to send against the fanatical Mahdists. The Bombay colonel followed orders. On November 5, 1883, his force of 7,000 infantry and 1,000 cavalry was ambuscaded by the Mahdi thirty miles south of El Obeid. Three hundred of the army of 8,000 escaped with their lives. Colonel Hicks received a spear through the neck.

It is worthy of note that here Britain again risked nothing in men, except for the leader of the expedition, Colonel Hicks, who had with him fourteen Europeans. After the El Obeid battle, and despite the warning inherent in its outcome, European invaders of Africa henceforth adopted the practice of conscripting native armies to pursue conquest, stiffened by European officers.

Official and civilian, London awoke to the chilling realization at last that the British might be losing caste in the Sudan, as in Egypt proper; and the seed of suspicion was planted that the African, Sudanese or Zulu, might conceivably resent conquest and—more alarming because more incredible—had also the courage and the numerical strength to resist invasion. British newspapers refused to publish first reports of the El Obeid massacre, although as early as November 13 the annihilation of Hicks' force was known to Paris and Berlin editors. The reluctance of Fleet Street to believe the news was characteristic of the entire nation. On the 14th, nine days after the rout, *The Times* reassured its readers: "It is announced today from the Sudan that *a very powerful native insurgent tribe, occupying a district near El Obeid, had made its submission to the governor of Khartum* [Hicks]." On the 17th, the same newspaper once again decried the detailed reports in the Paris press. Finally, on November 20, *The Times* conceded the loss of "eleven officers and 142 privates." And at last, on the 23rd, cables reaching Fleet Street from Cairo were so explicit that editors had to publish the destruction of Hicks' force in the Sudan as the truth, however inconceivable.

Thus *The Times*, stunned, aghast and realistic:

"No one at all familiar with Oriental character and with the modern phases of the Mohammedan faith can doubt that the blow which has fallen at El Obeid will give a shock to the authority of England throughout the East."

That Conservative organ and the provincial press demanded retribution, and charged that British garrisons in the Sudan were being deserted. Downing Street hurriedly denied any responsibility for the massacre: Granville told Fleet Street laconically that Hicks was merely a soldier of

From "Europe in Africa in the Nineteenth Century."

THE MAHDI

fortune (he had retired in 1880).* But the Gladstone ministry began to realize that Britain was so deeply involved in Egypt and the Sudan that evacuation of her troops was untenable. And inevitably, after the massacre of Hicks' force, the omnipotent bondholders cracked down on London.

The immediate sequel to the Sudan defeat of 1883 was another tragedy, even more shattering to British pride and prestige. The cabinet dispatched General Charles George Gordon to the Sudan where he had served three years as governor-general in the name of Ismail Pasha; he was to gather a native army, if necessary, to effect the withdrawal of Egyptian troops in the Khartum and other Sudan garrisons. Meanwhile, the British commissioners at Cairo were instructed by London to order the Egyptian Government to abandon the Sudan, at least south of Wady Halfa. It was too heavy a drain upon the country's finances on which the money-lenders of Europe had first claim.

Before Gordon arrived, General Valentine Baker, in December of 1883, made an attempt to relieve Sinkat and Tokar, in the northeastern Sudan along the Red Sea littoral. (The Mahdi's numerous victories had won him 200,000 rifles, nineteen cannon, and large stores of ammunition.) With 3,715 men, gendarmerie, Sudanese, blacks and Turks, Baker started toward Tokar. A small body of tribesmen ambushed the column at El Teb. Baker lost 2,375 men killed, including eleven European officers. How he escaped remains a mystery.

Sir Herbert Stewart in January 1885, attempting to rescue Gordon besieged at Khartum, met Hicks' fate. The British and French consuls at Khartum, fleeing the town, were also killed, after a manner which makes unpleasant

* *The Times* pointed out that whatever the stand of the Government, Egyptians would consider Hicks' expedition a British project, since led and officered by Englishmen.

Death of Gordon's Body Servant at Khartum.

reading. The heroic story of Gordon and the siege of Khartum needs no retelling. When the Arabs and dervishes, followers of the False Prophet, poured into the town they made short work of the British general who "met them at the top of the stairs. As he stood facing them, a Dervish plunged his spear into his breast." *

To make doubly sure the Unbeliever would fight no more, his head was severed. The date was January 26, 1885. Vic-

* *Gordon and the Sudan*, B. M. Allen, London, 1931.

toria, incredulous with the rest of England, found an outlet for her shock in an infuriated telegram to Gladstone wherein she remarked that "it is too fearful to consider that the fall of Khartum might have been prevented and many precious lives saved by earlier action."

iii

The Sudan was lost to the Khedive, which is to say it was lost to Britain, but whatever the discomfort of the Gladstone ministry, the British troops—chiefly from India with field-batteries from New South Wales and from Sussex—could not be withdrawn from Egypt. To do so was a political and military impracticality. There was still "an army locked up in Africa," Lord Derby reminded Granville. The Sudan was ablaze, and the fires of revolt might spread northward. It was incumbent upon the British commissioners to stabilize the Cairo Government, and to find fresh sources of revenue to compensate for the loss of the Sudan taxes. The public indebtedness was mounting, and jittery bondholders in Europe again sent emissaries to Cairo. They found consolation in the fact that the loss of the Sudan, if it deprived the Khedive of taxes, meant an end to the annual deficit of £200,000 it had cost the Egyptian treasury.

The financial hegemony of Britain at Cairo, and behind her of the Continental bondholders, was completed by an ingenuous loan project devised after Lord Northbrook, first Lord of the Admiralty, visited Egypt late in 1884 to inquire into its finances. His appointment to that mission, which proved a grotesque failure from the bankers' viewpoint, followed a conference earlier in the year, to attend which Sir Evelyn Baring, British agent and consul-general in Egypt, had hurried to England from Cairo. It is worth noting that as the Sudan problem became acute, the first concern of the

Powers was to summon a conference to consider Egyptian finances; and it is relevant to recall that Baring, later Lord Cromer and a cousin of Lord Northbrook, belonged to the family of London bankers, and during 1877–79 had served as British commissioner of the Egyptian public-debt office.

The conference ended in disagreement with the French, who stuck by a thesis that they should have effective financial representation in Egypt, as they had had during the Dual Control; similarly there was a disagreement among the German, Austro-Hungarian, Italian, Russian and Turkish representatives.* The upshot was that the cabinet sent Lord Northbrook to Cairo "to report and advise Her Majesty's Government, touching counsel which it may be fitting to offer the Egyptian Government in the present situation of affairs in Egypt." The special commissioner's particular attention was directed to the "present exigencies of Egyptian finance." The phrase is Victoria's.

"A bad day for me," the Admiralty Lord noted prophetically in his journal. But *The Times* was sanguine in generous, imperial vein, and saw an "excellent omen [in] the spectacle of the two Barings, the Dioscuri of the East, repairing together to the distracted land of the Pharaohs."

The clamorous voice of the Continental bankers could be heard in the Queen's exquisite reference to the "present exigencies of Egyptian finance"; it was in such restrained language that Northbrook's colleagues reminded him that, while the military situation was troublesome and dangerous, it was imperative to liquidate the financial tangle. If ever there was a thankless diplomatic task, Northbrook was given it. He was expected (1) to devise new sources of revenue in Egypt, (2) to guarantee the continuance of cur-

---

* For unadulterated acrimony couched in droll urbanities, see the account of the proceedings in *Great Britain, Sessional Papers, 1884,* vol. 89.

rent income, without the Sudan, (3) to satisfy the European bankers and their bondholders, (4) not to offend either the prerogatives of the British and French governments, (5) conciliate the Cairo Government, weary of British meddling, and (6), if practical, give a thought to the overburdened, triple-taxed and wretched fellahin.

In justice to Baring, whatever the weight of financial associations in Threadneedle Street, he had concluded from his connection with and administration of Egyptian finances that lightening of the burden of the fellahin was prerequisite of the collection of the usurious interest on the bonds. It was the realistic view of the money-lender who recognizes that the debtor must be kept afloat if he is ever to repay capital and interest. Northbrook, however, was clearly instructed to collect—"not to impede the normal and progressive development of her [Egypt's] financial prosperity," but also not to "curtail the rights of the creditors to their profit."

Evidently the logic of Baring's argument won over Lord Northbrook. He complied with the Ministry's recommendation, more correctly a desperate request, and permitted the diversion into the empty Treasury of revenues which since 1880 had been earmarked for the Caisse de la Dette, or sinking-fund, for the benefit of the bondholders. Without the emergency use of these funds, both Northbrook and Baring were aware, the Egyptian Government would collapse, and financial chaos ensue. All departments were literally starving, and the salaries of even petty officials and clerks were months in arrears. In defense of his move, Lord Northbrook wrote that his drastic step "was necessary to preserve the existence of Egypt" and to prevent the "collapse of the administration which must have followed if the army and officials had not been paid." *

* *Thomas George, Earl of Northbrook, A Memoir,* Bernard Mallet, London, 1908.

Howls of financial anguish immediately filled the air of Europe from St. Petersburg to London. The reverberations even reached Northbrook, writing his report in the deckhouse of *H.M.S. Iris,* enroute to Marseilles. The wily Gladstone was annoyed, and wrote to Granville that the Admiralty Lord "like Gordon went out to do one thing, and did another." (In the view of the Gladstone ministry, Gordon had been sent to the Sudan to effect the withdrawal of the British and Egyptian forces, but instead had elected to stay at Khartum; similarly, Gladstone reasoned, Northbrook had been dispatched to Cairo to collect, but instead had destroyed the creditors' sinking-fund.) What particularly upset the digestion of the prime minister, soon to be defeated, was Northbrook's proposal that the Egyptian revenue be made the security for a loan of £8,500,000—to be guaranteed by Britain. Particularly fulminatory was France, which saw the coming of permanent single control of Egypt by Britain. The Mixed Tribunals enjoined the diversion. Inevitably, another conference was summoned to survey the incipient wreckage. The result of that conference and negotiations in Europe was far-fetching. It gave birth in March 1885 to an extraordinary document, the effect of which was forever to solder Egypt to Britain. This was the London Convention, a document characteristic in spirit and purpose of the current attitude of Europe to Africa, and one which even the financier Baring described as "a triumph of financial cumbersomeness and ineptitude." *

Nevertheless, effective.

The seven Powers floated and guaranteed a loan to Cairo of £9,000,000, in return for which Egypt was bound:

1. To repay, with interest, £315,000 yearly;
2. To pay immediately indemnity for the burning of Alexandria (which had been provoked by the British bom-

* *Modern Egypt*, Lord Cromer, vol. II, London, 1908.

bardment and for which Admiral Seymour won an earldom);

3. Immediate payment of the deficits on the bonded indebtedness (i. e., the bondholders' interest) of the years 1882 and 1883.

The balance remaining to the Egyptian treasury of the £9,000,000, after these conditions had been met, was £1,000,000. The case is typical. The London Convention stipulated finally that if Egypt could not "pay her way" at the end of two years—that is, if the fellahin broke down—another international commission would move into Cairo. In any event, the British financial control and British troops remained. London consented to the provision for an international commission—to buy off French hostility. In a mood either of self-righteousness or virtuousness, or more plausibly, unconscious irony, Baring charged in his memoirs that "the French, supported by some other Continental Powers . . . looked almost exclusively to the interests of the bondholders."

To avert the danger of active intervention in Egypt by the other Powers, inherent in the London Convention, the British set to work energetically to make certain that Egypt in two years could "pay her way." At last Downing Street realized what had long been evident to Englishmen on the ground in northeastern Africa: that the potential wealth of the land of the Pharaohs was enormous—as the cotton development later was to demonstrate—and the strategic value of the country incalculable, as it could be made to command the southeastern corner of the Mediterranean, the two approaches to the Suez Canal, and thence the Red Sea route to India and beyond. Every political and economic consideration demanded that Britain remain top-dog in Egypt; any ethical consideration of what right England had at all in the country, or for that matter anywhere else in Africa, was of course irrelevant, and in the middle-class mind at home a thought both disloyal and impertinent. With the revealing directness characteristic of the best of his documents, Granville countered the renewed discontent of the Egyptians with the observation that "it should be made clear to the Egyptian ministers and governors of the provinces that the responsibility which for the time rests on England obliges Her Majesty's Government to insist on the adoption of the policy which they recommend; *and that it will be necessary that those ministers and governors who do not follow this course should cease to hold office.*"

No more accurate and honest summation of British policy in Egypt, with its underlying contempt for the fundamental rights of another people, has been made to this day.

A program of drastic economic reforms was launched immediately. The £1,000,000 remaining of the loan guaranteed by the Powers was expended on improvement in irrigation, a measure which in remarkably short time created sufficient revenue to "obviate the catastrophe of internationalism"—thus a British commentator whose faith in Egypt's need of British, or any other relatively juvenile, civilization is so unaffected and sincere as to provoke rollicking laughter. Sir Evelyn Wood, created "Sirdar of the Egyptian Army," conscripted a new military force from the stricken remnants of Arabi Pasha's veterans, permitting the withdrawal of a few British troops as an empty but conciliatory gesture to the Khedive; Sir Colin Scott-Moncrieff lightened the burdens of the *corvée*, which may be translated euphemistically as statute-labor, but is slavery in practical fact, and initiated the irrigation and other public works which proved fertile; Sir Edgar Vincent, the financial adviser foisted upon an impotent and helpless Cairo ministry, countermanded any farthing of expenditure of Egyptian funds on which he could not foresee realization of tomor-

THE BRITISH CHISEL

row's profit, and in so doing was following precise instructions from London.

By 1890 the lot of the fellahin had unquestionably improved. In the face of much vehement literature and "eyewitness" narratives to the contrary, and censure which came mainly from Englishmen themselves, a reasonably conscientious examination of credible accounts, records, and British and Egyptian documents, pro and con, of the results of the British administration in 1885–90 leads to the conclusion that the Egyptian peasant was better off materially than the decade before. But the argument that such improvement

Falls of the Nile.

extenuates or mitigates colonial invasion is specious from so many angles that there is no need to dwell upon it, except perhaps to refer again to the danger imminent today of a revolt of 140 black millions against a handful of Europeans not exclusively armed with weapons of wholesale death.

British administration in the five years wrought an improvement in sanitation, education and prisons, and eventually it allowed the partial suppression of forced labor, except for the seasonal conscription of natives to bolster the Nile banks during the annual floods. A budget surplus appeared in 1887. In Europe bondholders had less cause for hysteria.

iv

In the same five-year period there were three further penetrations by the British into Africa.

One was the introduction of the civilization of Shakespeare and Keats into Bechuanaland, today delimited as a region of 275,000 square miles directly north of Cape Colony, west of the Transvaal in central South Africa. The inroads northward and northeastward of the Cape administrators in the seventies, extending their "zone of influence," have already been remarked. In 1884 the dispossessed Boers proclaimed a protectorate over the country, establishing the republics of Goshen and Stellaland. In London this was regarded, as juridically it was, a violation of the London (Transvaal) Convention of 1884, which had held the Boers down to a slice of eastern Bechuanaland; but not without practical reasoning, the Transvaal President, Paul Kruger, declared the treaty infraction "a breach made in the interests of humanity." In the face of the protracted British disregard of the rights of the Boers, who in their occupation of South Africa at least had the right of priority, the breach was scarcely a valid pretext for the indignation and the expres-

THE BRITISH CHISEL

sions of self-righteousness it aroused in press and Parliament in London. Cecil Rhodes, then opposition leader in the Cape Colony Parliament, charged the Boers were supported by Germany, colonizing farther to the east, which no credible records deny. He found support both at Capetown and London for his opinion that "we must acquire the whole of the [Bechuanaland] interior." A powerful supporter was Sir Hercules Robinson, British High Commissioner, and the net result politically and militarily was that Sir Charles Warren was ordered by Whitehall to "liquidate" the errant republics. A bow is due this officer, in the light of previous and subsequent British campaigns in Africa, since he followed orders from London with slight casualties to the Bechuana the Boers had enlisted, and none to his own men. In September 1885 Bechuanaland, south of the Molopo river, was proclaimed a British protectorate (and a decade later inevitably annexed to Cape Colony).

The direction of the British swath of empire in Africa could now be foreseen by the dullest school-boy. "Colonial exigencies," "the Empire's necessaries," and "imperial trade outlets" were *clichés* of the five years and afterward. Nothing less than a clear path to Capetown from Cairo would satisfy civilian opinion in England, or the official minds of Downing Street and Whitehall that British pride and authority throughout the 5,000-mile length of Africa could be preserved. . . . Eventually, nothing else did. The Versailles Treaty, it will be seen, at last realized the imperial dream and set the stage, with France's latitudinal expansion in Africa, for tomorrow's Armageddon.

Shortly before Warren led a column north, the Rev. John Mackenzie, a missionary, was sent by the Cape Colony to effect a compromise. He was recalled in July 1884 because Rhodes and Robinson considered him pro-Bechuana, since he reported to the latter that "I consider that immediate annexation [of Bechuanaland] to the Cape Colony, introducing the reign of stiff law and procedure, utterly foreign to the ways of this people, would practically put the Bechuana . . . in the hands of a few sharp agents. . . . So far as I have mastered the question of the settlement of the country, immediate annexation of the country would be an evil to all parties." *

There followed the sale "down the river" of rebel Bechuana men, women and children, captured without resistance for lack of knowledge how and when or where to resist, for five-year terms as "farm servants indentured," at a Capetown square known as the Slave Mart. Montsion, chief of the Barolong near Mafeking in 1886, complained futilely to Cape Colony legislatures that the whites were obtaining a customary domination over the natives by the practice of distributing spirits. "The white people are selling brandy to the natives." †

A second penetration, to prove of vast strategic importance, was into Abyssinia, land of the Somali flanking the Red Sea and the Gulf of Aden, developed eventually into a British protectorate approximately the size of Missouri or Florida. Although man was indisputably extant in that region of Africa during the Stone Age, and dressed stones evidence a high degree of civilization, the missionaries and the Government were persuaded that the natives had crying need of British culture. Because the British East India Company required "harbor of their ships without any pro-

* *Austral Africa; Losing It or Ruling It,* John Mackenzie, vol. I, London 1887.

† Parliamentary Papers, C.—7932, p. 3. A detailed and documentary report of the results of the occupation and protectorate is found in an extraordinary pamphlet, *The Bechuana Troubles: A Story of Pledge-Breaking, Rebel-Making and Slave-Making in a British Colony,* H. R. Fox Bourne, London 1898.

THE BRITISH CHISEL

hibition whatever," its agents made private treaties with the Arab governor of Zeila early in the last century. When the Mahdi expelled the Egyptians and the British from the Sudan interior, and the control of the Khedive ended in 1884, warships appeared off the west littoral to protect sun-baked Suez. The inescapable protectorate was declared the next year over all the coast from Ghubbet Kharab to Ras Galwein; three years later, to keep French fingers out of Egypt, Britain ceded a part of the protectorate to France, including the Djibouti region. Administration of the protectorate was entrusted to the India Office for manifest reasons.

In geographical extent, Britain's Somali theft was minor, compared to her past annexations in south and in north Africa, or her subsequent appropriations in the east center of the continent. Treaties were negotiated with coastal tribes that, for intrinsic value of goods received, were less barefaced swindles than most of the documentary frauds which Europeans perpetrated in Africa: the customary technique in the acquisition of territory, devised in its most effable form by Stanley, was to promise a gallon of gin or rum if a chief could or would first execute an "X" for his particular region or kingdom. The protectorate has proved costly to Britain in lives and money, but British Somaliland then was thought to have a strategic value. Italian nervousness since the autumn of 1935 over a naval war with Britain has proved certainly its psychological value to Downing Street. . . . For the rest, the Somaliland Protectorate is interesting only for the incursions of that fearsome Arab, another Mahdi notorious in history as the "Mad Mullah," who combated British intervention for twenty years; at last, in 1920, he learned appeals to Allah were ineffective against the Royal Air Force.

The last British incursion of the period was a characteristic foray by Stanley, in reward for which he won back his citizenship and, for good measure, a knighthood. Stanley had energy, skill as an explorer and, if not an ounce of moral courage, that physical indifference to danger which is heroism to most of us. When newspaper-readers in England grew excited over the fate of Emin Pasha in Africa, a cry arose for Stanley, now a tired, run-down gentleman of forty-six. He interrupted a lecture tour in the United States —"my agent was in despair—the audiences were so kind— the receptions were ovations, but arguments and entreaties were [to me] of no avail." *

Stanley rushed back, and with Sir William Mackinnon in London raised a relief fund of £21,500. The chairman of the British India Steam Navigation Company, later the British East Africa Company, asked Stanley to combine Emin Pasha's rescue with a negotiation of treaties in the eastern lake regions. The ultimate negotiation of treaties by a man twenty years grayer in hair and wearier in body than his years should reveal, and profoundly sick of Africa, was the nucleus of the present-day Kenya Colony and Protectorate.

Stanley was still under contract to Leopold. But with the dexterity that was his genius he sailed from England in January 1887 in the employ of the King of the Belgians, Mackinnon's steamship company, the London *Daily News*, the "Emin Pasha Relief Expedition," and the Khedive of Egypt. The reason for the last association was that Emin Pasha, a German doctor named Eduard Schnitzer, was the poor Tewfik's governor of the Equatorial (lower Sudan) Province of Egypt. The Mahdi's victories had isolated him, as they had Gordon.

The terrible story of Stanley's expedition to save Schnitzer is told fulsomely in the account of the rescuer—a moving,

* *In Darkest Africa*, Stanley, vol. I, London 1890.

THE BRITISH CHISEL

detailed and horrible account. No one can tell it more tiresomely and yet more dramatically than Stanley.*

When Stanley returned to Zanzibar in 1889 with 246 alive of his party of 646, not including the dead and starved on the way, he had made thirty treaties in Britain's favor, which were subsequently given to Mackinnon's British East Africa Company. But in the five years Britain had far from preëmpted all that remained to be seized.

* Stanley's rescue of Schnitzer produced another of those dreadful pomposities between Europeans meeting in the African jungle. In his diary Stanley relates, under date of April 29, 1888, on the hostile shores of Albert Nyanza: "[A] rather small, slight figure, wearing glasses, arrested my attention by saying in excellent English, 'I owe you a thousand thanks, Mr. Stanley; I really do not know how to express my thanks to you.' 'Ah [Stanley declares he replied], you are Emin Pasha. Do not mention thanks, sir.'"

VII

–And Other Scalpels
[1885–90]

THE Italians were quick to follow the British raid into the "horn" of Africa, yet Rome did not move in time to seize a Somaliland territory as valuable strategically, a fact which General Rodolfo Graziani recognized with military embarrassment in the advance late last year on Addis Ababa from the southeast. Nevertheless if the Crispi ministry was slow to act, it moved in time to forestall British occupation to the east and south along the coast.

In 1885 Rome launched a colonial project which eventually led to the appalling defeat the next decade at the hands of Menelik II of Abyssinia (Ethiopia), but which also brought her, by means of occupation, concessions from Britain and France, and by lease, a Somaliland colony and protectorate of 194,000 square miles, or nearly one-third more than the extent of Italy proper.

In April of that year, after the Italians had followed the British example by occupying Massawa, the port of Eritrea on the Red Sea, Rome hoped to extend its holdings southward along the coast, to connect Eritrea with the projected Somaliland colony. Unfortunately for Italian colonial designs on East Africa, the British in the north and central lands of the Somalis blocked the way; and it has been noted previously that the French, in 1883, had declared that the extreme north, the coastal region lying immediately between the Red Sea and the Gulf of Aden, was theirs by virtue of a set of treaties (Djibouti was established in 1887). Seemingly to Rome, all that might be seized or occupied of Somaliland was that relatively barren and inhospitable territory south of the British: the problem of connecting Eritrea and the proposed new colony might be solved ultimately by hacking a corridor through eastern Ethiopia (a plan since elaborated to include the complete annexation of the empire of Haile Selassie).

Apart from Italy's desire for colonial expansion as an avenue to new markets and outlets for her population, an economic and social doctrine of imperialism she shared with six nations of Europe, Rome's determination to make room for herself in east Africa sprang in part from distrust and dislike of the French. The Italian Foreign Office had not forgotten the French grab of Tunisia in 1881. It saw France the major beneficiary at the Berlin Conference, from which Count Luigi Corti and Count de Launy had returned empty-handed, so far at least as territory was concerned; and Signor Depretis, the foreign minister, suspected that the Paris Government was extending secret support to Menelik. (That the suspicion was well-founded was evidenced eleven years later when it was disclosed that the Ethiopians had routed the Italians at Adowa and elsewhere with the aid of French arms and ammunition.)

One of the five warships employed in the Red Sea expedition resulting in the seizure of Massawa, the *Barbarigo*, was dispatched to Zanzibar in April 1885. Five years later, incidentally, the French and Germans were forced reluctantly to recognize a British protectorate over that island. Captain Antonio Cecchi, in command, was instructed to open negotiations with Bargash ibn Said, Sultan of Zanzibar.* Bar-

* Cecchi, an explorer, was the leader of Italy's abortive expedition to Zeila in 1877.

gash's sultanate extended northward as far as some of the ports of Somaliland, at least 250 miles from the island. The British, German and Portuguese consuls were dickering similarly with the Sultan. Cecchi succeeded only in obtaining commercial concessions, for he could not pay the tribute offered by the London and Berlin representatives, or demanded by Bargash. By 1889, however, Bargash's successor had come to terms with the Italians, and had placed the remainder of his dominion along the Indian Ocean, in Somaliland, under the protection of Rome. On November 19 the same year, in accordance with the farcical procedure laid down in the Berlin Act, Italy notified the Powers that "occupation is effective"; and substantially the present-day areas of British and Italian Somaliland were agreed to in a succession of treaties signed at Rome and London.* The Sultan in 1905 was to relinquish much of his northern coastal territory, extending ten miles inland and as far up the coast as Mogadiscu (where during the period June–November 1935 Italian troops were disembarked for the southeastern front in the present conflict) for payment of £144,000. Italian travelers and commercial agents in the protectorate were murdered frequently by the protesting natives in 1885–86, but a terrible wholesale slaughter occurred at Dogali in 1887—nine years before the annihilation of the Italians at Adowa. . . . Whatever the reason, Italy has found the black man a singularly tough and scornful foe.

Italian regular troops had their first major encounter with the Somali-Ethiopian warrior early in the year, and the few who survived acquired an abiding respect for his courage and prowess as a fighting-machine. Military campaigns

* The treaties may be found in detail in a British Foreign Office pamphlet, *Italian Somaliland*, Historical Section, No. 128, H. M. Stationery Office, London 1920.

in Africa do not fall within the immediate province of this political history, except where they directly concern events in Europe. But because this encounter caused the defeat of the Depretis cabinet, and also because of the Italian-Ethiopian conflict today, the reader may be interested in a passing note on the battle of Dogali.

The Italian encroachments along the Red Sea (Eritrea) and southern Somaliland alarmed the negus John, ruler of northern Ethiopia. His chief in Tigre province, Ras Alula, seized as hostages members of Count Salimbeni's "scientific" expedition to Massawa, which was in fact a filibustering expedition pure and simple. General Carlo Gené, Italian commander in East Africa, ordered a column sent to seize Saati, west of Massawa. This acomplished, the force, led by Colonel De Christoforis, pushed farther westward. Near the village of Dogali, De Christoforis was surprised by Alula (January 24). The force of 524 officers and men lost their heads, jammed their machine-guns and fled in panic. One trooper escaped unwounded. A total of 407 men and twenty-three officers were killed, and ninety-two men and one officer wounded. As an object lesson, Alula cut the ears and noses from most of the dead and wounded. . . .* The Depretis ministry fell in a howl of fury and frustrated pride,

* Alula retired to Asmara (now Italian) with a Major Piano among his prisoners. Later the officer was set at liberty to carry back a message from the Ras to General Gené. The message, written apparently in justification for the mutilation of the Italian casualties and also as a warning, is worth reproducing: "What has happened was caused by your tricks. Let us be friends as in the past. *Remain in your own country!* All the region between Massawa and here belongs to the Negus [John]." This reasonable argument was amplified by the Negus himself who wrote (Jan. 26) that "in the first place you took Wuaa [Massawa] and now you have come to Saati to erect a fortress. What object have you? Is not this country mine? Evacuate my country if you have come by orders. You bring what is abundant with you—cannon, muskets and soldiers."

and the way was paved for the historic premiership of Crispi. Despite the plain warning given Italy at Dogali, evident to her military experts, the Chamber of Deputies immediately appropriated 500,000 lire for reinforcements in East Africa, but with the cautious stipulation that there was not to be penetration beyond regions "adjacent to the occupied posts." For the next ten years Italians along the southern littoral of the Red Sea committed a long succession of native murders; the tribes responded in kind and, on festive occasions, with a cruelty surpassing in ingenuity even that of the Italian administrators.

At last, in 1889, a treaty was concluded with Menelik, ruling in the south, which included an extraordinary article (XVII) under which that Negus "consents to make use of the Government of His Majesty the King of Italy in treating of all matters that may arise with other Powers or Governments." When the King of Kings realized that this meant that he was giving over to Rome the conduct of his foreign relations, if not actually placing Ethiopia under Italian domination, Menelik denounced the treaty (1893).*

ii

After establishing herself on the West Coast, Germany's interest shifted to the east. As early as the sixties the nation was represented on that side of the continent by explorers and missionaries; between 1860 and 1865 a Hanoverian baron, von der Decken, explored the mainland domain of the Sultan of Zanzibar, and had told scientific societies at home that here was a profitable sphere for

* In his formal note to the Powers, denouncing the treaty, Menelik wrote, with appreciation at last of the significance of the instrument, that "under the cloak of friendship they [Italy] are seeking to divide up my country. I do not wish to strike at our relations with Italy, but my empire has sufficient importance not to require a protectorate and to exist independently."

German colonial expansion. Thenceforth Hamburg merchants established a flourishing trade with Zanzibar proper and with the mainland settlements, and it is revealing that the German consul at Zanzibar was always a Hamburg citizen, whose association with the Woermann shipping interests and other German export houses, as well as with members of the German Colonial Society, was intimate.

Like many another colony on the continent, German East Africa was established in part by a ruse played on the other Powers—trickery of the natives was regarded as necessary, if not desirable, if the black man was to be civilized. The origin of German East Africa may be told briefly:

In November 1884 three Germans arrived at Zanzibar from Hamburg, from where they had sailed as steerage passengers and, of course, without any official standing. They were Count Joachim Pheil, Dr. Karl Peters, a former instructor in philosophy, and a Captain Hermann von Wissmann, all traveling under false names. The British consul at Zanzibar, Sir John Kirk, smelled a rat, and asked his German colleague, Dr. Gerhard Rohlfs, to explain the real purpose of the visit: Peters, in particular, was well known as an explorer, geographer and advocate of German colonial expansion, and in his youth had studied "English principles of colonization" at London. The German consul, however, disclaimed hastily any belief that the trio was anything more than it pretended to be, and in the phrase of Sir Harry Johnston the Germans were "officially discountenanced by the [German] consul." . . . The British representative could not know that as early as 1875 Vice-Admiral Livonius of the German Navy had urged upon Bismarck, in a long report, the annexation of Zanzibar and the establishment of a German protectorate in East Africa. (Bismarck suppressed its publication, fearing diplomatic complications with Britain.) In any event, the German party disappeared into the mainland interior, to all intents and purposes to study flora and fauna.

Two weeks later Peters had negotiated treaties at Nguru, Usagara, Ukami and with the chiefs of adjacent regions in the interior, giving him concessions to a territory of 60,000 square miles, particularly rich in coal. The German flag was raised in East Africa. With a rather surprising degree of self-righteousness, Evans Lewin (former librarian of the Royal Colonial Institute) and other British writers charged that the chieftains in the Tanganyika region had no comprehension of the documents they signed at Dr. Peters' urging. This was doubtless true, but it was no truer of German agents than of British or French or Belgian. However that may be, one of the several treaties obtained by Dr. Peters may be reproduced here, for it is typical of many such instruments negotiated by Europeans in Africa—typical of the almost invariable fact that, save for rum, gin or possibly a Tyrolese chapeau, the native received nothing.

"Mangungo, Sultan of Msovero in Usagara, and Dr. Karl Peters, Sultan Mangungo simultaneously for all his people, and Dr. Peters for all his present and future associates, hereby conclude a Treaty of eternal friendship.

"Mangungo offers all his territory with all its civil and public appurtenances, to Dr. Karl Peters, as the representative of the Society for German Colonization [subsequently the German East African Company], for the exclusive and universal utilization of German colonization.

"Dr. Karl Peters, in the name of the Society for German Colonization, *declares his willingness to take over the territory of the Sultan Mangungo with all rights for German colonization, subject to any existing suzerainty rights (Oberhoheitsrechte*) of Mwenyi Sagara.

"In pursuance thereof, Sultan Mangungo hereby cedes

all the territory of Msoveri, belonging to him by inheritance or otherwise, for all time, to Dr. Karl Peters, *making over to him at the same time all rights.* Dr. Karl Peters, in the name of the Society for German Colonization, undertakes to give special attention to Msovero when colonizing Usagara.

"This Treaty has been communicated to the Sultan Mangungo by the Interpreter Ramazan in a clear manner, and has been signed by both sides with the observation of the formalities valid in Usagara, the Sultan on direct inquiry having declared that he was not in any way dependent upon the Sultan of Zanzibar, and that he did not even know of the existence of the latter.

"(Signed) Dr. Karl Peters
"Signature of Mangungo" *

In February 1885, back in Berlin, Peters made over his concessions to the German East Africa Company. The same month the ninety-year-old emperor William I proclaimed the extension of his "protection" over the territories seized by Peters, whom Emil Ludwig rather generously calls the founder of the German colonial empire.

Peters thereupon proposed to Bismarck that the German East Africa Company should also acquire southwestern Madagascar and the Comoro Islands, lying between the former and the mainland. Bismarck, never enthusiastic over the colonial program, said "that is the French sphere of interests, and I must not meddle with it."

Peters reasoned that "as the French had not fought for the recovery of Metz and Strassburg, it was not probable that Paris would fight for the territories he, Peters,

---

* Lewin and others charged that Ramazan, the interpreter, could not understand Peters clearly, much less read or write and, states Lewin, "the complaisant chieftains, in any case, preferred unlimited spirits to legal documents."

suggested grabbing." To which the Chancellor retorted characteristically, "Do you manage European politics or do I?" *

In August of the year a German squadron of four gunboats anchored off Zanzibar, Commodore Karl Paschen in command. The latter delivered an ultimatum to the Sultan to cease his hostile acts against Germany, which meant the Sultan's natural resentment against annexation, in which, it is now evident, he had the support of Britain. Bargash, confronted with German naval guns, submitted to the inevitable.

German administrators displayed no concern for the welfare of the Arabs or the Swahili coastal tribes in the protectorate, and by 1888 insurrection became general—not against the Germans alone but all Europeans. The administrators and nationals retreated to the coast. The British at Zanzibar grew alarmed and gave Capt. Wissmann, then Imperial Chancellor for German East Africa, 1,000 Sudanese troops. With this force and 200 German sailors and sixty German officers and non-coms, Wissmann suppressed the revolt and executed its leader, one Bushiri.

The conflicting interests of Britain, Germany and France in Zanzibar and the mainland opposite were eventually resolved in 1890 by a series of trades negotiated in Europe, best likened to the protracted bargaining at a rural mule-auction. The German East Africa Company paid the Sultan £200,000 for his title to the continental coast "within the German zone of influence" (the sum, be it noted, was paid over to the British who now had the Zanzibar protectorate and who generously permitted the Sultan to spend only the interest). In return for French acquiescence to the British protectorate over the island, London agreed to keep out of Madagascar and recognized a vast French "zone of influ-

* *The Germans and Africa*, Evans Lewin, chap. xi, London 1915.

ence" lying between Algeria, the upper Niger and Lake Tchad—roughly corresponding today to French West Africa. In an Anglo-German agreement of the same year, Berlin relinquished in part her claims to the great lake-regions (Victoria Nyanza, Tanganyika and Nyassa) but was guaranteed free access to them, and the northern boundary of German East Africa was drawn from the mouth of the Umba to Victoria Nyanza (in 10° S. Lat.) and across the lake to the eastern boundary of the Congo Free State. In return the German chancellor, General von Caprivi—William II had by now "dropped the pilot"—demanded Helgoland of Lord Salisbury. The German Navy had long believed that the North Sea islet was of vast strategic importance.

There was harsh criticism of the swap in both London and Berlin. Time was to prove, however, that the advantage was all Britain's, since under the Versailles Treaty she obtained mandate over German East Africa (Tanganyika Territory), and was able also to enforce the razing of the powerful German forts on Helgoland. In German Southwest Africa, Berlin obtained in the 1890 agreement access to the upper Zambezi, a 300-mile concession known as the "Caprivi Strip"; Britain obtained minor concessions in the Cameroons and German Togoland.

At the conclusion of the deal, Sir Henry Percy Anderson, head of the African Department of the British Foreign Office, and one of the negotiators, uttered one of those pious predictions which had become a fixed part of the procedure at European conferences depriving the blacks of their lands: the cynical practice seems to have been initiated by Leopold at his Geographical Congress in 1877.

"In the future," said Sir Henry, "British and German subjects will not be content with operating each in his own sphere, in a spirit of reciprocal exclusiveness, but . . . will take advantage of the improved situation, in which constant friction of interest with consequent acrimonious discussions should disappear, to join hands in developing the commerce of central Africa, in *civilizing* the natives, and in putting an end forever to the existence in any form of the Slave Trade."

iii

Of the French, however, Lord Salisbury demanded more than their recognition of the British protectorate over Zanzibar. In payment for the compliance of Downing Street to the claims of Paris to the vast and mostly arid (Sahara) region bounded by southern Algeria, the Upper Niger and Lake Tchad, England in the 1890 agreements demanded non-interference in the Lower Niger. To this demand the French agreed: the Government-subsidized trading-stations on the Lower Niger had not been able to compete with the British United African Company, and the Frenchmen were at still greater disadvantage when that company in 1890 received a charter from Victoria, becoming the Royal Niger Company.* Before another decade had passed the British and French were to come to the brink of war over the west frontier of Nigeria, for Paris flatly demanded an easy outlet on the Guinea Coast.

iv

As to Belgium, the expenditures of Leopold had finally exhausted even his exchequer. He stood in real danger of losing the Congo Free State altogether, or at least the control inherent in his sovereignty, by a forced sale to the

* It is pertinent to note that the charter was granted, in part, because of "large sums of money expended [by the United African Company] in acquiring cessions from the native chieftains."

French—under the preëmption clause giving Paris an option if the King were required to seek aid abroad.

But a man who could build a personal kingdom largely by political dissimulation was not to lose it for a momentary lack of funds to keep his administrators, engineers and agents alive. He would not lose it, in any event, without a fight to salvage some profit for himself. The stake was too great. If his ministers were indifferent to his pleas for money (in 1886 the total income of the Free State was only 74,201 francs), and the Belgian public suspicious over whispers of (1) abuses of natives in the Congo and (2) Leopold's private orgies, means of raising a loan must nevertheless exist.

In 1887, however, his financial worries had become so acute that he wrote Auguste Beernaert, the finance minister, that "we need money—or we will have to liquidate. . . . A liquidation would mean a sale to France. It might be advantageous to my personal finances, but it would be harmful to our neutrality. Neither Germany nor England would forgive Belgium for it. Thus it is essential to find money. I have shown myself ready to abandon my official budget, and thus make room for a large loan."

The reference to Belgian neutrality was astute. His reference to abandonment of his "official budget" meant, one may suppose, the suppression of plover or truffles at court banquets.

At length the Belgian Parliament with considerable reluctance from the Left parties authorized the King to float a bond issue of 70,000,000 francs, to which was attached a lottery feature to make it more attractive. Government funds were not, of course, used to buy the bonds, as official Belgium had no connection with or responsibility for Leopold's overseas kingdom. The issue, however, was not a success. As a remedy negotiations were opened with the Paris Government to permit sale of the bonds on the Bourse; these overtures were successful, but at a price: a hard-headed French Colonial Office demanded territorial concessions in the Congo and obtained them. Nevertheless the improvement in the sale was not spectacular.

By 1889 the King was in desperate straits, hounded by bankers to whom he was just another borrower. In tears the Queen told her Chamberlain that she was "appalled by the alteration in the features of the King and the state of depression in which she found His Majesty." But by July Leopold had saved himself by one of those agile jumps characteristic of that Belgian opportunist.

In his most sanctimonious vein he wrote Beernaert a letter which revealed openly that he no longer regarded the Congo Free State as an international venture, in the sense given it by the Berlin Conference, but instead as a project exclusively Belgian. Overnight he had reversed himself; no longer was the Congo a field for the united efforts of the civilized world. And he added:

"A country must grow or decline. . . . For thirteen years as senator, for twenty-four years as constitutional chief of State, I have been constantly preoccupied with saving the country from choking in its narrow limits and with *finding an outlet for her surplus production of men, things and ideas* [the old diplomatic euphemism for colonial theft]. . . . *I wish if* [Belgium] *consents to make it my heir in the Congo.*" *

---

* To this document there was a realistic postscript, revealing Leopold's complete disregard of the welfare of the natives. It read: "The annals of the Athenians, the Venetians, the Genoese, the Portuguese and the Dutch are worthy of our meditation. These small States, which had but limited provinces in Europe, knew how to create outside possessions and relations, which not only extended their commerce, but also *procured them the means of paying for their military expenses and maintaining their political existence.*"

The effect on the public of this implied bequest to the nation was electric. The obedient press was delirious in praise of the monarch's generosity. Stanley hastened to Brussels to receive from Leopold, in a box studded with diamonds, the insignia of the grand cross of the recently established "Order of the African Star." The explorer made a speech in English saying "Your King is the wisest of kings, he is a great man in every sense of the word. He possesses that true grandeur which rests neither on strength of arms nor upon might, but on ideas, generosity, love of country and of humanity." *

It would not occur to the gullible Stanley that Leopold's hand was forced by financial pressure, and that the bequest was purely a shrewd move to tap the coffers of the Belgian State.

The upshot was that Leopold published a will in which "We declare by these presents that We will and transmit, *after Our death,* to Belgium our sovereign rights over the Congo Free State as they have been recognized since 1884." The Government lent the Free State (i. e., Leopold) 25,-000,000 francs without interest. At the end of ten years Belgium could either annex the Congo or demand repayment of the loan. The agreement stipulated that sovereignty over the African State was to pass to a Council of Three, including the King. Thus both Leopold and Belgium were protected, and the danger averted of preëmption by the French.

v

Portugal in 1885–91 negotiated a series of treaties with Britain in which inevitably the Lisbon Government emerged more or less shorn territorially. Continuing to push northeastward after the Bechuanaland Protectorate was pro-

* As reported in *La Patriote*, Brussels, April 23, 1890.

claimed, the British grew nervous when Portugal—in 1887—claimed the entire territory between Angola (Portuguese West Africa) and Mozambique (Portuguese East Africa); or at least announced on paper the joining of those colonies. The deputy commissioner of Bechuanaland, Cecil Rhodes, did not consider "occupation as effective" in the Portuguese pretension, although Germany and France were agreeable—anything to check Britain. There was no time to lose, Rhodes argued. For £100 monthly and a supply of fire-arms, a chieftain named Lubengula agreed to turn a deaf ear to any but British agents, and permitted the British South Africa Company to search for mineral deposits.

The Portuguese were outraced. A Quai-d'Orsay spokesman, referring to the grab of Malabeleland and Mashonaland (subsequently Southern Rhodesia), made the accurate observation that the British South Africa Company now had possession "of the pick of Central Africa on both sides of the Zambezi." In the Anglo-Portuguese treaty of June 11, 1891, Lisbon submitted to the aforementioned separation of her possession on the west and east coasts by the annexations of the British. Portugal also agreed that the territory north of the Zambezi was "within the sphere of influence of Great Britain," and the same year the British proclaimed a protectorate over Nyasaland, later the British Central Africa Protectorate. . . . That was the end of Portugal's dream of a transcontinental empire in Africa.

vi

Just as Bismarck in 1884 had used Portugal as a stalking-horse for the Berlin Conference, so were the nations to use Lisbon again as a pretext for the Brussels Conference of 1890, although it was nominally summoned by Victoria. It was charged in Europe that Quilimane, a port in Portuguese

East Africa, was a depot for the slave-trade, from which slave-dhows regularly transferred chained blacks from the interior to ships bound for Arabia and Turkey. The authorities reportedly winked at the practice, or were negligent and lazy. This was unquestionably true, but Portugal was not the only nation to close its eyes to the pledges in the Berlin Act. Nevertheless by 1890 the more astute officials in the African divisions of the Europeon chancelleries realized that their own commercial interests, and the safety of their agents and nationals in Africa, required the destruction of the slave-trade. Exploitation of the native forced-labor and military conscription were something else again. . . . Ergo, the Brussels Conference.

VIII

Opéra Bouffe at Brussels
[1890]

THE summoning of another Africa conference at Brussels may be explained in two ways. One is that it was convoked under the presure of public opinion or the growth of an international conscience with respect to Africa. It is true that in 1889–90 the anti-slavery sentiment in the United States was strong, and in a variety of ways made itself felt in Europe. It is also true that Britain for more than fifty years had maintained a naval patrol off the coast of east Africa to suppress the Arab slave-traffic, but it is similarly fact that in 1883 *H.M.S. London,* with her squadron of small ships designed to pursue the slave-dhows up the creeks, was withdrawn. Their maintenance was expensive, and the results gained not encouraging. Downing Street substituted three vice-consuls, one on Lake Nyasa and the others on the coast, whose particular duties were to curtail the traffic, if possible.

The other explanation of the motives behind the Conference, called four years after that at Berlin, is considerably less altruistic. It is (1) that the Powers needed to place a tax upon liquor exports to Africa, not to protect the natives but to establish a tariff precedent for a continent which had never had trade barriers; (2), that the anti-slave-trade measures were primarily for the purpose of keeping the blacks under European control for their conscription later into colonial armies; and (3) that both the spirits and fire-

OPÉRA BOUFFE AT BRUSSELS 145

arms given the natives must be curtailed, or the Powers would risk an uprising which would expel all Europeans and their investments from Africa.

An examination of the day-to-day proceedings of the Conference, contained in white- and blue-books of half a dozen nations, presents ample evidence that the motives activating most of the delegates were a good deal less than benevolent, despite the ringing facility with which the plenipotentiaries spoke of "humanity," "civilization," and "the welfare of the populations of Africa"; similarly Mussolini so rerecently as December 1, 1935, asked whether "it is a crime to carry civilization to a backward land?" References to "civilization" have an unholy fascination to the imperialist of any generation. However that may be, the net result of the Conference, so far as the native was concerned, was to place him still further under the domination of Europeans, and to curtail his elementary rights and diminish his property correspondingly. As it developed, he was to drink more, and to fire a rifle oftener.

The diplomatic mechanics, or procedure, in calling the Conference are worth noticing. Since 1885 the British Colonial Office had not been blind to the practices of Leopold's agents in the Congo Free State. If British agents in Cape Colony and in the Bechuanaland Protectorate, in the south, and in Egypt in the north, had also been guilty of conscripting labor and of using spirits for "currency," at least their practices were not as open and flagrant as in the Congo Free State. Downing Street foresaw that the Belgian King was well on the way to building an empire of prodigious value, by practices which the British public could not be expected to tolerate within their own colonies. Both selfish and unselfish factors acted, consequently, in devising some check or brake upon the unconscionable occupant of the Palace at Brussels. Reference has already been made to another pretext for calling the Conference—that the Portuguese were passive to, if not actually encouraging, the Arab trade in slaves.

Nevertheless, Lord Salisbury could not afford to act in any manner that would imply open criticism of Leopold's policies in Africa. The initiative was therefore given to the House of Commons which called upon the Government "in view of the increasing and extending desolations in Africa caused by the Slave Trade, to take steps to ascertain the willingness of the Powers to meet in Conference for the purpose of devising measures for its suppression."

Accordingly, after negotiations between London and Brussels, "the Government of His Majesty the King of the Belgians, *in agreement* with the Government of Her Majesty the Queen of Great Britain and Ireland, Empress of India," addressed invitations to confer at Brussels. The stated object was to put "an end to the crimes and devastations engendered by the Traffic in African slaves, [to protect] effectively the aboriginal populations of Africa [and insure] for that vast continent the benefits of peace and civilization."

Leopold consented to the Conference because, with characteristic foresight, he realized that the traffic in spirits could only be controlled by the removal or the modification of the stipulation in the Berlin Act which prohibited the imposition of import duties in the Congo Free State and the Niger Basin. Normally, the free-trade provisions of that instrument would have remained in force for twenty years. Here, he reasoned, was an opportunity for sorely needed revenue. Moreover, by consenting to the Conference, and indeed appearing before the world as its promoter, or joint-promoter with Victoria, he was enabled to seem to concur with the campaign of the French Cardinal Charles Lavigerie, primate of Africa, who had long been agitating against the slave-trade, with the support of Pope Leo XIII.

The invitations were addressed to the United States, Ger-

OPÉRA BOUFFE AT BRUSSELS 147

many, Austria-Hungary, Denmark, Spain, France, Italy, Holland, Portugal, Russia, Norway and Sweden, Turkey, Persia and Zanzibar. Turkey and Persia received bids as the two chief importers of domestic slaves from Africa, and the Sultan of Zanzibar was asked to send a representative to Brussels because the slave-dhows were most active within his waters, despite the fact that in 1873 he had declared the importation of slaves illegal when pressure was exerted on him by Sir John Kirk, the British consul-general on the island.

Leopold also addressed an invitation to himself as sovereign of the Congo Free State. The Conference assembled November 18, 1889, and ended July 2, 1890.

It was soon apparent in the sessions that there were to be serious differences of opinion among the delegates, notably on the liquor traffic and the right-of-search of ships for slaves. Harmony was not improved by the fact that the Conference brought together again several of the horsetraders who bore scars of the bickering at Berlin four years before. The United States was represented by the irrepressible General Sanford.* He was supported by Edwin H. Terrell, the American minister at Brussels; Baron Lambermont and Émile Banning, now director-general at the Ministry for Foreign Affairs, were again on hand for Belgium; George Cogordan of the Quai-d'Orsay and Albert Bourée represented France; Lord Vivian, the minister, and Sir John Kirk were the British delegates. The delegates of the remaining

* The Florida promoter, incidentally, had an unhappy financial experience with his Sanford Exploring Expedition for Trade, organized at Brussels, June 28, 1886. In reward for Sanford's services in obtaining the United States' recognition of the Congo's sovereignty, Leopold induced the Comité d'Études du Haut Congo to purchase stock in the American's expedition. The project collapsed in 1888 after heavy expenditures; see *Histoire de l'État Indépendant du Congo*, Fritz Masoin, vol. i, p. 63, Namur 1912.

nations were, for the most part, their accredited envoys to Belgium. One of the Russian delegates was Admiral Nicholay Petrovich Rimski-Korsakov, uncle of the composer who was, incidentally, conducting at the Théâtre de la Monnaie during the early part of the sittings.

What might be described as Leopold's "conference technique" had come to full bloom by 1889—he had initiated these African parleys in 1876. The monarch knew precisely what to do. Replicas of the Order of Leopold were freely bestowed upon such as had not received one at previous assemblies: the others received the grand cross of the Order of the African Star. At the Palace banquet for the delegates, the truffles and plover were, for the one occasion, restored to the royal menu. The press of Europe reported that the King's ball and reception eclipsed anything in the richest days of Eugénie and Napoleon. In London *The Times* was more serious:

"Never before [it pointed out, November 30, conveniently forgetting the Berlin Conference] have the Continental Powers been brought into line for the purpose of making a joint effort against the slavery outrage upon civilization and humanity, and seldom has light been so opportunely thrown on some of the darkest regions—darker even morally than they are geographically and physically—of the Dark Continent." And elsewhere the leading organ of England referred to "the generous and philanthropic hopes of those who have long striven against the slave-trade, which is rarely compensated by the concert of European effort and opinion now tardily established."

Baron Lambermont was elected President, and the sessions began. It should be noted here that, in addition to the task of the delegates to restrict the liquor traffic, there were three forms of slavery to be studied. The first was the exportation of domestic slaves to the Mohammedan countries; a second was the seizure of slaves by rival tribes, for use as carriers and, in some instances, as human sacrifices; and the third was the common practice by Europeans of conscripting labor for a given term, i. e., forced labor, less brutally described sometimes as the "institution of indention."

In the following extracts of testimony, particularly those dealing with the trade with the natives in spirits, the reader will best evaluate the underlying motives of the discussions if the fact is borne in mind that the principle of tariff imposition in the Congo and throughout the young protectorates was the main, if hidden, issue; "the restriction of the liquor traffic" was merely a stalking-horse for recognition of the doctrine that modern trade would demand the erection of tariff walls in Africa. The phrase was, however, deeply satisfying to those innocents, members of the Society for the Prevention of Sale of Alcohol to the Native Races, who descended upon Brussels in hopeful battalions.

Early in the proceedings the Portuguese, led by Henrique de Macedo, exasperated the other Powers by seeking to inject territorial questions which were felt to be outside the province of the Conference. The Lisbon delegates regarded the Brussels assembly as the logical place in which to remind the nations that Britain had seized a vast territory in Central Africa (Mashonaland and Malabeleland), in the face of the Portuguese proclamation of "effective occupation" by themselves. This was, of course, true and Minister de Macedo had the prompt support of the French and German delegations. The British envoys, however, by no means proposed to see this outright steal made a Conference football, and Lord Vivian was successful in snubbing the gentlemen from Lisbon. The day following *The Times* archly dismissed the incident with the observation that "it is not desirable to afford the Portuguese an opportunity for raising questions which are really outside the scope of the Conference." *

Beaten by Rhodes in Central Africa, and outmaneuvered simultaneously by the British at Brussels, the Portuguese gave up, and prepared to hear themselves excoriated by more civilized nations as a people indifferent to the slave-traffic in east Africa.

All the old oratorical stops were pulled by the delegates at the inaugurating session. Prince de Chimay, the Belgian Foreign Minister, in the opening address had a deal to say of "the attainment of one of the noblest aims that can animate humanity." The tariff issue was sedulously avoided, for the press of the world was represented in the galleries. The *doyen* of the diplomatic corps at Brussels, Baron Gericke de Herwijnen of the Netherlands, was certain his colleagues would do their "utmost . . . by seeking the most efficacious means for putting a stop to the odious Traffic which has too long dishonored humanity." United States Minister Terrell, after referring to those inevitable "reservations" of Washington to protocols of European origin, told the Conference that "a country which has so long suffered from the ills of slavery, and which has not shrunk from one of the most bloody wars the world has known in order to free its territory from them forever, must feel beyond all others an immense interest in the work of this assembly." At the close of the first day's rosy addresses, and after the delegates had voted to inform the newspapermen of routine matters only—because "the members of the Conference recognize that it is the duty of all to assure the success of their labors by acting with discretion, without which success could never be obtained"—everyone hurried in virtuous mood to the cham-

* November 30, 1889.

pagne provided for them by Leopold at the Hôtel de l'Europe.

ii

The following sessions were devoted to the introduction by the delegates of evidence and data relating to the slave-trade in Africa and to "degradation of the natives by the sale and distribution of spirits." That the various envoys were not more than human, and despite their decorations were heir to the foibles of common mortals, was clear in their rather droll persistence that every nation except their own was enormously guilty. Most of the *dossiers*, in any event, cited chapter and verse, both as to the slave-trade and the liquor traffic.*

As to the *dossiers* dealing with the slave trade:

The French denied that any part of the slave-trade emanated from Madagascar where they claimed they had qualified agents stationed to prevent the traffic, but charged that most of the Arab traffic centered about Zanzibar—an attack on the British who held the protectorate over that island. They protested vigorously the British proposal for a convention under which the Powers would have the right to search one another's ships in the Indian Ocean in instances where slave-smuggling was suspected. Lord Vivian declared that the "slave-trade is carried on on a great scale in the Red Sea"—which elicited protests from the French, the Turkish delegates, and the Italians. M. Bourée presented

* The *dossiers* of the French, British, Portuguese and German plenipotentiaries may be found in *La traité des Esclaves (Renseignements et documents recueillis pour la Conférence de Bruxelles)*, Belgian Royal Academy, Brussels 1890. For the minutes of the more important sessions see Great Britain, Foreign Office, Africa, No. 7, General Act of the Brussels Conference, London 1890.

evidence to show that the number of French sailing-vessels in the Red Sea or the Indian Ocean was inconsequential. The Portuguese declared that, if it were true most of the blacks engaged in the trade bore Portuguese names, these were adopted patronyms, indicative only of the early visits to East Africa of the Portuguese—a remark calculated to irritate the British. M. de Macedo presented evidence acquitting his nation of permitting the traffic, including a letter written by Stanley (May 11, 1878) to the American Anti-Slavery Society, in which the explorer stated that "to be just, one must distinguish between the European Portuguese and the African Portuguese." The Italians proved intransigeant throughout, apparently for the sole reason of embarrassing the hated French: the chief delegate from Rome, Baron de Renzis, took exceptions and made reservations on every possible occasion that the French sought to soften or emasculate the severe penalties, the right-of-search, etc., advocated by Lord Vivian. The latter introduced reports from British consular agents and returned to attack the Portuguese who permitted the sale of fire-arms and munitions, he said, a fact which tended to neutralize the efforts of both his countrymen and the German nation to stamp out the traffic. The argument grew bitter. . . . The Russians, Austro-Hungarians and Spaniards added to the din, for the sheer joy of joining the fray and, doubtless, seeing their remarks in tomorrow's newspapers.

Be it said for the sincerity of the British delegates, they repeatedly steered the discussions back to the primary subject before the Conference, that is, concerted means of ending the traffic in humans. Lord Vivian and his colleagues were not only under official pressure from Downing Street, but throughout England and even on the ground at Brussels there were influential representatives of British public opinion clamoring for effective action. In part to satisfy them, as well as European philanthropists and others present as observers, delegates from all the Powers made lush references, interminably, to "humanity," "civilization," "protection of the aboriginals," "odious traffic," et cetera.

In the face of the political cross-purposes at work, the pettifoggery and the irreconcilable attitudes of several of the nations represented, it is cause for some astonishment that the delegates arrived eventually at agreement upon measures to check the slave-traffic. But the weight of public opinion against its cruelties, if not so sensible in Turkey, Persia and Russia, was felt in great or less degree elsewhere. Manifestly the delegates dared not fail at some agreement on exterminating the traffic in blacks, for failure would have jeopardized the chance of each chancellery to gain the right of tariff protection for its African holdings. Agreement on slave-traffic restrictions entailed a trivial sacrifice in diplomatic vanity—but was spectacular in public effect—compared to the opportunity of legislating a tariff under the guise of prohibiting or controlling the imports of gin and rum.

Nevertheless agreement was not reached on this one issue until July 2, 1890—the closing day of the Conference. In sum, the anti-slavery stipulations, "*effectively* protecting the aboriginal populations of Africa, and of assuring to that vast continent the benefits of peace and civilization," provided that:*

1. The African regions where slavery originated were to be placed under rigid control (Chap. I);

2. Slave caravans from the interior were to be interrupted and the slaves liberated (Chap. II);

3. The signatory Powers were given the right-of-search of vessels of less than 500 tons (a concession to the French)

* For full text in English, see *The Map of Africa by Treaty*, vol. II, Sir Edward Hertslet, London 1909.

within a "Slave maritime zone" extending on one hand between the coasts of the Indian Ocean (those of the Persian Gulf and of the Red Sea included) from Beluchistan to Point Tangalane (Quilimane), an area including Madagascar and extending to the 26th degree of south latitude (Chap. III); sea-borne slaves were to be liberated when found;

4. The signatory nations recognizing the existence of domestic slavery (Turkey, Persia and Zanzibar) agree to forbid the importation of slaves from Africa for that bondage, and agreed to legislate punishment for persons found trafficking in slaves and for mutilation of children or of *male* adults (Chap. IV);

5. An International Maritime Office was to be established at Zanzibar charged with the interception of slave-traffic by sea, and the Powers agreed to facilitate interception by the exchange of information.

It was far from a foolproof agreement, but a marked improvement over the parenthetical reference to the slave-traffic in the Berlin Agreement of 1885.*

iii

But unanimity upon controlling the traffic in spirituous liquors was far more difficult. Aside from the resentment and vindictiveness aroused among a half-dozen or more delegations over the slave-traffic recriminations at the Conference (inevitably a diplomat by profession is a dis-

* This agreement, together with the convention on export of spirits, munitions and fire-arms to Africa, which constituted the "General Act of the Brussels Conference," was signed July 2, 1890, by all the Powers represented. Ethiopia and Liberia signified their adherence in 1892, and the Orange Free State in 1896. But parliamentary ratification in France, because of the right-of-search stipulation, and in Germany and Holland, because of the liquor proscriptions, was long delayed.

senter, which is a polite definition of an opportunist), it was realized by everyone present that here in the liquor issue was the *raison-d'être* of the Conference. Measures to suppress the slave-traffic, and impress world opinion accordingly, might be pledged by rhetoric alone. Similarly it was felt by Britain and France that hyperbole would settle the liquor issue—so far as public opinion was concerned—and permit the Conference to direct its major efforts to drafting a convention permitting an African tariff.

And as it developed, such private groups as the Society for Prevention of the Sale of Alcohol to the Native Races and missionary organizations were satisfied with the ultimate convention. But the delegates of Germany and Holland, particularly, fought restriction energetically, to the disgust of other delegates who felt that an export trade in spirits was small potatoes, in the way of concession, compared to the opportunity of protecting other export industries by tariff.

As to the *dossiers* and debates dealing with liquor:

Lord Vivian evoked the pregnant issue by asserting that "in view of their operation upon the social condition of Africa, and their consequent *indirect* effect upon the Slave Trade, it will *probably* be desirable that the Conference should direct its attention to the restriction of the commerce in ardent spirits and in munitions of war."

The delegates awoke from their sessional slumbers. After weeks of oratorical nonsense about slavery, the crucial issue was now at hand. The British blue-book reporting the foregoing address observes laconically that "Lord Vivian's communication is received with interest by the assembly." Baron Lambermont, in the chair, obediently seconded the proposal, conceding that "nobody denies that the abuse of spirituous liquors supplied by Europeans is one of the chief causes of the degradation and destruction of the

Negro race. Public opinion has never ceased to denounce this evil: it now demands that the Governments represented at Brussels should come to some understanding with a view to staying its ravages." The Dutch representative at the session, Baron Gericke de Herwijnen, awakened to remark that, while he supported "to a certain extent the arguments put forward," no mention had been made in the agenda of this question. Hence, was it not improper for the assembly to discuss it?

On March 14 (1890) the British brought forth a draft proposal, the genesis of the convention eventually adopted. It stated in the preamble that "the improvement of the moral and material conditions of life of the African races is closely connected with the suppression of this [liquor] evil, which assumes more serious proportions as the ever-increasing liquor trade throws more temptation in the way of the ignorant natives."

The British proposal divided the African peoples into three groups. These were (1), "the races, estimated at 40,000,000 souls, who inhabit the Basin of the Middle Niger and the western Sudan and who . . . . are not consumers of spirits. It is of the utmost importance to prevent the demoralization of those races [within both the British and French zones of influence], for it is impossible to exaggerate the pernicious consequences of introducing strong liquors among the warlike and fanatical tribes. . . ;" (2), the "pagan tribes who inhabit the heart of Africa and who have not yet acquired a taste for strong liquor;" and (3), the coast population who *"are more or less in contact with civilization, and have therefore acquired the habit of strong liquors."*

With respect to the first and second categories, the British proposed absolute prohibition if the signatory Powers to the Berlin Conference would "coöperate effectively"; as

OPÉRA BOUFFE AT BRUSSELS 157

for the coastal Negroes, Lord Vivian said that Her Majesty's Government would suggest "the imposition of a minimum import duty on all spirituous liquors above a certain alcoholic standard, and by the imposition of an equivalent excise duty on spirits manufactured in the [African] country."

General Sanford, Count Alvensleben, representing Germany, and the aforementioned Dutch delegate joined forces in a bloc. In turn they asserted the draft proposal was, in their view, outside the province of the Conference, or asked that the discussion be delayed until instructions were received from their home governments.

In principle, the British draft had sense and appealing logic. For one thing, it satisfied public opinion, and for another it did not conflict with the interests of any of the British "Africa companies" whose export trade in spirits was negligible. But the vexatious phrase "above a certain alcoholic standard" was a bone of interminable contention as the spring months wore on. The Dutch, with a profitable trade in gin to the Congo and also to the coast of east Africa, took pains to remind the Conference repeatedly that under the Berlin Agreement no duties were to be imposed in the Congo or Niger basins for twenty years. Since Holland had no African colonies, The Hague had no reason to concern itself over the "warlike and fanatical tribes" whose exposure to rum alarmed Lord Vivian. The Germans were less adamant: the Woermann (Hamburg) lobby was reminded by Count Alvensleben that the Reich had already tasted insurrection in Africa, central and south. Nevertheless the liquor debate was protracted and bitter, and carried far into the nights over Leopold's champagne at the delegates' hotel. Dutch and Germans fought lustily and loudly to lower the proposed tariff and to increase the alcoholic content of spirits which might be admitted free of duty. The adroit

Sanford, in search of compromise, introduced some much-needed, if unconscious, humor into the debate by recommending "the exclusion of spirits unfit for use, by condemning and confiscating those that are found imperfectly rectified or adulterated." In other words, the blacks were to drink only the best and most expensive spirits.

Finally, however, the opposition was shouted down.

iv

At length the delegates who signed the "General Act of the Slave Trade Conference" agreed, apart from the anti-slavery measures, to an emasculated form of the British proposal. It provided:

1. Within a zone extending from the 20th degree north latitude to the 22nd degree south latitude, bound by the Atlantic Ocean on the west and on the east by the Indian Ocean, comprising the islands adjacent to the shore up to 100 miles from the coast, "the Powers shall prohibit [liquor] importation . . . in the regions of this zone where it shall be ascertained that, either on account of religious belief or from other motives, the use of distilled liquors does not exist, *or has not been developed.*"

2. *That the prohibition could be suspended . . . under conditions determined by each Government* (thus annulling any restriction).

3. On the coastal regions and beyond the forbidden zone, a tariff of not less than 15 francs a hectolitre at 50° Centigrade was to be levied, and increased after three years to 25 francs, if believed necessary.

4. An equivalent tax, as proposed originally by Lord Vivian, upon spirits distilled in coastal Africa.

It was also agreed that within the same zone fire-arms and munitions must not be imported because "the experience of all nations who have intercourse with Africa [has] shown the pernicious and preponderating part played by fire-arms in Slave-Trade operations, as well as in intestine wars between native tribes" (Chap. I, article viii).

Despite the oblique language of international law, the strictures against the slave-traffic were relatively effective —the stipulations provided for a supervisory office at Zanzibar, and for definite penalties against offenders. The liquor and munitions agreements, on the other hand, meant nothing save as *décors*. Today, as a generation ago, the Berber and the Bantu can get a gallon of rum as easily, and a good deal less expensively, than the New Yorker or the Londoner. Similarly the native can obtain, except in an extremely circumscribed district, a rifle as simply as his "civilized" brother in Paris or Berlin, and he need not concern himself with the red-tape of a license. Cartridges and liquor became common currency in Darkest Africa. That is the net result, so far as the native is concerned, of the Brussels Act nearly a half-century after its signature.

v

The revealing finale to the debate was the paragraph enabling the tariff. It was the last paragraph, and was quietly inserted into the agreement as a "declaration *annexed* to the General Act of the Brussels Conference." Under it the Powers agreed to a ten per cent *ad valorem* duty, not only on liquor but on any merchandise. That tariff was the underlying reason for the Conference, and it was enacted under the shrubbery of resolutions against slavery and alcohol.

IX

"Why Do You People Kill Me?"
[1890–95]

For all the high-flown oratory at Brussels, and the superficial impression it created that the Powers had awakened to a certain sense of responsibility toward Africa, the immediate after-effect was a redoubling of efforts by Europeans to seize more ground; and the native—Mr. Rudyard Kipling's "pore benighted heathen"—be damned. Since the sole reason for the Conference was the enactment of a tariff, whatever else an impressionable generation had been led to believe, the acquisition of more territory was first in the mind of every chancellor, for the larger the colony, the wider the area productive eventually of import duties.

The imperialist virus raced in the veins of every petty statesman, in whose mind the acquirement of land abroad, and particularly in Africa, was related in a vague, muddled way with the nationalism, or the peculiar "civilization," he represented: the perfect modern example of that casuistry is Mussolini. That peculiar vanity and illogic was not so true of Britain, whose imperial policy and practice in the closing decade of the nineteenth century was born of pragmatic thinking, a long experience, and the dispassionate view that the sole reason for colonies was trade; but to Germany and Belgium, and especially to Italy, Spain, Portugal and France, it was profoundly satisfying to defraud a tribe or tribes of so many hundred or thousand square miles, and to signify that theft by raising the flag. To Germans the confiscation of more territory was a somewhat mystic affirmation of the validity of the legend on the imperial standard—*Gott mit uns*—as well, no doubt, as proof that the new cry of *Deutschland über alles* was something more than the expression of a wistful, unrealizable desire. To the French mentality, official and civilian, the planting of the tricolor on the Upper Niger, for example, was irrefutable evidence that the Berber or the Touareg recognized the enlightened wisdom that that emblem symbolized—*liberté, fraternité, égalité.* Italians witnessed with happy complacence the planting of the emblem of the House of Savoy along the Red Sea, with its emblazoned F. E. R. T. (*Fortitudo eius Rhodum tenuit*—his strength held Rhodes).* Although the island had been lost to Rome for centuries, the motto signified that the strength of the Cæsars might still be exercised beyond the Peninsula. . . . If there is comic irony in that nationalist and peculiarly Latin attitude, it seemingly was not recognized as such by leading Continental editors and leader-writers of the day.

ii

Most energetic of all the chancelleries in extending their influence in Africa, chiefly because its financial resources were greatest, was the British Colonial Office. In 1884–85 members of the Church Missionary Society determined to export the Church of England to the Bantus and Hamitics,

* The Fascist slogan, "A noi!" adopted as the national motto in 1922 after the March on Rome, has the virtue of surpassing honesty. A free but not inaccurate equivalent in English is "All for us!"

who had hitherto needed no other god than old Katonda, the "supreme creator," an amiable, not overly-demanding diety. He was worshiped almost universally throughout Uganda, the region in eastern equatorial Africa lying between lakes Victoria and Albert, and between the Victoria Nile and Lake Rudolf. As a token of esteem for the labors of the British missionaries, the natives shot the bishop of Harrington through the neck, and reduced his Negro converts to fine ashes.

While that murder, in 1885, deeply touched the Christian conscience throughout the world, it was generally felt that Britain should have the exclusive privilege of avenging the bishop. Not only was that dignatory an English subject, but it was to be recalled later that under the Anglo-German agreement of 1890—which gave Helgoland to Germany— the Uganda district was regarded as within the zone of influence of the London authorities.

Busy rescuing Emin Pasha and on a fishing expedition for the British East Africa Company, and knowing something of the sentiment of the Uganda tribes, Stanley declined to intervene. Accordingly, the Colonial Office in 1890 dispatched Captain F. D. Lugard to "liquidate" the situation, which was a dangerous one for Europeans in the region. He conscripted a force of Sudanese, and with 250 rifles and a Maxim gun set out to establish order and respect for Europeans—the prelude to a protectorate. It was a perilous assignment, made more dangerous by the rivalries between the French Catholic missionaries and their British Protestant colleagues. In 1892, however, the Colonial Office lost heart, as well it might, and ordered Lugard to evacuate the territory.

"I left on June 16, and a letter signed by the great chiefs of all parties was sent after me, addressed to the Queen, imploring Her Majesty not to withdraw from the country [but]

"WHY DO YOU PEOPLE KILL ME?" 163

in England I found that Uganda was to be left to its fate. The influence of the Church Missionary Society was invoked, and the pens of a thousand writers in the press warned the Government that the feeling in favor of the retention of Uganda was too strong to be disregarded." * Captain Lugard neglects to mention that weightier than the lobby of the Church Missionary Society, powerful as it was, was that exercised by the British East Africa Company.

In London he informed the Colonial Office that "so far as I could judge, the trouble in every instance arose from aggressions on the part of the [French] Catholics." † For once in the history of the partition of Africa, the dispute between the Powers was not economic or political, but religious. Meanwhile, Captain W. H. Williams, Lugard's successor, telegraphed the British High Commissioner at Capetown that "it would be a *great thing* if the next Safari brought up a small Nordenfelt [machine-gun] or Hotchkiss carrying a percussion shell of about 2 or 3 lbs."

While denying categorically the French accusation that British agents and missionaries had sought to "alienate the religious dispositions" of the Uganda, Lord Salisbury consented nevertheless to pay an indemnity to the priests. The Paris Government, assuming the cudgels for the priests, was insistent—Church and State were still one in France—and Downing Street could not permit religion to confuse an issue which the cabinet regarded as purely colonial and territorial. Britain had more pressing trouble in Egypt, and the outlook in South Africa was threatening. Parliament appropriated £10,000 to mollify the priests, and in June 1894 the Union Jack was hoisted and Uganda declared a Brit-

---

* *Story of the Uganda Protectorate*, Gen. F. D. Lugard, London 1901.
† British Foreign Office, *Africa, No. 8, 1892, Papers Relating to Uganda*.

ish protectorate. That was the genesis of the present protectorate, which has an area of 94,204 miles, including 13,616 square miles of water—a rich producer of cotton, coffee, timber, hides, sugar, ivory and tobacco. It controls Victoria Lake, the great reservoir whence the Nile proper begins its long journey to the Mediterranean, just as the British today control Lake Tsana in Ethiopia, source of the Blue Nile.

iii

Ten thousand pounds was an insignificant sum to pay for the snatch of Uganda; it was also a trifling reparation to insure an interval of peace in east central Africa. For after 1890 the British recognized that storms were blowing up within their zones of influence in both north and south. The public and press at home might believe that British prestige in South Africa was such that there was no reason for concern, military or moral—indeed, if prestige might be gauged by the rapidity and apparent ease with which new annexations were effected, protectorates established and spheres of influence extended, one could logically conclude that the Union Jack was venerated by all the natives who had seen it wave, and yearned for by those of the benighted who had merely heard it described.

Fortunately for the British Empire, such muddled thinking was not characteristic of Gladstone, who had resumed the reins of power in 1892, of his Foreign Secretary, Lord Rosebery, or the Colonial Secretary, Lord Ripon. Fresh in their minds were the past defeats and the potential results of the policy of Downing Street toward Africa. They had not forgotten the attempted seizure of the Orange Free State, or the bald confiscations of Bechuanaland, Mashonaland, Zululand, the Transvaal and Natal. That succession of grabs in the holy cause of civilization had not created a native love for the British. Agents of the High Commissioner reported the tribal sentiment north and south of the Zambezi; the cabinet was kept well-informed. Wisely it prepared, or at least tried to prepare, for the imminent whirlwind which was to materialize in 1899. . . . If more saber-rattling was injudicious, what else might be done to avert—or at least delay—a general uprising? That concern is evident in many of the inter-ministerial memoranda, and in memoires.

Lord Rosebery made a shrewd proposal. He believed that a relatively safe and effective step would be the granting of self-government to Natal Colony. It was in line, moreover, with the recommendations of Sir Theophilus Shepstone, the Natal Secretary for Native Affairs, and the returns in the Natal council elections of 1890 had shown a majority in favor of a modified autonomy. The British police force there was impressive numerically and fairly efficient; most of the crime was of the nature of assault "between master and servant," generally provoked by the "caprice or insolence of an undisciplined native." * The common remedy for native insubordination was flogging.

At first dubious over the practicality of Lord Rosebery's suggestion, the Cabinet was reassured by the report of Colonel J. G. Dartnell, commandant of the Natal Mounted Police, who observed that crime was on the decrease—save for the horse-stealing from natives by Europeans; he added with pride that the natives now were contributing to Her Majesty's Government by being made to pay a dog-tax, although he admitted they did so with increasing reluctance. He regretted to inform His Lordship, the Colonial Secretary, that "the sale of spirituous liquors is, I fear,

* Natal Blue Book Supplement, *Departmental Reports*, 1892–93.

everywhere on the increase [due to] the want of discrimination shown by the Licensing Board in granting licenses which, it should be quite palpable, are only applied for, for the sale of liquor to Natives [and] also to the presence in our midst of a degraded type of European who associates with the Natives on terms of equality and who give passes for liquor, and *to the spread of education amongst the Natives* which enables them to write their own passes." . . . There could be no more eloquent testimony of the vacuity of the liquor restrictions in the Brussels Act than the report of this official (June 30, 1893), three years after the Act was signed. And there is a certain grim humor in Colonel Dartnell's observation that by virtue of education, i. e., the instruction given by European missionaries and others, the native was outwitting the purveyors of civilization by scrawling his "own passes." Orthographical education in Africa was to prove as much a boomerang to Europeans as firearms or rum.

But the Cabinet waved this aside. The cardinal point for Downing Street was whether self-government in Natal would lead to disorder, rebellion or to any weakening of British authority and prestige. The Gladstone ministry, in any event, decided to risk it, weighing the possibility of insurrection against the psychological advantage of granting self-government. It was fervently hoped that the move would place the home Government in a less despotic light, perhaps, and deflate the rebellious Boer and native sentiment in South Africa, which was unquestionably approaching the explosion point. The Colonial Secretary had good reason for concern, since there were more than 50,000 Europeans in Natal alone. . . . Self-government was approved in 1893, an electoral law adopted which made it virtually impossible for the native to obtain a franchise, or at least only an in-

"WHY DO YOU PEOPLE KILL ME?" 167

effective number of them, and the Gladstone cabinet breathed more easily and returned to its port.*

The gesture meant nothing to the Afrikander. While Europeans rejoiced in Natal, the first Matabeleland War burst out seven hundred miles to the north.

The Matabele chief, Lubengula, decided in 1893 that he had had enough of the British South Africa Company, after having permitted its agents two years before to make mineral surveys in Mashonaland: in return for this concession he had accepted a gift of 10,000 rifles and £100 a month. As Lubengula should have known, the British South Africa Company would not remain content with Mashonaland when there were gold, silver and copper also to be mined in adjacent Matebeleland. He gave the Company's agents a simple lesson in ethics, after declaring his resumption of sovereignty over the northern province, by punctiliously returning the 10,000 rifles, and serving notice he would no longer accept the £100 monthly, or anything else from the white man. With the fire-arms went a friendly note assuring the Company that "one Matabele with his *assagai* [light javelin] is a match for four Englishmen with machine-guns." Lubengula asked why he should permit the British South Africa Company to enslave the Mashonas when he had long since conquered that people and exploited their labor; he admitted he considered that people as "nothing less than cattle," which provoked hypocritical expressions of dismay from Europeans. He added that while Queen Victoria might have granted a royal charter to the Company, giving it authority over both Matabele-

---

* Four years later, in 1897, Parliament approved the annexation of Zululand to Natal, not the wisest political step: two years later came the explosion.

land and Mashonaland, Her Majesty had no right to speak for him or his people, or to sell them into serfdom to her subjects. Legalistically, Lubengula's argument was unassailable—he had promised only to shut his ears to the offers of agents of other Powers, and to permit the mineral surveys.

From the imperialist viewpoint, however, all that Lubengula's action meant was that an "insolent Black King" was opposing the Queen of Great Britain and Ireland, and looking for trouble by impeding the progress of civilization, i. e., the British South Africa Company's search for underground wealth—a project pushed energetically by its managing-director, Cecil Rhodes. Equally disdainful of Lubengula's opposition was a Scottish doctor, Leander Starr Jameson, the Company's administrator in Mashonaland.

Accordingly both sides prepared for war. The Company promptly received military reinforcements from England. Lubengula welcomed the offer of services made by an American filibuster named Whittaker who had organized a flying column of 330 men, all of British origin. The Matabeleland chief made a series of raids upon the Mashonas, his chattels. Gladstone judged correctly that Rhodes and Jameson were over-reaching themselves, and that their aggressiveness might light the spark of a general uprising. When the Mashonas fled to the Company's forts—the most formidable of them named after Victoria—Lubengula's *assagais* pursued them in clouds that darkened the African sky. There were a series of skirmishes, in character not unlike the Italo-Ethiopian "war" of 1935–36, the air-bombings of hospitals and civilians excepted. At last Gladstone supplanted Rhodes, who had hastened to the jungle front, with Sir Henry Loch, the high commissioner at Capetown. While advancing against the British, his warriors unimpressed by Maxims, field-pieces, Martini-Henry rifles, bayonets and revolvers, Lubengula kept up a lively correspondence with Victoria

"WHY DO YOU PEOPLE KILL ME?" 169

through intermediaries. On August 19, 1893, he asked her, reasonably enough, "Your Majesty, what I want to know from you is, *Why do you people kill me?* I am not hiding anything when writing to your Majesty." * Dr. Jameson considered the letter "illiterate." As a token of profound respect, the Black King on this occasion signed his state paper with his elephant-seal. Through Sir Henry Loch, Victoria chattily responded that "You have been misled. The Great Queen cannot consent that the Mashonas should be killed and children carried away as slaves, and she will tell her white people if these things happen they must be stopped and the men who do them punished." But the correspondence languished, due perhaps to the Queen's rather chilling epistolary style. Moreover, the High Commissioner at Capetown felt that it was somewhat *infra dig* for Victoria to exchange letters with the Black King of Matabeleland and Mashonaland, for on October 31 he advised Lord Ripon telegraphically that it was "not advisable to send any reply to Lubengula in the name of Her Majesty the Queen." And in a subsequent dispatch, he added a practical note by assuring the Colonial Secretary that "I will keep expenses [of the conquest] as low as possible."

Eventually, of course, Lubengula was deposed by the Maxims, and he conveniently died. Rhodes and his agents swarmed over Matabeleland. Possibly a thousand Matabeles were killed in the campaign. In May 1895 the Company's two territories were named Rhodesia by proclamation (more correctly, southern Rhodesia). Another uprising took place in 1896 as a sequel to the abortive Jameson Raid.† British

---

* British Foreign Office, *Correspondence Relating to Affairs in Mashonaland, Matabeleland*, etc., 1893.

† Jameson's Raid into the Transvaal (Dec. 28, 1895) brought him no thanks from Downing Street which promptly disowned him after his surrender to the Boers the following month—although the impetuous doctor had tried to do with 500 men a task which was

troops from Natal and Mafeking mopped up the following year, and thereafter Matabeleland and Mashonaland lost all geographical entity.

The rape of Matabeleland gave birth at Cambridge to a curious pamphlet, in 1894, written anonymously and titled "The Matabeleland Scandal." * Despite the burning rancor and heavy irony of its author, and the fact of anonymity which necessarily lessens the force of its argument, the publication is interesting as evidence that not all England was blind to the real nature of British policy in South Africa. Referring to the clash with Lubengula, the author wrote:

"The British Tiger has tasted blood, and returns to the banquet of blood, as usual, under the mask of the highest benevolence. . . . If any other European State ventures to annex a region in Asia, Africa or Oceania, there is an outburst of pious indignation on the part of the British Public: to Great Britain alone is reserved the right of invasion, confiscation, and annexation. The British are righteous in all their dealings: the French, Belgians and Russians are unprincipled land-pirates. . . . The device of Chartered Companies is an ingenious one; it is to supply a kind of buffer of crime. How can a Company have a conscience when it has no soul, and no backside to be kicked? This is a great truth, to which the Matabele bear unwilling testimony.

"The name of Lubengula will go down to posterity with

---

to cost the British Government three years of war and the employment of 2,500,000 men. War with Germany nearly resulted. Jameson served four months' imprisonment in England for leading the raid, despite Rhodes' intervention, but by 1904 he had staged a remarkable comeback as head of the Progressive Party, and that year became prime minister of Cape Colony.

* "By One Who Remembers the Punishment which Fell Upon Cain for Killing his Brother, and Is Jealous of the Honour of Great Britain."

"WHY DO YOU PEOPLE KILL ME?" 171

that of Boadicea, Caractacus and the Athenians and Romans who died to protect their country from the invader. . . . It is no new idea, no brand-new conception of Mr. Rhodes' fertile genius, to kill out as vermin so-called inferior races for the sake of their land and their gold. . . . The British Matron, reading her paper at the breakfast table, remarks that two thousand more Savages have been killed. 'A rise of ten percent. in Mine Shares,' is the retort of Pater Familias. My pamphlet will perish, as it deserves. One or two copies may survive on the shelves of the Library of the British Museum, and the two great Universities, to record the fact that there were a few voices in 1894 crying in the wilderness to denounce crime, even when committed by their own countrymen."

iv

But the British pushed on. If they had to fight to hold what had been seized in the two preceding decades, the Colonial Office did not forget the implicit duty of England to disseminate its code of manners and morals farther afield—if any fields remained not occupied by Belgium, France, Germany, Italy, Spain and Portugal.

The region immediately north and west of Lake Nyasa had been claimed by the Portuguese, who had been compelled to relinquish it under the Anglo-Portuguese treaty of 1891. Lord Ripon appointed a high commissioner, following the customary colonial technique. Meanwhile, agents of Rhodes penetrated beyond the nominal British "sphere of influence" north of the Zambezi, and a large territory west and north of the lake was obtained by native treaties for the South Africa Company. The Nyasa Protectorate was proclaimed in 1892, and the adjacent territories—now northern Rhodesia—was also obtained for the Company. Until 1896 the British fought the Arabs and Mohammedan

Yaos in the region, and to the public at home the slaughters were extenuated as unavoidable in the humane course of suppressing the slave-traffic. When criticism became acute, the Colonial Office reminded its critics that the "Arab War" was entirely private, and waged by the South Africa Company, not by official Britain. It is true that much of the slave-traffic was concentrated at the north end of Lake Nyasa.

The last Arab fort was razed by the Company in 1896. In the unofficial war to suppress the traffic in humans, a protectorate was carved from east central Africa which is today 40,000 square miles in area, and produces quantities of cotton, tobacco and coffee—the native laborers get the princely wage of $1.25 to $1.50 monthly.

Morocco was another area on the African map upon which England had her eye in the last decade of the century. In this she was not alone among the Powers; the French in fact had had precedence there for more than a century. But it was Britain which undertook, in 1892, to make the northwestern corner of Africa another international arena. Sir Charles Euan-Smith, minister plenipotentiary to the Sultanate, was sent to Fez with a mission to obtain a revision of trade restrictions. His confidential instructions from Lord Salisbury were "to preserve the independence and territorial integrity of the Empire of Morocco, *while neglecting no favorable opportunity of impressing upon the Sultan and his Ministers the importance and advantages of improving the government and administration of the country*." * Otherwise expressed, if Sultan Mouley Hassan could not effect an improvement, it was incumbent upon the British minister

* Great Britain, Foreign Office, *Correspondence Respecting Sir C. Euan-Smith's Mission to Fez,* Morocco, Nos. 1–2, 1892.

"WHY DO YOU PEOPLE KILL ME?" 173

to show him how—under the benign auspices of the Union Jack. There was some musical-comedy humor in the protracted negotiations. At one stage, after a thirsty march over the desert from Tangiers, Sir Charles Euan-Smith told the Sultan he "would look [to him] to take all measures for due protection and honor being paid to the flag." The threat to raise the flag was made, and backed up by gunboats off Tangier, because a crowd of Moors, resenting the tariff demands and other conditions made by the British, threw bricks at members of the mission as they wandered through the town on a fête-day—some of the stones bounced off the heads of a few Americans, incidentally, who were staying close to the British in the event of trouble. The minister reported to London that he was offered a bribe of $100,000 if he would sign an agreement acceptable to the Sultan, a charge not susceptible of proof since there were no witnesses save a native interpreter. The mission finally gave up in despair and exasperation. A good many English-language newspapers made the charge that the Sultan had been bribed by the French, which is not incredible but for which again there is no plausible evidence, despite the published insinuations of Lord Salisbury. The chief of the British mission told Downing Street by courier and by telegraph (May 15, 1892) that the Sultan was evidently annoyed that he, the minister, had not brought some "presents" from Victoria. . . . Possibly the British Government was momentarily hard-up, although Sir Henry Loch in the south was assiduously keeping military "expenses as low as possible." In any event, the Sultan was plainly disgruntled when Sir Charles Euan-Smith informed him through the Moorish Minister for Foreign Affairs that "I was sure His Majesty the Sultan would receive the representatives of the Queen with all due and proper means of respect, and with reference to the 'presents' I gave him to understand that it was not my intention to take any presents for the purpose of publicly presenting them to His Majesty."

British diplomacy is usually more adroit.

Although the Fez mission was an inglorious failure, it has significance in its clear implication that Britain was ready to compete with France and Spain in northwest Africa. Britain was almost certainly blocked by a deal between another Power and the Sultan. Lord Salisbury washed his hands of the affair finally with the godly comment that the mission "has unfortunately been attended from the first by misrepresentations which have seriously compromised its success. It is not necessary to inquire with what object these intentions were framed, or from what source they have come. It is sufficient that they have obtained a considerable amount of credence in Morocco, and that currency has been given to them by various organs of European opinion. [The mission] was conceived and carried out in a spirit entirely conformable to the policy which Her Majesty's Government has uniformly pursued, of upholding the Moorish Empire, and *discouraging all efforts either to diminish its extent or to precipitate its fall.*"

That was all very well for the public records of the British Foreign Office, but it provoked only chuckles in the Continental chancelleries, and high laughter particularly on the banks of the Seine.

v

The penetrations of the other Powers in the five years after the Brussels Conference were far less extensive. That lack of predatory enterprise was due to the depleted coffers of colonial offices on the Continent, as has been remarked, to fears of political entanglements or, as in the case of Spain especially, to sheer inertia. Nevertheless, the territory un-

"WHY DO YOU PEOPLE KILL ME?" 175

occupied or not already annexed by Europeans—or not falling within their respective spheres of influence—was every year narrowing in extent; and immediately after the five-year period here under discussion, when Italy sought a more prominent place in the sun she believed it necessary, then as now, to invade Ethiopia.

Before considering the European background of the Adowa massacre, in 1896, the moves of the nations other than Britain may be noted briefly. In 1891 French agents had brought most of the Shiré river, the greatest of the Zambezi tributaries, under their domination, although they were eventually to be forced to relinquish the region to Britain, Germany and Portugal—the French Colonial Ministry was seeking conquest somewhat too far afield: the Shiré district was all of two thousand miles from the French Congo, if somewhat closer to Madagascar. The latter, parenthetically, was formally annexed in 1896, after the bombardment of Antanànarìvo, the capital, and is still without representation in the French Parliament.

If there were any serious doubts in the Third Republic of the morality of African invasion, that skepticism was dissipated by the fate which befell Paul Crampel. That explorer, traveling between the Ubangi (a Congo tributary) and the Shari river, issuing at the south end of Lake Tchad, in French Equatorial Africa, attempted to unite the possessions of Algeria, French West Africa and the French Congo. Reasonably enough, the natives opposed this gigantic steal (finally accomplished in 1900 by the juncture of three columns led respectively by Émile Gentil, Foureau-Lamy and Joalland-Meynier). A mussulman chief named Senoussi, into whose district Crampel had come, ordered the Frenchman shot. In the indignation this provoked in France, there were no undertones of consideration of the feelings of the Lake Tchad tribes—the dominant cry was to avenge

Crampel, and teach the natives that murder is not condoned by civilized Europeans. British, French and Germans divided up the lake shores in 1890–93 in a series of treaties —the German share going to France in 1919—in the mistaken belief that that body of water had potential value as a waterway to the north.

The French added to their holdings by another annexation—on the west coast. This was Dahomey, today incorporated into French West Africa, lying between the British Gold Coast and Nigeria. To pacify the King of Dahomey, he was granted an annual pension of £800 in 1890, in return for which Paris obtained a colony more than 41,000 square miles in extent: formal annexation came in 1894, after the French had expelled the expensive King, and found a puppet monarch in his young brother. (In 1900 the French found that he, too, was intriguing against their Resident, which seems both plausible and logical, and he in turn was exiled to the Congo.) They pushed farther north, occupy-

French agents descending the Niger.

"WHY DO YOU PEOPLE KILL ME?" 177

ing the Timbuctoo area (at the great northern bend of the Niger) in 1893–94. There was much sanguinary unpleasantness with the natives, and a small French force perished. Rather surprisingly, the British, in control of the Lower Niger, did not protest the French occupation of the town. Perhaps their agents knew the temper of the tribes to the north.

The Belgian, German, Italian and Portuguese confiscations were even less important. The German explorer Georg Schweinfurth had made vague claims for Berlin to the regions bordering on the river Welle, an upper Congo tributary he had discovered. Leopold brusquely disregarded the claims, and the King's agents established posts along the stream. In addition, Belgians captured in 1892–94, and for the most part razed, all the Arab settlements along the Lualaba, or upper Congo, ostensibly as a measure to stamp out the slave-traffic: the fact was that the traffic by the Arabs had reached such proportions that Leopold had reason to fear he would be unable, when the time arrived, to conscript the labor battalions he would need himself. . . . German colonial ambitions, despite the energy and eager support of Wilhelm II, met with setbacks. When Dr. Karl Peters in German East Africa resorted to the subtle practice of executing women to preserve his authority—crimes definitely proved against him—the Kilemanjaro tribes displayed a mild resentment, however cheap life was in Africa. The Wilhelmstrasse, with protests pouring in from all parts of the world, had the good sense, and the precaution, to order the doctor home, where he was tried on a misdemeanor— "misuse of power"—and stripped of his commission. Similarly there was trouble in German South-West Africa where, in 1894, the Hottentots revolted and murdered several German farmers, their wives and children. But the Fatherland, never a success at colonization, persevered and remained undeterred by violent British and French criticism of its methods; much of the criticism on both sides of the Channel was manifestly propaganda, and by modern standards far from skillful.

After her Somaliland (Ethiopian) grab, Italy was momentarily content with pushing northwest into the interior, and established a post, in 1895, at Lugh, on the Jub river, near the 1935 Italo-Ethiopian frontier on the south; then as now, Rome dreamed of a corridor, if not all of Ethiopia, so that Eritrea and Somaliland would be geographically one. The War Ministry believed that Lugh might prove a strategic jumping-off place for the campaign of the next year. The Portuguese deposed a half-dozen Zulu chiefs in their Mozambique "dependency"—a felicitous euphemism now coming into favor as less susceptible to misinterpretation than "protectorate" or "zone of influence"—awakening at last to the convenience of the slave-traffic as a pretext for extending colonial control. The Spaniards were the last to realize the practical value of those amiable ambiguities in the Brussels Act relating to the slave-traffic. . . . By 1895 the tribes farthest in the interior recognized the so-called Black continent was no longer theirs.

X

African Caporetto
[1896]

FRANCESCO CRISPI of Italy was born a Sicilian, and he possessed both the cunning and the temper characteristic of his people. When he learned that Menelik II had denounced the treaty of Uccialli, in 1893, the Italian premier nearly lost his mind in a paroxysm of Latin rage. The year before he had triumphantly notified the Powers of the signature of the treaty—Article XVII of which in the Italian version made Ethiopia an Italian protectorate, since the Emperor had ostensibly agreed to consult Rome upon matters concerning "other Powers or Governments." But after the death of Johannes, and the coronation of Menelik as emperor of all Ethiopia, the latter himself notified the Powers of his succession to the throne—a procedure, to Crispi's narrowing eyes, violating the Uccialli agreement.

In his notification to Europe, Menelik "announced his own coronation, lamented his isolation, and hoped for an opening upon the sea for the importation of fire-arms." * Queen Victoria and Kaiser Wilhelm—the former "courteously," the latter more "pungently," to use Menelik's adverbs—replied that in view of the treaty of Uccialli it was improper for the Powers to communicate or to negotiate with the Negus, except through the agency of Rome. The King of Kings, with an understandable amount of pride,

* *Storia diplomatica dell' Etiopa,* Carlo Rosetti, Turin 1910.

was first humiliated and, after a day's rumination, amazed. He called for the Italian and the Amharic texts of the treaty, and learned to his horror that the terms of Article XVII in the two versions were not identical. The Italians, he charged in a letter to King Umberto, had played him a foul trick.

"When I made that treaty of friendship with Italy [he wrote the monarch] in order that our secrets be guarded and that our understanding should not be spoiled, I said that because of friendship our affairs in Europe might be carried on with the aid of the Sovereign of Italy, but *I have not made any treaty which obliges me to do so, and today I am not the man to accept it.* That one independent Power does not seek the aid of another to carry on its affairs, Your Majesty understands very well."

Infuriated, Crispi remembered his gift to Menelik in 1888 of five thousand Remington rifles as the price of Menelik's neutrality in case Italy declared war on the Negus Johannes, in northern Ethiopia. Now these fire-arms, the Sicilian foresaw, might readily be used against Italians.

Another instance of the boomerang effect of the various instruments employed by Europeans to subjugate the African.

Yet Menelik's defection, as it seemed to be in Crispi's mind, had its bright and Machiavellian aspect. If the Emperor persisted in negotiating directly with the other Powers, and particularly for "an opening upon the sea for the importation of fire-arms," Italy might well be justified before the world in a military invasion of Ethiopia. A treaty, in fine, is an international contract.

With few but Italian exceptions, modern writers of the events preceding the Adowa rout are convinced that Menelik was sincere in his consternation, and that he wrote in good faith to the head of the House of Savoy. There are more than superficial reasons to support that conviction.

Even after the signature of the Uccialli treaty, Crispi felt that Ethiopia was not sufficiently mortgaged to Rome. He therefore proposed to Menelik's special envoy to Italy, Ras Makonnen (father of Haile Selassie), the signature of an "Additional Convention," which was duly negotiated October 1, 1889. Under its terms, Menelik was to accept an Italian loan of 4,000,000 lire—for military or agricultural purposes, as he saw fit. One half of the loan was to be paid the Negus in silver at Addis Ababa. The remainder was to be placed on deposit in Italy, to be used for the purchase of supplies which Ethiopia was constrained to buy within the Peninsula. The Rome Government guaranteed the loan that was eventually floated by the National Bank of Italy. In return, Menelik not only agreed to recognize the sovereignty of the King of Italy to the Red Sea colonies, but he had to pledge the Harar Customs House receipts—Ethiopia's chief source of foreign revenue—as security for the loan. . . . It was colonial confiscation by economic mortgage, a novel instrument of invasion but in objective not different from conquest by machine-gun, gin or Tyrolese hats.

The set-up for Rome was perfect. If Menelik failed to meet his notes, Italy had the right to the exclusive administration of the Customs House and the diversion of its receipts, which meant control of Ethiopian finances, i. e., Ethiopia itself. On the other hand, if Menelik met his stiff payments regularly, Crispi reasoned that any territories acquired by the former, by virtue of the loan, would necessarily be added to the Italian protectorate implicit in the Uccailli treaty.

It was heads Crispi wins, tails Menelik loses.

After the Negus denounced the treaty, he recognized the trap. In his first moves, in which there was something of hysteria, students of the modern history of Ethiopia recognize Menelik's integrity. He had been rebuffed by Victoria and the Kaiser, due to what he believed was, on the evidence, Italian chicanery. He therefore refused any more loan installments due him from the National Bank of Italy, although they were pressed upon him assiduously, and began to make pitifully small repayments on the money already expended.

But a diplomatic bargain, an international contract, is more difficult to break than a civil one—despite, one should add, the World War obligations. Not only was Crispi's political future at stake, but the colonial prestige of Italy as well. The politico-psychological situation in Italy, after Menelik denounced the treaty, is aptly summarized by Ernest Work, former American adviser to Haile Selassie:

"In [Italy's] eagerness to have a 'sphere,' she had taken over Ethiopia in haste without having Menelik understand—perhaps not wishing him to understand—Article XVII, as Italy had written it. Now they could not bear the thought of giving up the *protectorate*. They were ready to make almost any sort of arrangements as to boundary that Menelik might wish, if only they might *protect* him. Italy just must have somebody to protect. All the others had, so must she have." *

Thus Crispi in Rome, and Count Pietro Antonelli at Addis Ababa as special envoy, moved heaven and earth to negotiate a new agreement with Menelik. In the abortive document finally signed at Addis Ababa on February 6, 1891, the Negus in comic fashion paid Italy back for slipping over Article XVII. On this occasion the Emperor took special pains that the one valid copy of the substitute treaty should be in Amharic, in which tongue Antonelli had not had benefit of Berlitz. As alternatives to Uccialli, Menelik had pro-

* *Ethiopia, A Pawn in European Diplomacy*, Ernest Work, Macmillan, New York 1935.

posed (1), signature of a supplementary treaty upholding the Uccialli agreement with the exception of Article XVII; or (2), a treaty upholding the Amharic version of the old treaty—i. e., leaving the Negus free to avail himself of Italian advice in Ethiopian foreign affairs *when and if he chose to do so;* or (3), preservation of the old treaty in both versions: a proposal which in ambiguity and circuition was worthy of Turkish diplomacy at its best.

Weary of the protracted discussions, the lack of *ravioli,* cheese and Chianti, the Italian count agreed to the last proposal—at least Italy could hold to her own interpretation of the 1889 agreement, in dealing with the Powers, while Ethiopia could not evade the explicit stipulation that she would permit no other nation to make a protectorate of her or any part of the country.

To understand how Antonelli signed the document he did, it must be assumed the ambassador was either in a diplomatic fog, or that one of Menelik's minor accomplishments was a facility at sleight-of-hand. Antonelli reported to Rome that he had signed the third proposal. When, however, he summoned his translator, the latter informed him laconically that, on the contrary, the treaty signed was the first of Menelik's proposals, the one destroying Article XVII.

One may imagine Menelik laughing homerically under his royal *ombrello rosso* in Addis Ababa. . . . The Negus had proved to his own satisfaction that if Italy two years before had tricked him into signing the Uccialli treaty, he could similarly trick an ambassador whose knowledge of Amharic did not extend beyond "yes" and "no." Antonelli returned to Rome in a white heat of Latin fury. When he had regained his speech he told Crispi and Rudini, the Foreign Minister, that French conspiracies at Addis Ababa were responsible for the entire comedy of errors and frustration. Again there were no tears along the Seine.

ii

Certainly French agents were busy between Djibouti and Menelik's capital. Gallic historians of Franco-Italians relations have never become lathered in denying the interest at the time of the Quai-d'Orsay, although there were and still are heard feeble refutations from politicians, notably deputies from the southern tier of *départements,* who benefit from any improvement in trade relations between Paris and Rome. Not only were French agents active in prejudicing Menelik, but France later was to lend him tangible aid against Italy by supplying fire-arms and ammunition.

The evidence that France intrigued against Italy in Ethiopia, as she unquestionably had against Britain in Morocco, is overwhelming and no serious historian would undertake to disprove it. Its interest here is that it provides another indication that the partition of Africa was executed in the several chancelleries, and not in the main by commercial agents and explorers in Africa.

The disgruntled Antonelli charged also that the French agents had offered Menelik 40,000 rifles to hold out against Italy, a credible allegation in light of the many French rifles the Ethiopians carried before and after Adowa.* The "Green Book" of the Italian Foreign Office for 1891 includes a claim by Antonelli that the French offered Menelik a substantial annual payment if he would permit the establishment of a French trading-station on Lake Assal (the great salt depositary ceded to French Somaliland in 1897— shortly after Adowa, it should be noted), the Negus to maintain his sovereignty over the region.

The offer was alluring. The French were not asking a protectorate, were not demanding that the Quai-d'Orsay be

* Italian Foreign Office, *Documenti Diplomatici,* No. XVII (1890–91).

entrusted with the conduct of Menelik's foreign relations, and were not engaged in saber-rattling; and besides, they had had the good sense to address the emperor as Negus Negusti (King of Kings), and not, as was the pointed Italian custom, merely as "Altezza." The difference may seem trivial and academic, but therein was one of the origins of Menelik's hatred and distrust of the Italians who would not recognize him as an independent sovereign. But for this gratuitous humiliation, there might have been no Adowa nor, it is conceivable, an Italo-Ethiopian conflict today.

There were other French blandishments and promises, besides the reported bribe of 40,000 rifles. It was charged that French agents had obtained the ear of Tigre princes and chieftains who, for one or another consideration, reported back to Menelik, with studious intent, that *i suoi amici Italiani sono gente che val poco* ("Your Italian friends are people of small valor").* That this activity was inspired and financed by the French Foreign Office is self-evident to anyone acquainted with the procedure and tradition of that rationalistic institution. Other anti-Italian measures in France were more open. Jean-Louis Deloncle, under-director of the Ministry of Colonies, a deputy and one of the French delegates to the Brussels Conference, obtained a copy of the Italian "Green Book" of May 26, 1890, which among copies of other documents included the Rome version of Article XVII of the Uccialli treaty. He sent it to Menelik who learned thus—and from Victoria and the Kaiser also—that he was a vassal of Italy. In the face of this, Menelik raised no objections when a M. Chefneux, an artillery officer in mufti, arrived at Addis Ababa with the bland innocence of the tourist on his face and fifteen machine-guns in his baggage. Despite vehement Italian protests, Chefneux was permitted entry.

* *Documenti Diplomatici*, No. xv, p. 264.

Soon after Deloncle's dispatch to Menelik of the "Green Book," French agents swarmed into Addis Ababa, and to settlements and villages along the caravan route to Djibouti, with manifestly garbled extracts of this Italian document—translated into Amharic. "From morning until night," the fuming Antonelli cabled Rudini, "they [the French] repeat to His Majesty, 'You see, we have reasons to warn you [to] distrust the Italians.' " To make matters still pleasanter for the count, French and other agents—reportedly Russian—had persuaded the Negus that by sharp practice the National Bank of Italy had swindled him, even after he had refused further payments. The present writer finds no credible evidence in support of that charge, but nevertheless the accusation was made.

Its patience exhausted, the cabinet determined upon another tack—in which lay the genesis of war. After the signature of the Uccialli treaty, the Foreign Office at Rome had notified the Powers, in accordance with the agreement reached in the Berlin Act, that Italy had proclaimed a protectorate over Ethiopia. With the exception of an equivocal acknowledgment from France (where it was asked in the Chamber of Deputies precisely what Italy meant by "Ethiopia"), the Powers raised no objections. After the fruitless negotiations with Menelik, Rome concluded that since Britain, Germany and Austria-Hungary were friendly to the protectorate it followed that Ethiopia's remonstrances against protection were inconsequential and not worthy of serious consideration by a civilized nation.

That was realistic, political logic to the Italian mind.

As a prelude to the employment of force in seizing Ethiopia, Italian forces in 1894 expelled the Mahdists from Kassala (in the eastern Sudan, near the present frontier of Eritrea) from which point Rome could threaten Menelik from his northwest frontier. Britain submitted her thanks to the Italian commanders, and Rome and London negotiated a treaty (May 5) permitting the Italian forces "a temporary occupation for military purposes." Although the British had retreated from the Sudan after the capitulation of Khartum, that vast area adjacent to Egypt still remained, of course, within their zone of influence: it was a question with Downing Street of merely how soon the War Office and Kitchener might feel it safe to move back again. As a further reward for booting the Mahdists, or Dervishes, from Kassala, the British consented to allow the Italians to include within her Ethiopian protectorate the Harar (eastern) district of Gallaland, directly behind British Somaliland.

But the Quai-d'Orsay, it appeared, never slept. The French Foreign minister, Gabriel Hanotaux, backed up by Georges Clemenceau, the finance minister, acidly reminded Downing Street that Britain was not qualified to "cede" any part of Ethiopia to anyone (certainly not to Italy!), could not pledge non-interference, and recalled a Franco-British convention of 1888 under which both Powers agreed not to seek a protectorate over Harar—a trading-center vital to all the Powers in east Africa. The British could not argue away the legitimate French objections—legitimate insofar as they had a treaty basis. Accordingly Paris once again checkmated Italy in Ethiopia. Moreover, England had also suffered, if intangibly, by her attempt to make a present to Italy of territory certainly not within her zone of influence, for it bred in Hanotaux's mind a lasting distrust of his trans-Channel neighbor, a suspiciousness that had no small part in the events which nearly provoked war five years later over Fashoda.

Nevertheless, the French were losers also in the quarrel: as so often happens at diplomatic horsetrades, all the parties are out of pocket. Since 1882 leading French writers on foreign affairs had urged repeatedly that so far as France was concerned, Italy should have Ethiopia, Tripoli or almost anything else within reason, provided only that Rome left the Triple Alliance. The successive rebuffs administered by the French to the Italians in east Africa were not calculated to persuade Rome to forsake Germany and Austria-Hungary, although the Italians were never enthusiastic over that alliance.

In the face of the French snubs, Crispi recognized the necessity of seeking joint action in east Africa with the British who were, at least momentarily, in a grateful mood over the capture of Kassala. Because of reports that the Mahdists planned another uprising, a Major San Miniatelli was sent to Egypt to discuss with Kitchener coöperation against the Dervishes—Kitchener had then just been appointed sirdar of the Khedive's army. The French were displeased with this overture, and with the promising auspices under which that British-Italian conference began, but the next two years were to prove that Britain would accept "coöperation" to save her own chestnuts from the fire, but not to save anyone else's, and assuredly not Italy's. Baron Adolf von Marschall, the German Foreign Minister, was giving Crispi sound advice when he warned him that Downing Street was using Italy for her own ends.*

The three-cornered international bickering over Ethiopia was now heightened by the perversity of Russia, which decided to enter the arena obliquely, chiefly to annoy Germany, alarm Austria-Hungary and encourage France †—otherwise, St. Petersburg had no concern in Africa. In 1894–95 all sight had been lost of the original dispute,

* *Die Grosse Politik der Europäischen Kabinette* (1871–1914), Johannes Lepsius et al, vol. viii, p. 463, No. 2063, Berlin 1922–26.

† In 1894 Russia and France had signed a secret military convention.

which was the right of the Negus to rule over his own people, and their right to remain free of subjugation by Europeans. Russian agents joined the French in Ethiopia, and Rome was particularly irritated by the arrival at Addis Ababa of a "Russian Scientific Expedition," a mission whose avowed interest was strictly religious but which, at least to Italian eyes, appeared excessively well-armed for a body of men ostensibly devoted to a peaceful study of the faith of the natives.* What its members sought, it developed later, was a coaling-station, although Ethiopia had no coastline, but their ostensible interest was the study of the Amharic religion in which, they claimed, there were similarities to theirs.

By 1894 it was evident to observant Italians that their government would be compelled to invade Ethiopia, if only as a face-saving gesture—as it was with Mussolini in October 1935, when the present invasion began. It is clear from Crispi's own memoirs that he felt Italy would be fortunate if she was not forced into war either with France or Russia, or both, over his projected Ethiopian adventure. And suddenly, in 1895, the Italian premier realized miserably he was too far committed to withdraw. In frantic haste, fearing entanglement with Paris or St. Petersburg, he turned to his allies of the Triple Alliance.

Diplomatically and militarily, all he received from Germany and Austria-Hungary was a cold douche. Chancellor (Prince) Hohenlohe instructed Bernhard von Bülow, ambassador at Rome, to tell Crispi bluntly that the mutual-aid stipulations of the Triple Alliance might not be invoked if Italy became involved in a war with France and Russia over Africa. For his part, the Austrian ambassador to Rome, Baron Petti, reported wearily to Vienna that "I have al-

* *Modern Abyssinia*, A. B. Wylde, London 1901.

ready had to listen to Italian lamentations, in every key, that they have been the victims of the Triple Alliance." *

There was one passing solace, it seemed to Crispi, before the debacle. By a secret treaty of May 5, 1894, negotiated between the premier and Sir Francis Clare-Ford, Italy and Britain had delimited—on paper—their respective zones of influence in east Africa. On the treaty maps, Ethiopia vanished from sight, and was replaced by a region called "Italian Abyssinia," stretching from the frontiers of Eritrea southeastward to the western line of Italian Somaliland: Menelik's empire was completely abolished—and what was then labeled Italian Abyssinia, i. e., virtually all of Ethiopia, is substantially the objective of Italy today. This again was a violation of the 1888 agreement between France and Britain, and spies of the former soon learned of the secret agreement. The British evaded the charge of treaty infraction by responding that while the 1888 convention prohibited either party from "ceding" any Ethiopian territory to another Power, the treaty did not prevent England from approving the pretensions of another nation to a zone of influence in Menelik's kingdom. This was, patently, the baldest quibbling, and Downing Street realized it had blundered seriously.

Inevitably, the British reversed themselves overnight, and Crispi learned to his consternation that material British support of his project in Ethiopia would not be forthcoming—despite Kassala, despite every wile Crispi had used, and political sacrifice he believed he had made, to drive a wedge between London and Paris. In Paris, M. Hanotaux allowed himself a sardonic grin over his *vermouth-cassis*. It was his second checkmate of Anglo-Italian efforts to swallow Ethiopia.

* *The Secret Treaties of Austria-Hungary*, Alfred F. Pribram, Harvard University Press, Cambridge, 1920–21.

AFRICAN CAPORETTO 191

iii

So to the Italian mentality, war was certain, which is to say it was politically desirable and would doubtless end profitably, even without British support. Late in 1895 the first skirmishes began—with another defeat of an Italian force which should have been seen as prophetic. . . . While Crispi had turned this way and that, Menelik's campaign to cement the tribes under one leadership had been remarkably successful—remarkable in light of the gifts and promises of Italian agents. The Negus found nothing so effective in winning pledges of loyalty from the tribes as the currency he gave to a song he composed from an African aphorism—"Of a black snake's bite you may be cured, but from the bite of a white snake you will never recover." * The melody has lingered.

iv

The clouds of dismay about the Italian Foreign Office lifted late in 1895 when it was reported from Aden that Menelik had been struck dead by lightning. It seemed that this intelligent act of God might solve Italy's problem, for without the organizing genius of the King of Kings it was highly probable that Ethiopia would be torn by civil warfare among the various princes north and south. Somewhat awkwardly for Crispi and the Italian war ministry, it developed that Menelik was extremely alive, and vigorously preparing for battle.

A few modern historians have given Menelik his due. There can be no doubt of his ability as diplomat and military leader—in both fields he was fortunate in obtaining competent Europeans, if not always disinterested ones, to advise and guide him. But British and Italian writers of an-

* *Memorie d'Africa*, General Oreste Baratieri.

other generation variously portrayed the Negus as an arch-criminal, a pitiless slave-driver, a political negotiator lacking even the ethics of European diplomats, and a cannibal to boot. Because it reflects the amusing egotism of one self-confessed "English gentleman" of the 'nineties, and also because it mirrors the imperialist attitude typical of a large class of Europeans, the following evaluation of Menelik by Augustus B. Wylde may be cited—if only, indeed, for its unconscious humor and inconsistency: *

"I firmly believe at present that no paper ties or promises that the king [Menelik] has ever made would be recognized by him if they stood in the way of his interests . . . and his life of intrigue that he has led makes him a match for the most able diplomatist of any nation, *so it will be very difficult to corner him.* . . . He may learn a lesson from those [the members of a British mission] he is now brought into contact with, as he never before saw *an English officer or a gentleman until our mission and the present English representative* [the over-modest Wylde himself] and may learn that there are other types of character than those he has formerly seen and been brought into contact with. No one who has had any dealing with King Menelik can doubt that he has many good points . . . but still he could have prevented the wholesale mutilation after the Adowa battle."

Evidently in the mind of Vice-Consul Wylde, Count Antonelli—a cardinal's nephew—was not a gentleman measured by British standards.

v

Militarily, the battle of Adowa has little significance, although it has been the subject of exhaustive studies by Italian, British, French and American cavalry and infantry

* Wylde was British vice-consul for the Red Sea region in the 'nineties.

tacticians whose problem has been to explain the blunders that made the slaughter possible.* Compared to the everyday butchery that often occurred in the space of a few seconds during the World War, the Adowa casualties were relatively unimportant. The primary import of Adowa was political, and in that sense twofóld: its outcome demonstrated to Europe that Ethiopia, and the black man in general, could not be dismissed lightly, and it halted the Italian advance in East Africa for nearly forty years.

Ras Mangasha, prince of Tigre province, was the illegitimate son of Johannes whom Menelik had succeeded. Ras Makonnen, who had gone to Italy as Menelik's special envoy in 1889, made overtures repeatedly during 1885 to the Italians in Eritrea for peace terms, as did Ras Mangasha. Neither expected peace, and it is doubtful they desired it, but it was part of Menelik's political and military strategy to lead the Italians on. The various frontier parleys came to nothing: Menelik demanded that the Italians relinquish Asmara, while General Oreste Baratieri, governor of Eritrea, declared that peace could be discussed only after the Negus had approved *in toto* the old Uccialli treaty, that is, consented that Ethiopia become an Italian protectorate. In any event, the general would not withdraw his forces from Asmara nor give up whatever other territory he was occupying in Tigre province, which had been wrested in August 1885 after the Italians defeated Mangasha. The Italians had also occupied Adowa, farther south, and before the end of the year (1895) Mangasha with Makonnen's aid had defeated an advanced Italian post at Makale. On that occasion

* Two technical accounts may be cited for those interested: *La Bataille d'Adoua*, by Lieut.-Col. Petitin, which appears in the Journal des Sciences Militaires, ser. 10, vol. ix, pp. 255–83, Paris 1901; and *The Battle of Adowa*, by Major Bernard Smith, U. S. Cavalry Association Journal, Sept.–Oct., pp. 33–41, Washington, D. C., 1935.

Makonnen had permitted the battalion to retire with full military honors after the troops took an oath never to bear arms again against Ethiopia. The Italians were lucky to escape with their lives, due solely to Makonnen's forbearance—perhaps he recalled the honors lavished upon him years before in Italy; the oath, subsequently broken, should be remembered in view of the mutilations which horrified the world. The freed officers reported back to General Baratieri that the natives were equipped with Hotchkiss rapid-firing guns, superior to the Italian muzzle-loading mountain-pieces. They also reported, according to Wylde's account, that they had learned the guns were obtained from the French via Djibouti, and that many of Menelik's men admitted frankly they had been trained in their use by French and Russian officers at Addis Ababa. . . . Baratieri was nervous and demanded immediate reinforcements from Italy. Clearly he saw he had a major battle, not a series of skirmishes, on his hands.

Baratieri's flurry of messages to Rome finally percolated into the War Ministry which persuaded Crispi to soften his demands on Menelik. On February 8, 1896, he began a strategic retreat: he informed the alarmed governor of Eritrea, who was also commander-in-chief, that Italy now proposed peace if the treaty of Uccialli was accepted in the Amharic version, and if the Negus would cede that part of Tigre province—virtually all of it—occupied by Baratieri's forces. Menelik laughed, understanding readily that Crispi had been literally deserted by the Powers. He laughed more vociferously when, plainly in desperation, Crispi at last suggested that there would be no Italian invasion if only Menelik agreed not to cede any part of his empire to another Power. The Negus's answer took the form of ordering forced marches to defend Makale and dispatching scouting parties toward Adowa.

Baratieri's own account of the campaign, although in part a somewhat hysterical defense of his acts, written after dishonor was heaped upon him, discloses convincingly enough that he was loath to attack without a greater force. Yet the fact remains he had a formidable and, for the most part, well-trained body: in the actual engagement outside Adowa, his troops totaled 17,700 (14,519 infantrymen and 3,181 artillerymen), and fifty-six guns; of that total, 10,596 were Italians, or sixty percent. Menelik's highly individualistic "army"—every native was his own commander—numbered about 90,000, with almost that many rifles, perhaps ten thousand spears, and forty-two guns. Included in his force were 8,600 mounted riflemen. Menelik's forces were untrained in the European sense and very loosely organized. But, it may be pointed out, they were fighting on their own soil.

During the month of February there were sporadic clashes between Italian (native) scouting-parties and Menelik's advanced and highly mobile posts—clashes almost invariably resulting in a rout of the Italians.* At length Crispi's frayed nerves gave way under political pressure. A reluctant Chamber of Deputies had voted him an appropriation after an impassioned plea in which he based his request on the supposed craving of the people for a restoration of Italian military prestige. But Baratieri, crawling westward day after day over the difficult terrain between Adigrat and Adowa, had accomplished nothing. And in exasperation, on February 25, Crispi cabled the general this historic death-warrant:

"This is a military phthisis and not a war. . . . Small skirmishes in which we are always facing the enemy with inferior numbers—a waste of heroism without any corresponding success. . . . It is clear to me that there is no

* Bernard Smith, *op. cit*.

fundamental plan in this campaign, and I should like to see one formulated. *We are ready for any sacrifice in order to save the honor of the army and the prestige of the monarchy."*

On this incredible and incriminating document the premier is silent in his Memoirs, compiled from diaries, by his nephew. The compiler notes merely in a final aside that "unfortunately the Crispi ministry was swept away in consequence of a *battle lost in Africa.*" * No mention by Crispi of the dead—nor where their bodies lay rotting after a "battle lost in Africa."

Thus Baratieri's hand was forced by Rome. At Sauria, from which the attack was to be launched upon the main body of Ethiopians, fifteen miles southwest, the general hopelessly issued these orders to his army:

"The bayonet is to be used on every possible occasion;

"In the firing-line a close formation, that is, a thin line, shoulder to shoulder, is to be employed;

"No firing is to be ordered at a greater distance than 500 meters and, except in unusual cases, volleys are to be employed;

"The men with the commissariat column are to take part in the action, as many as possible of them advancing into the lines;

"As soon as the fighting begins, the reserve cartridges are to be distributed from the commissariat."

Oreste Baratieri was as competent a commander as any in Italy, despite the horrible outcome of Adowa, for which Crispi must share most of the responsibility. Knowing what he did of the force confronting him, of the terrain, of his halting supply-columns and frail lines of communication, it may be supposed that he wrote the conventional proclama-

* *The Memoirs of Francesco Crispi*, vol. iii, edited by Thomas Palamenghi-Crispi, London 1910.

tion on the eve of battle (February 29) in bitterness and despair, certain that slaughter was inevitable. That dismal *bravura* read:

ORDER OF THE DAY NO. 5

Addi-Dichi (near Sauria)
February 29, 1896
SOLDIERS!

For fifteen days you have impatiently waited for the Abyssinian attack.

Since they dare not come at us, we are going to them!

Their great numbers need not intimidate you. Your superior arms and your discipline will triumph over their disorganized and poorly equipped masses.

Have you not already defeated them in twenty encounters?

We will employ *échelon* formations against which their efforts will prove in vain.

Stay within control of your officers, and they will lead you to victory.

Soldiers! believe that all Italy has its eyes upon you; with the aid of the God of the armies, we will hurl these savages back to their mountains.

Your general trusts in you; count upon him!

vi

The advance was made overnight. Immediately everything went wrong, the advancing columns losing touch with one another because of misinterpretation of orders. The first action, after the fifteen-mile march, began at dawn on March 1, against the slopes of Mount Garima where Menelik's forces were in a strong defensive position. A little more than three hours later, at 9:30 A. M., the Italian forces who had escaped death or major wounds were fleeing back toward Sauria. Baratieri's right, center and left had been shot full of holes, and he was himself hurrying away from the closing jaws of Menelik's pincers. By 10 A. M. "all control was at an end [he reported to Rome in his first dispatch] and no orderly retirement could be organized. It was in vain that the officers tried to halt the soldiers on any of the successive positions because the enemy, bursting in on them, and the cavalry darting about below, were sufficient to throw them into confusion. It was then that the real losses began; the soldiers, as if mad, threw away their rifles and ammunition with the idea that if they were taken without arms they would not be emasculated, and almost all threw away their rations and capes."

An early Caporetto in miniature.

Italian casualties: 6,000 dead of the force of 17,700, 1,500 wounded, 2,000 prisoners, altogether 9,500. Ethiopian casualties, 11,000 of which 5,000 were dead, of a force of 80,000. Among other officers the Italians lost two generals, together with all their fifty-six guns and 11,000 rifles. Italian native prisoners, wounded and unwounded, Moslem and Christian, who had fought at Makale or elsewhere against the Ethiopians, suffered the penalty of emasculation or other mutilation, usually amputation of the right hand and left foot.* At least eight hundred Italian natives were mutilated, and an Italian colonel who had fought at Makale, and been released, was summarily shot.

Adowa stunned and nauseated Europe.

Baratieri was arrested at Asmara, and subsequently tried at Massowa by a military court-martial for "having inexcusably ordered an attack upon the enemy's force in circum-

* The joints of wrist and ankle were severed, and the stumps plunged into boiling fat to stop the flow of blood. Wylde, who visited the battlefield soon after the massacre, reported to the *Manchester Guardian* that he saw piles of hands and feet, as well as the bodies of wounded prisoners who had been left to die—or their end hastened mercifully by an *assagai* thrust.

stances which rendered inevitable the defeat of his command, for abandoning his post in action and retreating sixty miles on March 2 without knowing their (his generals') fate." The six generals comprising the court acquitted Baratieri of criminal intention or penal responsibility, in part because of Crispi's telegram, but in their final verdict they "deplored the fact that the command of the Italian troops should have been confided to an incompetent leader."

Nor did Crispi escape. On March 5, appearing with understandable nervousness before the Chamber of Deputies, he was hooted. In the streets, mobs screamed for his life—his telegram had been made public. The university was closed to prevent student rioting. Socialists cheered Menelik. Literally thousands of Italians fled across the three frontiers to escape service in Africa. There were sanguinary clashes between police and populace in all the cities and larger towns. At Pavia a mob tore up the railroad tracks to prevent the departure of troop replacements. The filtering reports of the emasculation of white soldiers by black infuriated the nation. There were demands for impeachment of Crispi and his cabinet for "immorality."

General Baldissera, who supplanted Baratieri, was ordered to open peace negotiations with Menelik or Ras Makonnen. The Negus would have proved less difficult and unbending but for the capture, in the midst of the negotiations (September 5), of the Dutch freighter *Doelwijk* by the Italian gunboat *Etna*. The ship was seized in the Red Sea, and her papers disclosed she had been chartered by Carrière Fils et Cie., a French export house. Below decks there were thirty thousand rifles consigned to Djibouti. Menelik declared the confiscation illegal. His back stiffened. He tore up the Pope's plea to release the Italians he held prisoner. Eventually, on October 26, Ethiopia and Italy signed a treaty of "peace and friendship *forever*."

It scrapped the Uccialli treaty. Italy recognized Ethiopia as a "sovereign independent State." Italy was forbidden to cede any of her Eritrea territory to another European Power. The Eritrea frontier returned to the former line made by the Mareb, Mouna and Belessu rivers. All Tigre province, of course, reverted to Menelik who, incidentally, ruled that the new treaty would be valid only in an Amharic and a French version—he would have no more to do with Italian diplomatic circumlocutions.

Apart from the fury aroused in Italy over the Adowa disaster, there were recriminations elsewhere in Europe. The Wilhelmstrasse complained to Downing Street that Britain, complacent when the Italians had seized Kassala and willing to "cede" Gallaland to them, had deserted Italy in the face of emergency. Britain replied that, just before hostilities began, she had offered Rome permission to transport troops through British Somaliland via Zeila, to attack Menelik in the rear, *provided the French raised no objections.** The inference is that France had objected, and vigorously—if one recalls M. Hanotaux's distrust of England. The British Foreign Office added, in its alibi to Berlin, that neither could England have offered financial aid to Italy without provoking a howl of protests from City bankers, and that in any event British collaboration would have invited an attack by Menelik on Zeila. There the bickering ended.

But the defeat of the Italians provoked no dismay at St. Petersburg. The Czar, who had sent eighty Red Cross nurses to Addis Ababa, expressed his delight over Menelik's military prowess by bestowing upon the "Lion of the Tribe of Judah" his highest decoration, the Grand Cordon of the Order of St. George.

* *Die Grosse Politik,* vol. xi, p. 239.

XI

Sudan Idyl
[1896-98]

IN Italy as elsewhere the moral strictures against the coterie responsible for the Adowa carnage subsided in a few months—an emotion so furious could not, in the nature of man, be prolonged forever. By the end of 1896, published and spoken philippics against Crispi, Baratieri and company were rare. That ubiquitous individual known as the man-in-the-street forgot Adowa.

But not the men in the chancelleries.

The political portents of Adowa were infinite. Generally speaking, they may be reduced to the conviction, among the offices of the colonial and foreign secretaries—apart from the chastened Italians—that Ethiopia could be conquered. . . . The Italians had suffered a military accident, and even in Rome it was agreed their diplomacy before Adowa had been atrocious. But the projects and the motives at play in the various capitals, so far as East Africa was concerned, were not identical, save in the sense that all the Powers hungered for more territory—if any remained, in the ambiguous phrase of the Berlin Act, that was not "effectively occupied." The post-Adowa viewpoint of Britain, France and Germany, whose economic stake was greatest, may be summarized thus:

Britain. Menelik's victory raised convenient alarms in the foreign and colonial offices that (1) an attack might be launched by Ethiopia against British Somaliland, and (2), that joining with the Mahdists, the Ethiopians might rise in a rebellion against all Europeans, and endanger British-controlled Egypt on the north, and the recently proclaimed Protectorate on the south. Was the time at hand to recapture the Sudan?

France. The Quai-d'Orsay, as well as the nation at large, not only distrusted Britain and suspected her of designs upon Ethiopia, but the Government felt that, in return for its covert but effective aid to the Negus against Italy, Menelik should be favorably disposed to territorial and economic concessions for the French. (At one point the distrust of Britain reached a point that charges were published, as in *Le Petit Journal* of Paris, that the British were at the bottom of the Dreyfus scandal.) In addition, there was a large body of official and private opinion that the Third Republic, recovered from its growing-pains, should now extend its African holdings across the continent from west to east, more specifically into the Sudan where, in the opinion of M. Hanotaux, for example, the British could no more claim "effective occupation" than they could pretend that it fell within their "zone of influence"—save for the natives, it was a No-Man's-Land. That being so, was this not a propitious moment to send a column to the Upper Nile?

Germany. The Wilhelmstrasse feared with good reason that its East African Protectorate would be encircled by British territory which would cripple their trade. The fear was so real that Germany was willing to join forces with the French, in the beginning diplomatically and at last militarily, against Britain—an extraordinary concession, to say the least.

Three years before Adowa, the French had launched a diplomatic campaign, directed against Britain, to recover some part of their former influence in Egypt, lost the summer of 1882 when they declined to join in the bombardment of Alexandria. President François Carnot had not hesitated to urge that the most effective method of forcing negotiations would be for a French force to occupy some Egyptian or Sudan territory. Moreover, the French desire to obtain ground north of Lake Victoria, if a clean sweep from the Atlantic coast was not feasible, became more pressing when it became known that Rhodes, Joseph Chamberlain and others were planning a Cape-to-Cairo railroad. Such a British project was of course a formidable threat both to French and German ambitions in Africa.

Paris and Berlin, in consequence, agreed quietly to collaborate diplomatically against Britain, to destroy any imperialist projects in Downing Street of a 6,800-mile swath through Africa, north to south, under English domination. The spearhead of their attack was upon Article III of the Anglo-Congolese treaty of 1894, in which Leopold leased to Britain a Congo corridor between Lake Albert and Lake Tanganyika. That would give her a right-of-way to the Mediterranean, once she had "pacified" the Sudan.

So bitter was France over the concession that war became imminent. At Brussels the French, infuriated over this maneuver to exclude them from the valley of the Upper Nile, sharply reminded the Belgian monarch that they had the exclusive right of preëmption in his Congo State, under the bargain of 1884. Leopold was affable, but he pointed out he had neither sold nor conceded any territory to England. All he had done, he insisted, was to lease a paltry strip twenty-five kilometers in width.

The French had no illusions as to the importance of that "paltry strip." And their continuing attack upon Leopold and the British was not subtle. Criticism rocked the Chamber of Deputies. Eugène Étienne, a deputy from Algeria, boldly declared for the benefit of other chancelleries that:—

"Today we are submitting to affronts and encroachments of the Congo Free State, but above all we have been too long exposed to the opposition, the continual hostility, of the British Government."

While striving to persuade Leopold to repeal the objectionable article in his treaty with the British, the French did not overlook another means of combating the British. One was founded on President Carnot's somewhat extreme proposal to send an expedition to the Nile. M. Hanotaux, not in the slightest intimidated, asked and obtained from the Chamber of Deputies an appropriation of 1,800,000 francs to send a large military party, led by Colonel Louis Montiel, from the French Congo northeast to the Nile. The French colonial technique of cutting off the hinterland of a Power seeking an African holding—as exemplified by their movements in the instances of the Gold Coast, Lagos, Gambia, the Upper Niger, Morocco and Tripoli—was to be employed again.

War seemed once more a matter of hours. To judge by the newspapers of the day, the tension then between France and Britain over Africa was as great as that between Britain and Italy in January 1936. By what narrow margin hostilities were averted will be seen. At both London and Paris the nationalist press blazed with inflammatory editorials. Lord Dufferin, in 1895 the British ambassador to the French capital, summoned his coach and hurried to M. Hanotaux's office next door to the Chamber, after that body had voted the credits. A French expedition to the Nile—was His Excellency the Foreign Minister in his right mind? M. Hanotaux was not to be outbluffed, at least on his home-grounds. Lord Dufferin said that the French project was the equivalent of an ultimatum. Unperturbed, M. Hanotaux pointed to the speech of Sir Edward Grey, Under-Secretary for Colonies, in the House of Commons (March 28, 1895) in

From a woodcut by William Nicholson

CECIL RHODES

which that official had said that "the advance of a French expedition under secret instructions, right from the other side of Africa into a territory over which our claims have been known for so long, would be not merely an inconsistent and unexpected act, but it must be perfectly well known to the French Government that it would be an unfriendly act, and would be so viewed by England." * Which utterance, incidentally, was greeted with cheers. M. Hanotaux said that, to his mind, Sir Edward Grey's speech constituted an ultimatum, and not the projected Montiel mission.

Germany chose this psychological moment to join forces with the French against Britain. The threat proved effective momentarily, for translated in military terms it meant that should hostilities break out in Africa, the Reich in German East Africa might attack Uganda and Bechuanaland while the French, joining with Menelik, might move into the Sudan or might descend the Niger, or both. The German stand was about identical with the French: the Wilhelmstrasse maintained that Article III violated the German-Congolese treaty of 1884 (in which Belgian sovereignty was recognized). In the objections of both nations based on their 1884 treaties with Leopold, France and Germany had some degree of justification under international law. M. Étienne, who served as the foreign minister's mouthpiece in the lower house of the French parliament, expressed the legal position clearly enough when he said that "this [Anglo-Congolese] treaty placed the Free State in a position of conflict, I hope *peaceful*, but certainly a position of conflict with the public law of Africa." † Meanwhile, to bear down still more forcefully upon Downing Street, Baron von Marschall instructed

---

* Great Britain, Foreign Office, *Correspondence With the French Government Respecting the Valley of the Upper Nile, Egypt No.2* (1898).

† G. Hanotaux, *Le partage de l'Afrique-Fashoda*, Paris 1909.

his ambassador at London to mince no words in telling the British Government that "withdrawal of the [Anglo-Congolese] agreement, *and without delay,* is the only way to avoid complicating the European situation. England will learn that she cannot treat us as she chooses, and it will give her reason to prefer our friendship to our ill-will."

Another point of similarity between the French and German positions, *vis-à-vis* Britain's Cape-to-Cairo maneuvers, was von Marschall's warning that "we must refuse [if England did not back down] to be responsible if the Egyptian question is raised. . . . Compensation will not remove the difficulty for us; what England would have to sacrifice would be very considerable."

In other words, if England did not agree to the repeal of her lease of a salient Congo strip, France and Germany would summon a conference to discuss what right, under international law, Britain had to occupy Egypt. In the face of the strong protests, which might lead to a European or to an African war in which he would lose both at home and abroad, Leopold had a sudden attack of political nerves.

He asked the British to consent to the withdrawal of the troublesome article.

Britain backed down, an act of imperial discretion, and lost her Congo corridor. The Franco-Germany victory, however, was not without its drawbacks. It hastened the British decision to give Kitchener his marching-orders into the Sudan. And the fact remains, whether due or not to the British retreat, that the French Government diverted the Montiel Nile mission to the Ivory Coast, possibly to calm the fears of Grey and others. Incidentally, the threat which Grey had made against France in the Commons, which had been the subject of a diplomatic protest by Ambassador de Courcel at London to Lord Kimberley, the Colonial Secretary, and had provoked anger in the Quai-d'Orsay, was forgiven by M. Hanotaux when he received an oblique apology from Kimberley, characterizing the warning of his assistant as "merely the words of a simple Under-Secretary of State." (The "simple Under-Secretary" in twenty years was to send Germany the ultimatum that, one school of historians maintains, resulted in the World War.) That back-treading communication to the French ambassador was made after M. Hanotaux told the Senate that Grey's speech postulated "a sort of Monroe Doctrine applied to a considerable part of Africa." So far as the Sudan was concerned, the French at the time argued that if it belonged to anyone it was to the Khedive and that he, in turn, was under the suzerainty of Turkey. Ergo, the Sudan belonged to the Sultan, and not to Britain. (And if the Powers were to agree, implicitly or explicitly, that Turkey had no moral or other right in Africa, then the Sudan belonged to whichever of those Powers first achieved "effective occupation.") But conveniently the French reversed themselves—in their pretension that the Sudan was the Khedive's—after the Fashoda imbroglio.

ii

Montiel, in any event, was shunted away from the Nile expedition, probably because his party was so impressive numerically and in equipment that the French feared provoking Britain to a Sudan campaign. Nevertheless, that was what happened. Less elaborate expeditions were sent out quietly by the French to the Upper Nile, with the avowed objects of scientific study or merely as "civilizing missions." Late in 1894 Théophile Delcassé, new Minister of Colonies, received a report from de Brazza, then governor of the French Congo, giving word of a rumored British expedition moving north of the Uganda Protectorate under General Sir Edwin Henry Colville. As he had before his race against

Stanley, de Brazza warned that there was no time to be lost, and strongly recommended the dispatch of a lightly equipped and highly mobile column by way of the French Congo. To Hanotaux he wrote with abundant confidence that "if we wish the valley of the Nile we have only to go there and take it; treaties, numerous though they be, change nothing." In this there is an echo of Stanley's inability to consider political realities; both explorers had the naïve, if relatively commendable, viewpoint that the partition of Africa had chiefly to do with the natives, and had no connection with diplomatic poker in the capitals of Europe.

Victor Liotard was sent to the Upper Ubanghi (the great northern tributary of the Congo), ostensibly as governor of a territory ceded in 1894 by Leopold to France (to which, curiously, Britain and Germany made no violent objections). The district was not distant from the Sudan frontier; and in reality Liotard's mission was to make a flying raid to the Upper Nile and somewhere and somehow dig in and raise the French flag. Louis Mizon, a naval lieutenant, was sent to Addis Ababa to ascertain the mood of Menelik. Similarly, a Captain Clochette was ordered to proceed to the Nile via Djibouti-Addis Ababa. Late in 1895 the Government, guarding strictly against ostentation, prepared another expedition to the Nile, to be led by Captain Jean Marchand who was to supplant Liotard—the latter had failed to get farther than 250 miles beyond the confluence of the Welle and Bomu rivers (Ubanghi tributaries). Marchand, in whose ability to beat the British to the Upper Nile the Government had great confidence (he ended the World War a divisional general), sailed from Marseilles June 25, 1896.

But Lord Salisbury had not been idle. Twelve days after the Adowa massacre—on March 12—he had cabled Lord Cromer (then Sir Evelyn Baring, of the banking Barings),

SUDAN IDYL

Consul-General at Cairo, that Britain proposed to reoccupy the Sudan, after a decade's hesitation. Egyptian prosperity was dependent upon control of the headwaters of the Nile, and she could not permit the French to obtain such control, as it was clear to London—and the tactless Grey!—they *were* attempting to do. Not only must the French be blocked once and for all, but the Khalifa—the True Prophet of the Only God, and the Mahdi's successor—must be destroyed, along with his emirs.

For a reason never officially disclosed, Downing Street preferred a palpable fraud to honesty in making the announcement, on March 12, that the cabinet had determined to recapture the Sudan. The reason for the deception was probably fear of complications with the French who, to British eyes, continued intransigent. The editor of *The Times* on March 12 was given at Downing Street a copy of a telegram with a Cairo dateline, purportedly a Reuters dispatch, announcing that the Government had decided to expedite a force for the conquest of Dongola province in the Sudan. *The Times* correspondent never filed the dispatch and neither had the Reuters correspondent. But for political reasons which remain unexplained, Lord Salisbury wished to give himself a line of retreat if his announcement should lead to another diplomatic *contretemps* with France—that is, he could claim, reasonably enough, that an official statement of that importance was authentic only if and when issued at London, and that he could not be responsible for reports emanating from Egypt. It may be surmised both Reuters and *The Times* consented to the deception. When the fake Cairo dispatch appeared in the latter on the morning of March 13, and was inevitably relayed back to the point whence it had never originated, "no one was more surprised than the gentleman who represents *The Times* in Cairo." *

* *Towards Khartumn*, A. Hilliard Atteridge, London 1897.

Lord Cromer in "Modern Egypt" contents himself with observing that the decision to order Kitchener southward "was taken and publicly announced with somewhat excessive haste. . . . The absence of consistency, which is so frequently noticeable in the aims of British policy, is indeed a never-ending source of embarrassment to those on whom devolves the duty of carrying that policy into execution."

But the Dongola expedition, and the Sudan campaign generally, was a financial as well as a military undertaking. The London bankers who invested in Government securities did not propose that Britain alone should defray its cost. On the other hand, the Continental bankers who represented the investors in Egyptian bonds, or who had themselves investments in public-works at Alexandria and Cairo, howled bitterly when Britain proposed that since Egypt had a proprietary interest in the Sudan, Cairo should be made to pay for the reconquest of the Upper Nile—the more so if the British were magnanimous enough to undertake the military direction of the campaign and to send out white troops. Downing Street was singularly deaf to the argument of the Continental bankers that Britain should bear the cost since, it was evident to all, if the Sudan were recaptured it would revert to England.

The British Government won the argument, but not easily. The French and Russian commissioners of the Egyptian Debt, representing those of their nationals who were bondholders, obtained an injunction forbidding the payment of sums from the Caisse de la Dette or special sinking-fund of the Cairo Treasury. Immediately Lord Cromer had recourse to the judges of the Court of Appeals. That body upheld the injunction. Eventually Cromer's financial genius solved the difficulty by an arrangement which was to give the British Treasury a handsome profit. London extended the Cairo Government a loan of £800,000—at 2.75 percent. interest:

SUDAN IDYL   211

thus the Egyptians paid for the Sudan reconquest themselves, and paid as well a substantial rate of interest to London for the dubious privilege, as it developed, of giving over Sudan control to an English governor-general (who makes all laws and regulations) and his British district commissioners. But Lord Cromer, dwelling upon the readiness with which a paternalistic home government made the loan to Egypt, regarded the transaction as an "episode . . . to which both Englishmen and Egyptians may look back with pride and satisfaction."

In this account of the diplomatic background of the theft of Africa, military campaigns must of necessity be treated parenthetically.

Kitchener concentrated an expeditionary force of 8,200 British and 17,600 Egyptian troops, with forty-four guns and twenty Maxims on land, thirty-six guns and twenty-four Maxims afloat, and with 2,469 horses, 876 mules, 3,524 camels and 229 donkeys. There was a river flotilla of three armored screw gunboats, seven armored stern-wheel gunboats, and five steam transports. It was a military concentration the like of which in equipment Europe had never seen before. Nearly all the Powers sent military attachés to observe the fighting.* There were scores of "war correspondents" who in that day, by the way, engaged in the actual fighting: a *Times* correspondent (Hubert Howard, with the 21st Lancers) was killed by a British shell, and

---

* Winston Churchill, attached to the 21st Lancers, wrote that on the eve of the battle of Omdurman Baron von Tiedemann, the officer of the German General Staff assigned as observer, turned to him and said enthusiastically: "This is the first of September. Our great day and now your great day—Sedan and Sudan." The future First Lord of the Admiralty adds that "I laughed at his ponderous wit; nor have I since been able to decide whether or not it cloaked a rather bitter sarcasm."

another *Times* representative and the envoy of the *Daily Chronicle* were both severely wounded in a cavalry charge.

On March 14 (1896) Kitchener began moving south, accompanied by the gunboats. The railroad was pushed southward. The advance was marked by a succession of British victories, due chiefly to the skill in modern military warfare of what Churchill describes as the "educated men of a civil-

British Field Telegraph, Nile.

izing Empire." * The decisive battle was that of Omdurman (September 2, 1898) where the Khalifa's army was virtually destroyed—his casualties were 20,000 of which number 10,560 were killed and 5,000 taken prisoner. British and Egyptian losses were less than 500. After Omdurman a storm of criticism arose against Kitchener who, it was charged, had not acted to prevent the shooting of prisoners, wounded and unwounded. But the Government vindicated him after an inquiry. The Sirdar of the Egyptian army had

* *The River War.*

SUDAN IDYL

been sent south to destroy the Khalifa and mahdism, and he accomplished that end with thoroughness and dispatch. He had avenged Gordon by recapturing Khartum and he had recovered nearly all the territory that Egypt had lost. A flying-column under Sir Reginald Wingate caught up with the Khalifa at Um Debreikat (November 24, 1899) where the prophet calmly awaited and met death, huddled on a sheepskin with his emirs. . . . The dervish dominion at an end, and British dominion began.

Inevitably, Britain demanded some tangible reward for Kitchener's accomplishment. It was quite beside the point to the imperial mind that (1) the Nile expeditionary force was more than 70 percent. Egyptian (2), that it was in the main equipped by Egypt and (3), its expenses paid by Egypt from a loan upon which Cairo was paying interest to London.* The cardinal—and only—point to consider was that control of the Sudan meant control of the Nile which, in turn, was the economic key to Egypt. By no means could or would Britain relinquish the Sudan, once the dervishes were destroyed, to its original possessor, or permit another Power to threaten the flow of the Nile. The major cause of official British concern over the current Italian invasion of Ethiopia arises over the threat to Lake Tsana, headwaters of the Blue Nile and not, of course, to any altruistic adherence to the League Covenant.

The genesis of the British control today of both Egypt and the Sudan lies in the Sudan Agreement of January 19, 1899, "Between Her Britannic Majesty's Government and the Government of His Highness the Khedive of Egypt." Since the bombardment of Alexandria in 1882 the British had effectively dominated Egypt, but the conquest of the

---

* "It is true that the Egyptian Treasury had borne the greater portion of the cost."—Lord Cromer, who signed the subsequent treaty with the Cairo Government, in *Modern Egypt*, p. 113, vol. ii.

Sudan irrevocably mortgaged the Cairo Government to London.

The appalling mass of treaties relating to the partition of Africa through which this writer has waded is, for the most part, written in that turgid and bombastic style which delights the legal mind. There is, however, a refreshing and naïve directness about the Anglo-Egyptian agreement of 1899 relating to the Sudan. It begins:

"Whereas certain provinces in the Sudan which were in rebellion against the authority of His Highness the Khedive have now been reconquered by the joint military and financial efforts of Her Britannic Majesty's Government and the Government of His Highness the Khedive;

"And whereas *it is desired to give effect to the claims which have accrued to Her Britannic Majesty's Government, by right of conquest, to share in the present settlement and future working and development of the . . . system of administration and legislation;*

"It is hereby agreed:

"[Art. III] The supreme military and civil command in the Sudan shall be vested in one officer, termed the 'Governor-General of the Sudan.' He shall be appointed by khedival decree *on the recommendation of Her Britannic Majesty's Government,* and shall be removed only . . . with the consent of Her Britannic Majesty's Government."

Other articles of the treaty made Egyptian laws inoperative unless approved by the British, enforced the flying of the Union Jack with the Egyptian flag, and forbade the recognition of consular agents of any nation without "the previous consent of Her Britannic Majesty's Government." . . . A forthright, cards-on-the-table document, written under the direction of the astute Cromer. At Omdurman, where he made a speech in July 1899 to the assembled sheiks—after the destruction of the Khalifa's army—Lord Cromer said:

SUDAN IDYL

"You see that both the British and Egyptian flags are floating over this house. That is an indication that for the future you will be governed by the Queen of England and the Khedive of Egypt." * The order in which the names of the two rulers occur in the address was significant. The British Consul-General in *Modern Egypt,* is jauntily frank about the spirit underlying his speech: "there could be no mistaking the significance of these words, and there was no desire that they should be mistaken. They meant that the Sudan was to be governed by a *partnership of two, of which England was the predominant member.*"

iii

The meeting of the British and French at Fashoda in the Sudan (today Kodok, about 400 miles south of Khartum) is minimized by most historians as an "incident." The diplomatic setting has been obscured by the somewhat dramatic circumstances of the meeting between Kitchener and Marchand, and the narrowness by which a European war was averted has been forgotten. An identical "incident" today in Africa in which war would not be averted, might reoccur so readily that Fashoda has a special pertinence to the present conflict in Ethiopia, and to the continuing menace of world war.

Sailing from Marseilles in June 1896, Marchand landed at Loango (French Congo) the following month, and gathered his party of seven French officers and noncoms and 120 Senegalese riflemen. He had two small steamers and three aluminum barges. His mission was to win the friendship of the Mahdists and to establish "effective occupation" somewhere in the Upper Nile valley. The privations suffered by the small party, voyaging some 2,600 miles in a

* *Modern Egypt,* vol. ii, p. 116.

race to beat Britain to the Lower Sudan, make scarcely credible reading. Marchand nearly died enroute. The expedition went up the Ubanghi and down the Bahr-el-Ghazal (Upper White Nile), arriving at Fashoda some eighteen months after leaving the Atlantic coast.

Although Marchand had built more boats, he was in a dangerous position. He did not know the extent of the Mahdist defeat, or that they were being pursued southward by Kitchener. He sent his steamer 250 miles up the Bahr-el-Ghazal to his nearest supply-depot, and began a letter home, whistling to keep up his courage.

"I have now, in the Basin of the Bahr-el-Ghazal—that is, of the Nile—an all-powerful position," he wrote. "I have seven barges or steel boats, a steamer underway, fifteen canoes made by my *tirailleurs,* able to take me wherever I wish in the Basin of the Nile, where the first French steamer has now penetrated in spite of obstacles and every hostility.

"But do not think that our position is altogether an agreeable one. First of all, we are dying of hunger." *

Five days after his victory at Omdurman, and two months after the raising of the French flag at Fashoda, Kitchener heard that a European party had emerged from the jungle and reached the Upper Nile. Word came to him through the captured crew of one of the Khalifa's boats who reported that their craft had been fired on by "black troops commanded by white officers under a strange flag." Bullets embedded in the boat testified that the Mahdists were not daydreaming.

Kitchener decided to waste no time. The Mahdi prisoners could not describe the flag, but the Sirdar guessed it was either Italian or French, and most probably the latter. With five gunboats, two Sudanese battalions, two companies of Highlanders, an artillery battery and four Maxims, he set

* *Bulletin de la Société de Géographie de Lyon,* 1899.

SUDAN IDYL

off up the river. On September 18 the gunboats moored a short distance north of Fashoda, and Kitchener sent his aide-de-camp ahead with a message addressed to the unknown "Chief of the European Expedition." That emissary, be it noted, was the present Lord Robert Cecil, third son of Lord Salisbury.

In the painfully formal negotiations and interviews that followed between the chiefs of the two armed parties, there was again observed that drawing-room deportment that—recalling Livingstone, Stanley, de Brazza and others—was seemingly *de rigeur* when Europeans met by accident in Africa. Marchand, his French aides and the black *tirailleurs* awaited the messenger silently, the leader hoping that European enforcements might be at hand, for he soon expected another Mahdist attack. He greeted the young Englishman with a bow and a salute, and tore open Kitchener's letter. It read in part:

"Sir:
"I have the honor to inform you that on the 2nd September I attacked the Khalifa at Omdurman and, after destroying his army, reoccupied the country.
"Considering that the report of the presence of Europeans is probably true, I have thought it my duty to send you this letter in order to inform you of the events which have recently taken place, and of my approaching arrival at Fashoda.
"I have, &c.,
"Herbert Kitchener, Sirdar." *

To Marchand, racked by fever, worn by an eighteen months' fight across the continent, the implication was clear enough—Get out! This he had no intention of doing. His reply was equally uncompromising:

* British Foreign Office, Parliamentary Papers, *Egypt No. 3* (1898).

"*Mon Général:*

"I have heard with the greatest satisfaction of the occupation of Omdurman by the Anglo-Egyptian army. . . . I shall no doubt be the first to offer the very sincere congratulations of a Frenchman to General Kitchener. . . . Having fulfilled this agreeable duty, I consider it necessary to inform you that, by order of my Government, I have occupied the Bahr-el-Ghazal . . . as well as the Shilluk country on the left bank of the White Nile as far as Fashoda. I signed on the 3rd September a treaty with Sultan Kour Abd-el-Fadil, Grand Mek, placing the Shilluk country under the Protectorate of France. . . . I sent copies of the Treaty to Europe.

"I take note of your intention to come to Fashoda, where I shall be happy to welcome you in the name of France.

"With assurances of my profound esteem, &c.,

"Marchand."

The issue was clearly drawn in this first exchange. The meeting of the two men on September 19, however, was a model of *politesse*. Churchill reports that Kitchener, dis-

"Dr. Livingstone, I presume?"

SUDAN IDYL

embarking at Fashoda, shook hands formally with Marchand, and said with all the spontaneity of another Stanley:
"Sir, I congratulate you on all you have accomplished."
"But no, *mon général*. It is not I [pointing to his Senegalese], but these soldiers who have done it." (Back in London Kitchener said, repeating this remark of Marchand's, "Then I knew he was a gentleman.")

The Sirdar, it seems, steadfastly refused to look at the French tricolor flying over Marchand's headquarters, fearing that to do so would constitute, or at least imply, military recognition. Kitchener, Wingate and Colonel H. W. Jackson, with Marchand and his second-in-command, Captain Germain, repaired for a conference aboard the *Dal.* That meeting marked the culmination of Anglo-French rivalry in Africa, after the nations had confronted each other in Morocco, Egypt and the Niger country. Kitchener formally protested the raising of the French flag (still shielding his glance from that emblem); and with the formidable expedition under his command he could do so with authority. But even with only a half-starved force of 120 riflemen, Marchand would not retreat.

"And what, Captain, if Her Majesty's Government should insist that I expel you?"

"We are soldiers, *mon général.*" Comes the epic, devastating gesture, that fatalistic French shrug, accompanied by a weary raising of the eyebrows, hands raised expressively from the elbows, a spreading line of scorn along the lips.

Apparently the *général* felt that relations were becoming strained. M. Dutreb * asserts that Marchand has since said that a drink saved the day and averted immediate hostilities between Britain and France. The Sirdar,.so the account goes, felt compelled to admire Marchand's philosophical indifference to the certain massacre of the French force if the

* M. Dutreb, *La Mission Marchand*, Paris 1922.

British opened fire. *Bien émotioné,* we are told, the Sirdar walked over to Marchand, placed his hands on the Captain's shoulders, and said:

"Sir, will you permit me to offer you a whiskey-and-soda?"

Kitchener's spirituous amenities evidently cleared the air, although it may be assumed that Marchand would have preferred a milder apéritif. The British officer insisted upon raising the flag just outside Fashoda proper (formerly the Egyptian provincial capital)—but he was careful to hoist only the star-and-crescent of the Khedive, and not the Union Jack.* Colonel Jackson's ready French and manifest admiration of Marchand's feat, also made for easier relations, although for three months the two forces lived side by side in a state of urbane hostility. Eventually it was agreed that neither side would take military measures against the other until Downing Street and the Quai-d'Orsay had thrashed out the legal issues involved.

Kitchener returned down-river, leaving Colonel Jackson in charge. To get into closer touch with Paris, Marchand departed via the Nile for Cairo, enroute stopping at Omdurman to visit the scene of the slaughter where, realizing what might have happened to his small force, he was moved to tears. But had he then known the situation back at Fashoda he would have called off his journey to Cairo and hurriedly returned upstream.

Captain Germain had been left in command of the French party. That officer believed that Kitchener had outbluffed Marchand, and he saw for himself an opportunity to make a grand gesture *pour la patrie.* To Colonel Jackson's notes

* In *The River War* Churchill states both flags were raised, "amid musical honors and the salutes of the gunboats." Only the Egyptian flag was raised by the cautious Kitchener, evidence that he was not altogether sure of the legal position of Britain at Fashoda.

begging him not to do anything to endanger the *status-quo*, Germain returned answers which can be described at best as flippant and at worst as arrogant. He sent parties to make treaties to the right bank of the Nile, and ordered the French steam-launch north beyond the point which Marchand and Kitchener had agreed to respect as a temporary frontier until Paris and London had sought a solution. As a final, foolhardy act, the captain threw up trenchworks along the river. The Anglo-Egyptian gunboat crews trained their guns and Maxims, and cleared decks for action.

Had either side pressed home a trigger, a European war would almost certainly have resulted. Marchand arrived back at the proverbial eleventh hour, and censured Germain. With grim humor the isolated French leader wrote to Paris, "One hundred and twenty men against forty thousand [the entire Anglo-Egyptian force]! Is it not *drôle* enough to the extent of side-splitting!" Suddenly, and with a significance that was not lost upon any of the chancelleries, two German gunboats appeared at Algiers and received a fulsome welcome from the French Governor-General.

Paris and London meanwhile were making little progress over their diplomatic chess game. To Lord Salisbury's emissary at Paris, Foreign Minister Delcassé declared that the Khedive had long since abandoned the Bahr-el-Ghazal region, and that Fashoda was another No-Man's-Land; moreover, he argued, Marchand had arrived at Fashoda weeks before the Anglo-Egyptian force, and accordingly the district belonged to France. But the British Prime Minister met this defense by insisting that historically the Sudan belonged to Egypt, and that militarily it belonged to the conquering nation. Out of the maze of diplomatic argument the one salient fact emerged: the British forces outside Fashoda were overwhelmingly superior to the French. And when Delcassé was convinced that Britain would fight for Fashoda, with results that left no room for doubt, he backed down. Sir Michael Hicks-Beach, Chancellor of the Exchequer, made a threat in the Commons, for French consumption, that "Britain would recoil before nothing." In Paris, English businessmen declined new orders, fearing a moratorium. The French Atlantic Fleet gathered unexpectedly off Cherbourg, and a few hours later the squadrons raced through Gibraltar with lights doused. Once again British gunboats appeared off Alexandria.

So—Delcassé retreated. The Paris Government announced on November 4, 1898, that it "had resolved not to maintain the Marchand mission at Fashoda. This decision was taken by the cabinet after a profound examination of the question." An embittered and disillusioned Marchand evacuated Fashoda on December 11, his only trophy the flag of a dervish whom he had routed outside the town. And that sorry emblem was recovered for him by Kitchener's 11th Sudanese Regiment. As a final humiliation, the Frenchman had to borrow from Colonel Jackson sufficient ammunition to safeguard his retreat via Ethiopia to Djibouti. On March 21 of the following year the French and British signed an agreement under which the whole drainage system of the Nile was reserved to England and Egypt, while France's sphere of influence was to include all of northern Africa west of the Nile that was not then occupied by another Power—a vast if arid territory. German and Italian protests were overridden.

iv

The extent to which the Kaiser might have gone to support the French against Britain (and, incidentally, his grandmother) may be judged in a curious letter he wrote to the Czar, after the Fashoda fiasco.

"What on earth has possessed them!" he exclaimed, referring to the French. "After such a first-rate, well-arranged and plucky expedition by poor and brave Marchand! They were in a first-rate position, and able to help all of us others in Africa who are in need of strong help!"

XII

"Let the Storm Burst!"
[1898-1902]

IF it is axiomatic that colonial penetration never springs from philanthropic motives, it is equally a truism that predatory economics are invariably behind modern-day empire-building. Besides seeking a market for Belgian exports, Leopold confiscated the Congo for its ivory and rubber; France took over Algeria, Tunisia and Morocco for their phosphates, iron, zinc, timber and agricultural potentialities; the Reich seized the territories that became German East Africa and Southwest Africa for their stockraising acreage, diamonds (discovered in 1908 in the southwest protectorate) and minerals; and Britain pocketed Egypt and the Sudan for their yield of cotton and mineral wealth. It is no mystery why in 1871 the London Government appropriated the diamond-fields of the Orange Free State.

However much ingenious argument has been built by British and other apologists to prove that the South African War of 1899–1902 was, in the final analysis, an altruistic necessity, it requires no ingenuity whatsoever to find the economic motive which moved the Salisbury Government to undertake the final conquest of the lands remaining to the Boers. The "altruistic necessity" in this instance took the form of gold, needed to guarantee the position of England as the world's richest nation in that metal.

The immediate genesis of the South African War was the

"LET THE STORM BURST!" 225

ultimatum delivered by the Transvaal Government to Conyngham Greene, British agent at Pretoria, on October 9, 1899. To understand the factors which brought the Boers to that desperate pass, it is necessary to go back briefly fifteen years.

In 1884, the year of the London Convention which granted autonomy, gold in profitable quantities was discovered in the Transvaal in De Kaap Valley and two years later on the Witwaters Rand. Soon thereafter it was recognized that in the Rand region was the world's richest gold-field. Here two points should be noted: (1), that had the Rand discovery occurred only a year or even six months earlier, the British would never have consented to the London Convention and (2), that the *uitlander* (foreign white) population of the Transvaal—or the South African Republic, a title cherished by President Kruger—in 1884 was 45,000 and in 1899, fifteen years later, had swelled to 345,397. Apart from the native Dutch (i. e., the Boers), the increase in white population was due in greatest part to the hordes of British, German, French and American prospectors and wage-workers in the fields of the Witwaters Rand, west of Johannesburg, and the Reef to the east. Of the *uitlanders* the British were by thousands in the majority.

Moreover, the majority of shares in the gold-fields were held by Cecil Rhodes' Consolidated Gold Mines of South Africa—the richest on the Rand, from which he alone derived between £300,000 and £400,000 yearly—the British South Africa Company, Messrs. Eckstein & Company, and by lesser companies in which French, German, Dutch and American capital represented the minority stockholders. A still smaller minority investment was that of the Transvaalers themselves, who since the discovery of gold had shown no enthusiasm for what a gold-rush would and did mean— the descent of lawless gangs of undesirables from Europe and America. The Boers had had a foretaste of mining-camps after the discovery of diamonds in the Kimberley region, and the responsible element was determined not to encourage the mining of gold. As far back as 1879 they had forbidden such mining, after isolated deposits were found, fearing the baleful effects of a mining population. Subsequently, in 1889, they sought to check the exploitation of the

Flag of the British South Africa Company.

mines, and the immigration spelled by that exploitation, by making the sale of dynamite, essential to the mines, a government monopoly. Inevitably, means were found to circumvent each new restriction of President Kruger's, the commonest of which was bribery, which is no compliment to the Boers. Every new restriction, it should be added, was aimed primarily at the British for whom the Boers had an abiding and profound distrust.

In the face of the rapidly multiplying *uitlander* population, Kruger in 1882 had obtained passage of a law which withheld the franchise from any foreigner who had lived less than five years in the Transvaal, a reasonable measure designed chiefly to exclude freebooters and other fortune-hunters who, while they paid the greater part of the taxes, had been known to skip the country—after obtaining substantial credits—when stakes petered out. In 1894, further to protect the Transvaal from a disproportionate *uitlander* (majority British) voice in their political affairs, the Boers upped the franchise qualification to fourteen years. With unquestionable logic Kruger reasoned that a shorter period would mean the loss of the hard-won Boer independence to the British. He had, moreover, the legitimate argument that no other State, nor any theory of international law, considered it the obligation of any government to enfranchise aliens, however large their payments to its exchequer.*

The clamor from the British mining interests was immediate and deafening. Were subjects of Queen Victoria, who were paying a substantial part of the Transvaal revenue, to have no voice in the Volksraad, the legislature at Pretoria, which had the power to enact laws still more restrictive? There were jingoes, fearful of their pocketbooks, who demanded immediate war. But under the London Convention, Britain had no right to intervene, although it was evident that eventually under the pressure of Rhodes *et al,* and the embracing imperialist philosophy of Joseph Chamberlain, who became Colonial Secretary the following year, the Transvaal wealth in gold would make intervention and annexation an "altruistic necessity." As in Egypt, the Sudan and the Orange Free State, the natural wealth of the Transvaal might be effectively used in the "interests of civilization" only by British methods and under British auspices.

* For a legalistic argument upholding this view, see "A Vindication of the Boers" by "Diplomat," in *Briton or Boer* (a symposium), New York 1900. The opposite view is argued in the same volume by Sydney Brooks, an associate of Rhodes and Joseph Chamberlain, and subsequently editor of *The Saturday Review.*

In light of what happened, there is profound comedy in the words of Lord Salisbury shortly after he had committed Britain to war.

"I would go further and say," he told the House of Commons, "that England as a whole would have no advantage from the possession of gold-mines, except so far as her Government *conferred the blessings of good government upon those who had the prosecution of that industry.* Every industry that is prosecuted successfully breeds commerce. . . . But that is the limit of our interest. We seek no gold-fields. *We seek no territory."*

The *uitlanders,* which numerically is to say the British, may be said to have taken a leaf from the American Revolution. With at least surface justification they complained and protested against taxation without representation—or, at least, without adequate representation, in their opinion, in enacting legislation affecting their investments in Transvaal gold. In justice to many of these complainants, it should be observed that, apart from the gold-field controversy, the Pretoria Government showed a considerable genius in rubbing British sensibilities the wrong way—a technique not unlike that employed by the French in their post-war treatment of Germans in Alsace-Lorraine and the Saar: since 1881 Dutch was made the only medium of education, and public transactions in the courts and elsewhere could only be in the mother-language of the Boers. This was a gratuitous nuisance and offense, and it scarcely made for amiable relations between Boers and Englishmen in a country where, it was conservatively estimated in 1895, foreigners owned half the land and nine-tenths of other property. And the *uitlander,* whatever his freebooter methods and his lack of interest in the country *per se,* could argue with some degree of validity that he had as much right in the Transvaal as the

Boer, so far as the native question was concerned. To many foreigners the argument of the Boers that they certainly had the fundamental right inherent in priority, in "effective occupation," was a quibble.

In view of the strained relations existing in 1892 between the two factions, it is a cause for surprise that war did not occur in South Africa at least seven years before it did. To effect the "reforms" they wanted, the *uitlanders* organized themselves into a Transvaal National Union, headed by J. Tudhope, a former minister of Cape Colony, and James Leonard, a former attorney-general of the colony—both of them, of course, British subjects, as was by far the majority membership. Seven of the Union's members called upon Kruger in September 1892 to make known their suggested reforms. After Leonard had outlined them in his most placating prose, the dour Kruger turned on the delegation and said:

"Go back and tell your people that I shall never give them anything. I shall never change my policy. And now let the storm burst. . . ."

Kruger's anger may be explained by an earlier "incident" which, it appears, he never forgot nor forgave. Two years before, in 1890, the Transvaal President had visited Johannesburg when it was still a gold-rush town. As a pointed mark of disrespect, *uitlanders* on that occasion tore down and destroyed the Transvaal flag flying over the home of the local mayor. Far more calculated to inspire suspicion and hatred of the British was the arrogance of, and the duplicity underlying, the Jameson Raid (and fiasco), which even the *Manchester Guardian*—then less belligerently "liberal"—attacked as the act of "the financial giants who . . . dream in Empires, and who set themselves to realize their dreams by dangerous and treacherous intrigues. The

Jameson Raid exhibited and expressed the united force of these two streams of tendency, the gold-seeking and the Imperialist." *

ii

For fully two years before the abortive raid, Germany had displayed a lively interest in the row between the British and the Boers in South Africa. In 1895 Kruger had sent Dr. Leyds, his Secretary of State, to Berlin on a mission to win German sympathies for the Transvaal. Kaiser Wilhelm II was delighted with the Boer envoy but was careful to treat him as a private visitor, for fear of offending England. He and his ministers foresaw that joint German-Boer action might check the British. After Jameson's capture (January 2, 1896), the Kaiser sent his celebrated telegram to Kruger, a message which nearly provoked an Anglo-German war:

"I express my sincere congratulations that, supported by your people without appealing for the help of friendly Powers, you have succeeded by your own emergetic action against armed bands which invaded your country as disturbers of the peace, and have thus been enabled to restore peace and safeguard the independence of the country against attacks from the outside." †

* And added, July 25, 1899, less than three months before the outbreak of war, "The fact is that no case exists to support our claims of any right to interfere in the internal government of the Transvaal. . . . To insist that we have suzerainty implicitly contained in [the London] Convention, from which it is explicitly excluded, to read into that suzerainty an utterly unprecedented power to interfere in the internal government of a country whose independence we have explicitly guaranteed . . . constitute an aggravated insolence of demeanour which, persisted in, can hardly fail to bring its own punishment if the government of this world rests upon any foundation of morality."

† In his *Memoirs* (1922), pp. 79–82, Wilhelm charges that he signed the historic telegram only when the cabinet compelled him to. There is an extensive literature devoted to the cabinet meeting,

To which Kruger responded immediately, with unaccustomed exuberance:

"I express to Your Majesty my deepest gratitude for Your Majesty's congratulations. With God's help we hope to continue to do everything possible for the existence of the Republic."

The Kaiser's telegram sent England at large into an imperialistic rage, and even the royal family reacted in the frantic manner of a mother whose darling has been kicked in the teeth by the inebriate next door. The arch *Morning Post* looked down its patrician nose and rumbled that "the nation will never forget this telegram, and it will always bear it in mind in the future orientation of its policy." The *Saturday Review* was moved to belligerence in Latin: "Germania delenda est." The fifty-four-year-old Edward, Prince of Wales, urged his royal mother to give her grandson in Berlin "a good snubbing" (the phrase is his own). However much upset, Victoria admonished Edward that "William's faults come from impulsiveness, as well as conceit. Calmness and firmness are the most powerful weapons in such cases." * On January 5 she contented herself with telling "My dear Willie" that "I must now also touch upon a subject which causes me much pain and astonishment. It is the Telegram you sent to President Kruger, which is considered very unfriendly towards this country, not that you intended it as such, I am sure—but I grieve to say it has made a most unfortunate impression here."

To which "Willie" replied in a long letter to "Most Beloved Grandmama," on January 8, that "Never was the

---

and the burden of evidence, including that adduced by German historians, indicates that the Kaiser alone was responsible for the telegram and that he expressed annoyance when his ministers forced him to make the original text less provocative.

* Sir Sydney Lee, *King Edward VII*, vol. i, London 1925.

Telegram intended as a step against England. The reasons for the Telegram were 3-fold—First, in the name of peace as such, which had been suddenly violated, and which I always, following your glorious example, try to maintain everywhere. . . . Secondly, for our Germans in Transvaal and our Bondholders at home with our invested capital of 250–300 millions and the local commerce of the [Natal] Coast of 10–12 millions, which were in danger in case fighting broke out in the towns. Thirdly, as your Government and Ambassador had both made clear that the men were acting in open disobedience to your orders, they were rebels. . . . Now, to me, rebels against the will of the most gracious Majesty the Queen, are to me the most execrable beings in the world, and I was so incensed at the idea of your orders having been disobeyed . . . that I thought it necessary to show that publicly. . . . I challenge anybody who is a Gentleman to point out where there is anything hostile to England in this." *

The one honest note in this *billet-doux* is the Kaiser's anguish over German investments in the Transvaal. The rest was sheer persiflage, good for a laugh in Downing Street and possibly a chuckle from Victoria. The extent of Wilhelm's duplicity is sufficiently revealed in a letter he expedited to the Czar on the same day that he telegraphed Kruger. Clearly he was ready to pounce on the Transvaal if he could be certain of French and Russian aid.

"Now suddenly the Transvaal Republic has been attacked in a most foul way, as it seems, not without England's knowledge," he wrote to young "Nicky." "I have used very severe language in London and *have opened communications with Paris for common defense of our endangered interests*, as French and German colonists have immediately

---

* The full text of this comical paper may be found in Frederich Thimme's *Europäische Gespräche*, May–June 1924, No. iii, p. 243.

"LET THE STORM BURST!"

joined hands of their own accord to help the outraged Boers. I hope you will also kindly consider the question. . . . I hope all will come right but, come what may, I shall never allow the British to stamp out the Transvaal." *

Every day for a fortnight, war between Britain and Germany appeared a matter of hours only, as inevitable as hostilities between England and France had appeared four years before. How serious the war threat was, Lord Salisbury admitted frankly in 1898—doubtless as a warning to Berlin—when he said that "war would have been inevitable from the moment that the first German soldier set foot on Transvaal soil. No Government in England could have withstood the pressure of public opinion; and, if it had come to war between us, then a general war must have developed." The parallel between the situation then in South Africa, and that existing today in east Africa, needs no emphasis.

The German War Office, it was learned, planned to send a force of 500 colonial troops from German East Africa to Delagoa Bay (the Portuguese port in Mozambique) together with a naval detachment from three German cruisers lying outside the bay. At least two developments stopped Germany: the foreign minister at Lisbon declared promptly and vigorously that no German troops would be permitted transit through Mozambique for a march on Pretoria (where it was proposed to put the force at Kruger's disposal), and Baron de Courcel, the French envoy to London, announced that in the event of hostilities, "France would observe towards us a most benevolent neutrality." † This, despite the distinctly cool relations then prevailing between the two chancelleries.

* *The Kaiser's Letters to the Tsar*, 1920.
† Baron Hermann von Eckardstein, quoting Salisbury in *Ten Years at the Court of St. James, 1895–1905*, pp. 85–86, London 1921.

Britain rushed a flying-column into the Transvaal, reminding the Powers that the London Convention stipulated that she had jurisdiction over the foreign affairs of that Boer republic. Thus neither the Jameson Raid nor the Kaiser's telegram had serious results, but the latter nevertheless was in good part the cause for two diplomatic conclusions, one in Downing Street and the other at Pretoria. The first was that the British must annex the Transvaal, and soon, and the second was the belief of Boer leaders that if such annexation was attempted, Germany would prove an ally.

iii

The *uitlanders* were disarmed and disbanded, after Jameson's capitulation, early in 1896 when Sir Hercules Robinson, the British High Commissioner, warned that if foreigners at Johannesburg failed to relinquish their rifles "they will forfeit all claims to sympathy from her Majesty's Government and from British subjects throughout the world." The Jameson Raid, however, had definitely ended any hopes of reconciliation between Boer and Briton. And after the Raid, Kruger and other Boer leaders were taking only reasonable precautions when they began tightening restrictions against the foreigners. In justice to the latter, it should be said that not all the Boers approved, at least in practice, of the fairly drastic measures which the Pretoria legislature adopted.

The Volksraad enacted an Aliens' Expulsion Act, providing for the deportation of *uitlanders* who violated the laws or were otherwise deemed "undesirable." (An equivalent measure was in force in England and in most European countries, but the Transvaal foreigners, and most vehemently the British, complained that the law could be invoked by Boer officials as a pretext to rid the country of

From a cartoon by Leslie Ward
in Vanity Fair

DR. LEANDER STARR JAMESON

"LET THE STORM BURST!"

uitlanders with substantial investments in the Rand and elsewhere.) Similar criticism was made of the 1897 immigration law, designed to exclude paupers, persons with infectious diseases and other "undesirables"—but anyone whom Kruger feared, the foreigners charged, could be kept from entering the Transvaal by the trumped-up diagnosis of any quack that a given individual suffered from a communicable disease. A new law relating to the press was susceptible of curbing the free speech of the English-language newspapers, and another measure required a license for all outdoor meetings. *Uitlanders* immediately wailed of "Persecution! Oppression!" That plaint from the subjects of Her Britannic Majesty in South Africa had somewhat ironic overtones. . . .

In point of fact, the Aliens' Expulsion Act was invoked once only before the outbreak of war, and then with universal approval, in the case of a convicted murderer; of three outdoor meetings suppressed, two were pro-Kruger assemblies; press censorship or the muzzling of unbridled opposition newspapers was found impractical and useless, and the immigration law was repealed when adjudged in violation of the London Convention. So much for the four measures which the *uitlanders* held up as examples of Boer malevolence. Foreigners had more justifiable grounds for complaint over Kruger's removal from office of Chief Justice Sir John Kotze, who had served at Pretoria twenty years and long been a defender of a bar independent of the executive (i e., Kruger) and the legislature.

The indifference of President ("Let-the-Storm-Burst") Kruger to the repeated *uitlander* protests, coupled with the disdain of the Volksraad to the petitions regularly submitted to it by the foreigners, to which should be added finally the effect of their accumulating commercial interests, decided the leaders of a second "Reform" movement to appeal to Victoria for intervention. A petition was forwarded to London March 28, 1899, bearing the signatures of 21,684 British subjects. The gold-mine owners and majority shareholders were careful not to attach their signatures to the document. A counter-petition signed by 23,000 Boers also went to London. The former stressed the old complaint of the absence of the franchise, or the difficulties of obtaining the right to vote, the language restrictions, and included an artless reference to "the making [of laws] of which we can never have any voice, and *in the enforcement of which we have no interest.*"

Sir William Butler, acting High Commissioner, urged against the dispatch of the petition, which he regarded as maladroit politically, and warned Chamberlain not to regard it "too seriously"; Rhodes, he added, was the "scene-shaker" behind the agitation. However, it was precisely what Chamberlain wanted and needed—a formal bill of complaint against the Pretoria Government, signed by an impressive number of British subjects.

The reply of Chamberlain to the petition, addressed to Sir Alfred Milner on May 10, 1899, has been the target for a vast quantity of criticism, much of it from the United States, from France and Germany. The widespread sympathy overseas with the Boer cause may be said to date from that dispatch, which Boer sympathizers agreed in the main was designedly phrased so to outrage the Pretoria Government that war would prove inescapable—as it did five months later.*

---

* Literally hundreds of pro-Boer pamphlets were published before, during and after the hostilities. A curious example is *The Boer War, Its Parallel with America's Great Struggle: An Appeal to Christian Americans,* published in 1901 at New York by the Pan-German League; a form of Gallic vituperation as comic as it was irresponsible may be found in a lively booklet, *Les Crimes*

The Chamberlain dispatch:

"It results from this review of the facts and conditions on which the Petition is founded, as well as from the information derived from your [Milner's] Despatches and from other official sources, that British subjects and the *uitlanders* generally in the South African Republic, *have substantial grounds for their complaint* of the treatment to which they are subjected. . . . Her Majesty's Government, however, attach far less importance to financial grievances than to those which affect the personal rights of the *uitlander* Community, and which place them in a condition of *political,* educational and *social inferiority to the Boer inhabitants* of the Transvaal."

The Chamberlain *pronunciamento* concluded with a recommendation that Milner confer with Kruger "in the hope that you may arrive, in concert with the President, at such

---

de John Bull: Les Anglais sont-ils une nation vraiment grande? . . . Non! (Paris 1900), the profits of which ostensibly went to the Boer cause; apart from John Bull's crimes in the Transvaal the author of this opus also reported that "drunkenness, card-playing and betting are more prevalent among the English than any of the nations which pretend to be civilized." Charles S. Keyser was the author of another pamphlet, *The Republics of South Africa* (Philadelphia 1901), a copy of an address before The Netherlands Society of Philadelphia. For each pro-Boer pamphlet there were fully three or four pro-British booklets approving the intervention, or the subsequent annexation, on grounds ranging from religion to economics. An eccentric piece of special pleading for England's cause came from the Rev. W. A. Bartlett, of Utica, N. Y., who in a lecture there (November 7, 1899) thundered that "the war was *sprung* on the British when they were least prepared for it! The question simply resolves itself into this, should an unprogressive, ignorant, *religious* people [the Boers] have the right to block the progress of civilization?" Not the least droll aspect of this philippic is the fact of its citation as "American Opinion on the War" in a pro-British work, *Britain and the Boers,* by Lewis Appleton, London 1899.

an arrangement as Her Majesty's Government could accept and recommend to the *uitlander* population as a reasonable concession to their just demands."

The conference opened May 31 at Bloemfontein, capital of the Orange Free State whose President, M. T. Steyn, hoped that a compromise more favorable to the Transvaal might be arrived at upon neutral ground. The meeting ended five days later in a deadlock. Somewhat superfluously the High Commissioner observed upon its demise that "this Conference is absolutely at an end, and there is no obligation on either side arising out of it."

In a dispatch to the Colonial Secretary, publication of which was withheld, Milner reported that the case for intervention was overwhelming. The British would not accept Kruger's proposal to grant the franchise upon a seven years' residence, although this was only two years above the minimum asked by Milner. The reason for the British refusal was not the difference of two years, but Kruger's appended stipulation that henceforth any matters in dispute between the two parties—Britain and the Transvaal—must be submitted to an arbitration tribunal headed by a neutral. This neither Chamberlain nor the Widow of Windsor could swallow as it meant, obviously, a weakening of British authority in the Transvaal.

The Bloemfontein Conference had, however, some compensation for Kruger. It is evident, in light of events in October, that he had won over the President of the Orange Free State as a military ally. After the Conference, Steyn hurried to the German consul with whom he placed orders for Mausers and cartridges. Another four months passed in futile negotiation, agreement or any compromise desired by neither side, whatever the lip service paid to peace. Sir Robert Baden-Powell began raising troops in Bechuanaland and Rhodesia; there was discussion in the House of Commons of an expeditionary force of 10,000, and British agents sought to block delivery of the Boer order of rifles and ammunition by exerting pressure on the Portuguese, through whose port at Delagoa Bay the fire-arms must pass. Milner dispatched reinforcements to strengthen the town guard in Kimberley, and Boers of both republics moved toward the Natal frontiers.

The Transvaal ultimatum was delivered to Conyngham Greene at Pretoria on October 9. It was sweeping, and its phrasing was perhaps not felicitous diplomatically, but it cannot be denied that it left wide open a door to peace had the Salisbury Government acceded to its demands, which were:

1. Arbitration of all points in controversy;
2. Immediate withdrawal of all British troops on the Transvaal frontiers;
3. British troops reinforcements, which had arrived in South Africa since June 1, should be withdrawn within a reasonable time (while the Transvaal pledged itself not to make any attack upon British possessions during the peace negotiations, and to withdraw its frontier guards if the British complied);
4. That British troops on the high seas should not be landed in any part of South Africa.

It is conceivable, on the basis of available records and memoirs, that the British might have consented to the first three demands. But the last asked more than British pride could stomach.

An answer was required within forty-eight hours. Salisbury cabled Milner the following evening that "you will inform the Government of the South African Republic, in reply, that the conditions demanded . . . are such as Her Majesty's Government deem it impossible to discuss."

So the die was cast. The Orange Free State had joined

in the ultimatum, after its legislature had approved collaboration with the Transvaalers, and on October 12 the whistle of Mauser lead near Kraaipan proclaimed the start of the South African War.

iv

The war was over officially in two and one-half years, and it endured that long because the British discounted the military qualities of the Boer. Nevertheless its final result, even in the face of the successive Boer victories at the start of hostilities, was not questioned by European observers. Articles of peace were signed at Pretoria May 31, 1902.

The British dead, exclusive of those who died of disease, totaled 5,774; there were 22,829 British wounded. The Boer dead was slightly more than 4,000. In the concentration camps established by Kitchener for Boer prisoners, their families and natives (a total of 250,000, of which nearly 90,000 were natives), 4,000 women died and 16,000 children. The herding of refugees and prisoners in these camps—like so many cattle before slaughter—which for the greater part lacked the most rudimentary hygienic provisions, brought outraged protests from British and foreigners alike.

The total dead as a result of hostilities and of the pestilential conditions in the concentration camps was approximately 30,000, which represents the price in lives for British control of their investments in Transvaal gold. The financial cost to the London Government is usually estimated at £150,000,000—roughly five times, for example, the total amount spent by England and Wales on all forms of education in 1913, and nearly twice as much as was spent in 1933. The territorial gain to Britain was 160,097 square miles. The figures alone are dull, but they break up graphically: every dead Boer or native cost the British Treasury

"LET THE STORM BURST!" 241

approximately $200,000; and every square mile, $5,000.

The treaty demanded surrender of all Boer forces in the field, their submission as subjects of King Edward VII, insured the civil rights of the burghers, provided for the teaching of Dutch in schools where desired by parents, optional use of the two languages in the courts, a civil administration to succeed the military when and if feasible (the ostensible prelude to self-government), and a British grant of £3,000,000 in reparation for farms burned and other property destroyed by order of British commanders (who had recalled the efficacy of General Sherman's march to the sea a generation before).

The Union of South Africa, comprising the four self-governing colonies of the Cape, Natal, the Transvaal and the Orange River Colony, was proclaimed May 31, 1910. The British governor-general is empowered to dissolve the legislature, and serves as commander-in-chief.

v

The annexation of the two colonies was a victory for Salisbury and Chamberlain. But the necessity of justifying the cost in lives, money, property and in British prestige brought many farcical rebuttals from Tories and other imperialists, nettled by the thunder of Liberal criticism at home and abroad. Before Salisbury resigned the premiership, soon after peace was signed, he felt it incumbent to say, in apparent extenuation of the Government's conduct, that "all commerce that is produced is to the advantage of England, and all industries and commerce flourish better under that good government which she furnishes, than any other regimen in the world"—a singularly frank if ingenuous remark when considered in relation to the gold industry of the Transvaal. The Duke of Devonshire, the Lord President of the Council, was shocked to learn that the Transvaal Boers believed "we cherish some designs hostile to their independence." The Earl of Selborne, Under-Secretary of Colonies, complained irascibly that "the whole of [Transvaal] influence in the world at large has been used constantly, on every opportunity, against our interests, and it is no fault of the statesmen of the Transvaal that they have not succeeded before now in embroiling us with some European Power." Sir Michael Hicks-Beach, the Chancellor of the Exchequer and a House of Commons fire-eater, was slightly more whimsical: *"Without any provocation from us,"* he argued, "the Transvaal Government sent us the most impudent message [the ultimatum] that was ever sent to any country, requiring Her Majesty to withdraw her troops." But Sir Edward Grey, the former Under-Secretary in Downing Street who, it will be recalled, had nearly involved England and France in war a few years before, reached perhaps the sublimest heights of fantasy. "The war is," he insisted in capital letters, "a War against an Oligarchical and Oppressive Government, but do not let us forget it is a War for Freedom also."

The South African War was a god-send for David Lloyd George. For his pro-Boer speeches in and out of the House, he was mobbed so frequently in 1900–02 that he made the front-pages with monotonous but profitable regularity. In 1905 the prime mover in the seizure—fourteen years later —of Germany's African colonies, triumphantly entered the cabinet in the wave of Liberal enthusiasm that marked the reaction against the political regime which had stripped the Boers of their national identity.

XIII

Turret Diplomacy
[1905-12]

DIPLOMATICALLY, as in other respects, Wilhelm II had a tough hide. He had been given the snub direct after the Jameson Raid, coupled with a warning of "hands-off" from Britain, and the snub indirect after Fashoda. To one of his obdurate temperament—or "impulsiveness" in Victoria's more charitable opinion—neither was calculated to lessen the Kaiser's imperial *folie de grandeur,* or that of his chief advisers, notably von Bülow, who had become Chancellor after long service as foreign minister.

Early in 1905 the German Government announced that the Kaiser would pay a visit to Morocco. The year before the French and British had concluded an accord respecting Morocco and Egypt, which is as good an example as any, in the partition of Africa, of the cynical attitude of the Powers toward native rights on that continent, and of the bare-faced horsetrading among the chancelleries concerned. The Anglo-French Agreement of 1904 (signed April 8), the genesis of the Entente Cordiale and thus one of the major contributory causes of the World War, provided that:—

1. France recognize the "paramount interests" of Britain in Egypt, and agree to make no demands of the London Government to end the occupation, or to interfere otherwise;

2. As compensation, Britain conceded the "paramount interests" of France in Morocco, save that strip held by Spain.

The same year France concluded a similar agreement with Italy, granting the latter freedom of action in Tripoli in return for Rome's pledge to stay out of Morocco.

It is worthwhile noting at this point that the agreement was considered a piece of practical politics, since the British had checkmated the French at Fashoda, while the French had frustrated the expedition, in 1892, of Sir Charles Euan-Smith's column to Fez.

There were other provisions in the agreement affecting Siam, Madagascar, the New Hebrides and Newfoundland. The two foregoing articles, however, were the most important so far as Europe was concerned, and of those then made public: the secret articles will be cited presently.

Although on the face of it, the deal appeared to be a practical arrangement, publication of its text aroused criticism on both sides of the Channel—not to mention the anger it provoked at Berlin. French critics in and out of parliament pointed out that whereas the British occupation of Egypt was an accomplished fact, French occupation of Morocco was distinctly something else. Paul Doumer (the President assassinated in 1932), then chairman of the Chamber's budget commission, complained that "France has given a sight-draft, and in exchange has been given one that may be cashed only on maturity." To which shrewd observation he added, in envious vein, "Egypt! How many glorious souvenirs this name evokes in us, from St. Louis to Richelieu, from Richelieu to Bonaparte, from Bonaparte to Ferdinand de Lesseps! Egypt, this ancestress of nations which the great Mehemet Ali called the 'little sister of France.'"

Similarly in England, though less acid, the barter was

attacked as prejudicial to the country, and critics did not foresee that Britain was to fare much better than France. Lord Rosebery, the former Foreign Secretary, told the Liberal League that "no more one-sided agreement was ever concluded between two Powers at peace with each other. I hope and trust, but I hope and trust rather than believe, that the Power which holds Gibraltar may never have cause to regret having handed Morocco over to a great military Power." *

Despite the extensive parliamentary opposition in France, the agreement was confirmed, and Delcassé had the last word. He told the Chamber that the interests of French bondholders had been guaranteed in Egypt, the status of French societies and schools preserved at Cairo and Alexandria and, of paramount importance, that France had obtained a free hand in Morocco, the fulcrum of her empire in Africa.

"The convention is equally advantageous to both nations, since each obtains satisfaction on the points concerning them most. And it is very fortunate that it should be thus, because the arrangement, rather than being a cause for quarrels, has had for its object the wiping away of everything which might counterbalance the powerful interests which command England and France to live in confidence and good understanding."

The motive for the Kaiser's visit to Tangier, then, is plain enough. Yet it appears that when the yacht *Hamburg* had reached Lisbon, enroute to the Mediterranean, Wilhelm expressed his misgivings over the forthcoming visit to the

* The French agreed in the convention, however, not to erect fortifications on the Moroccan coast dominating passage through the Strait of Gibraltar. M. Aflalo, the Sultan's agent for British affairs, author of an anti-French indictment of the agreement (*The Truth About Morocco*, London 1905), asserts the British had little reason to hope the French would keep their word.

German ambassador. When the cabinet at Berlin learned that the Emperor was suffering from a seizure of diplomatic chilblains, von Bülow telegraphed Wilhelm that "the affair had already gone so far that it was impossible to recede without completely disavowing his advisers." *

The Kaiser hesitated no longer. His hand had been forced not only by the cabinet but by the remark of Herr von Kuhlmann, the German chargé-d'affaires at Tangier, to the French consul that "you are making a mistake not to come to an agreement with *us*. The Imperial initiative is going to intervene." He had added, moreover, that von Bülow denied that the French Government had notified the Imperial Government of the Anglo-French accord, which included a thirty-year guarantee of the commercial open-door in Morocco. (The documentary evidence that Germany had been duly notified through the French ambassador at Berlin is overwhelming, but at the time—1905—it was vehemently denied by Germany, since a pretext had to be found for the Kaiser's visit, as well as a motive sufficiently plausible to explain his speech at Tangier.)

Meanwhile, at Fez and elsewhere in Morocco, there was marked enthusiasm over the approaching visit. From hour to hour agents telegraphed the Quai-d'Orsay of the Moors' sentiments, engendered chiefly by the Anglo-French agreement, and of the anti-French feeling in Germany. Maurice Paléologue, the deputy director of political affairs (more cryptically designed as the "special business" of the Foreign Office), noted in his diary on February 20, 1905, that the "German press is beginning to discuss Morocco again, with the obvious intention of inflaming public opinion against us"; on March 24 that "public opinion in Germany is beginning to get heated. . . . The pan-Germans are talking

* Guibert and Ferrette, *Le Conflict Franco-Allemand*, Paris 1905.

war. . . . The *Magdeburger Zeitung* is threatening France with invasion"; and on March 27, four days before the Kaiser's arrival, that "the inhabitants of Tangier are getting very excited over the approaching visit of the Emperor Wilhelm. On instructions from Fez, the local authorities are preparing to give him a brilliant reception; they are displaying a degree of enthusiasm and energy which belies their reputation for lethargy. Morocco obviously looks on Wilhelm II's visit as the advent of her savior." *

When the Kaiser disembarked in the late forenoon—made somewhat timid by the choppy bay—the elaborate reception accorded him, the flags, the enthusiasm of the Moors and also, of course, the shouts of German residents, may well have vexed the French and British representatives. Nor were Wilhelm's words, more in the nature of an exhortation than an address by a monarch in a foreign land, calculated to disarm the French. The Sultan's envoy made an obsequious address of welcome, after which the Kaiser rode on horseback to the German Legation where he told a group of his subjects that "It gives me great pleasure to greet you as the gallant pioneers of German commerce who are helping me to maintain and develope the interests of the Fatherland in *a free country*."

This was, manifestly, a German *aide-mémoire* for French consumption. So far as the French and British were concerned, Morocco was anything but a free country, at least in their interpretation of that Empire in the convention of the year before. This was not, however, all that the Emperor planned to say, after von Bülow had telegraphed him *carte blanche* to Lisbon. At the diplomatic reception, where he was welcomed perfunctorily by Count Rene de Chérisey, second secretary of the French Legation, Wilhelm "clicked his heels

* Paléologue's entries may be found in *The Turning Point, Three Critical Years, 1904–1905–1906*, London 1935.

and thundered out, emphasizing every word" (according to the description sent the French Foreign Office):

"It is to the Sultan in his position of an independent sovereign that I am paying my visit today. I hope that under the sovereignty of the Sultan, a free Morocco will remain open to the peaceful rivalries of nations, without monopoly or annexation, on the basis of absolute equality.

"Yes, Monsieur [to Count Chérisey], Morocco is a very fine country, especially from the commercial point of view. So I hope that the nations of Europe will know how to safeguard efficaciously their economic interests here. Speaking personally, I am determined to see that German commercial interests are respected."

ii

The belligerent spirit and delivery of the address were not cheering to Delcassé, but its chief effect in Paris was to stiffen the back of that official. His colleague Paléologue wondered "how will he handle it all? . . . With an impulsive creature like the Kaiser, anything may happen. He is so highly strung, so apt to say something which our honor cannot let us ignore, or to do something which suddenly faces us with the irreparable." On the other hand, Baron de Courcel, the former ambassador to London, was inclined to regard the Kaiser's *coup de théâtre* at Tangier as the swashbuckling of a small boy with a wooden sword, who would run off if any of the Powers called his bluff. "I regard Wilhelm," he told Paléologue, "as a mountebank and coward who, at the critical moment, always runs away from the consequences of his own actions." . . . A prophetic analysis or, if you prefer, a good guess.

But the Kaiser was not planning to run away, at least not immediately. Before the Moroccan crisis was over, he came closer to precipitating a world war than at any time in mod-

ern European history before 1914. As an outcome of the
Tangier visit, Germany's first move was to prevail upon the
Sultan, then amiably disposed toward the Kaiser, to refuse
to adopt the political and economic reforms urged by France
—and supposedly by Britain. Count von Tattenbach was dispatched to Fez to exert pressure on the Sultan, who finally
agreed with the German special envoy that "he [the Sultan]
had made no concessions to the French, but had been awaiting the arrival of the German minister before reaching any
decision." *

The Kaiser's visit, therefore, had borne some fruit. The
Sultan on May 27 told Saint-René Taillandier, the French
minister, that he would not consent to any changes until these
were first discussed by the signatory Powers of the Conference of Madrid (1880). After successfully navigating the
diplomatic shoals in the path of the agreements with Britain
and Italy respecting her freedom in Morocco, France found
this demand—patently of German inspiration—a serious
check.

The Wilhelmstrasse was jubilant. It now remained necessary only to shelve Delcassé, who was proving as implacable toward Germany as his predecessor, Hanotaux, had
been toward Britain. So far as the French foreign minister
was concerned, there would be no conference over Morocco
with Germany.

Nevertheless, Germany obtained Delcassé's scalp, and
with more skill in political propaganda and diplomacy than
is characteristic of the Wilhelmstrasse. Her ally Italy informed the French ambassador at Rome that the Government had received information—from ostensibly authoritative sources—that Paris had given the Sultan an ultimatum
to leave Germany severely alone. The Italian Government,
possibly retailing the information in good faith, added to

* German White Book, No. 10, p. 262.

the French ambassador, M. Barrère, that from the same quarter it had learned that if France should move troops into Morocco, or otherwise indicate readiness to establish a protectorate, German armies simultaneously would move westward across the Vosges Mountains. Barrère expedited the report to Paris, and the Chamber of Deputies, and Frenchmen generally, were seized with paroxysms of fear. . . . The Franco-Prussian War had not been forgotten, and the Dreyfus Affair had not given the country a profound faith in the army.

The ultimatum and the German threat of invasion were, it soon developed, diplomatic fairy-stories.* Government and press in France learned, however, that there was no fiction in the massing of German troops in Baden, not far from the French frontier, in Württemburg, Westphalia and in the Rhine provinces, and that all leaves had been rescinded for the Royal Prussian Guard. Nor was it fantasy that the Krupp and the Ehrhardt works had received orders in 1905 which would completely replace German armaments.

Overnight a campaign of invective arose against Delcassé who, it was argued, had so exasperated Germany that once again France was confronted with the threat of invasion—thus ran the criticism. At this psychological moment, the German chancellery sent Prince Henckel von Donnersmarck to Paris to confer privately with Premier Maurice Rouvier to whom (according to *Le Gaulois* of June 17) he said:

"If you are of the opinion that your Minister of Foreign Affairs has engaged your country in too adventurous a course, acknowledge it by dispensing with his services, and especially by giving a new direction to your foreign policy. We are not concerned with M. Delcassé's person; but his policy is a menace to Germany; and you may rest assured that we will not wait for it to be realized. . . . Give up the

* Georges Reynal, *La diplomatie française*, Paris 1915.

TURRET DIPLOMACY 251

minister whose only aspiration is to trouble the peace of Europe; and adopt with regard to Germany a loyal and open policy."

Delcassé remained adamant against a conference in which Germany would be represented, urging upon the cabinet that no foreign country had the right to intervene between France and Morocco (nor particularly to seek the removal of a cabinet member). But the ministry voted against him, and Delcassé resigned. Germany thus had won both preliminary objectives . . . so pleased was Wilhelm that he hurried to von Bülow's house in Berlin and made him a prince on the spot, in reward for ousting Delcassé. In her jubilation the new Princess von Bülow told intimates that "We didn't ask for his [Delcassé's] head, they offered it to us." It seems not altogether implausible that Delcassé's dismissal from the Rouvier Ministry originated in that lady's head.

Even immediately before Delcassé's ejection, on June 6, so serious was the Franco-German situation in British eyes that King Edward was sent to Paris to give the appearance of solidarity between the lion and the cock. The King would not believe that von Bülow's insistence upon a conference over Morocco was mere bluff. So far as was practical he would support the French, particularly for the sake of the Entente, but he privately told de Courcel in Paris that "You must settle this Moroccan business quickly. Sponge it off. . . . *Schwamm darüber!*" *

Germany now was applying more than diplomatic pressure. Newspapers openly favored war as the cheapest and most effective way to obtain satisfaction. With good reason, the conviction prevailed in the Reich that the German armies could go through France like a knife through cheese. Bismarck's former organ, the *Hamburger Nachrichten*, suc-

* A few days later, at Marienbad, King Edward refused flatly to confer with Kaiser Wilhelm, his nephew. See *Edward VII at Marienbad* (chap. XXII), by Sigmund Münz, London 1934.

cinctly expressed the view of the Wilhelmstrasse:

"In the opinion of our Government, we must achieve a success in Morocco at any price. Otherwise the prestige of the Empire will be seriously damaged, as Germany will have suffered a humiliating reverse for the first time since Bismarck's day. This means that Germany must be rushed into war to make good the shortcomings of her diplomacy."

After Edward's visit, Theodore Roosevelt believed war so imminent that, despite the traditional hands-off policy of Washington, the President decided to intervene. It should be recorded, however, that his intercession followed receipt of a letter from the Kaiser. He summoned Jules Jusserand, the French ambassador, to the White House.

Jusserand reported back to the Quai-d'Orsay that President Roosevelt had said to him:

"The Emperor Wilhelm has just written me a personal letter in which he says that he is demanding a conference to settle his dispute with France, and that *the refusal of his request involves the risk of war*. He tells me that your English friends are inciting you to resist, and further that you have made a defensive and offensive alliance with England. . . . I find it extraordinarily difficult to advise you, but I wonder if you wouldn't choose the lesser of two evils by agreeing to the conference."

Two days later, June 19, Jusserand reported to his Foreign Office that President Roosevelt added:

"France ought to adopt a conciliatory attitude toward Germany. You must know that I'm not the sort of man to yield to threats. But there are many concessions to be made, without loss of honor, to avoid a war. I would not hesitate if I were in your place. You'll have to give some sort of sop to the Emperor Wilhelm's unbounded vanity."

On June 16 the German Government had come as near to sending France an ultimatum as was diplomatically pos-

TURRET DIPLOMACY 253

sible in the absence of a definite declaration of hostilities. The German ambassador had given Rouvier—who was acting both as premier and foreign minister—a communication which stated that "the Imperial Government cannot discuss the program of the [proposed] conference with France until the Government of the Republic has formally accepted the invitation to be represented at it."

And Rouvier, who at heart as much disliked the conference project as Delcassé, was "bowled over," according to Paléologue, and exclaimed in despair: "This makes me believe what the Emperor said in his letter to Roosevelt—if we don't agree to the conference, war will be inevitable."

Paléologue labored until 2 A. M. the following day, sending instructions to French agents in Belgium, Luxemburg and Switzerland to post men immediately at frontier points to watch for German mobilization. A telegram was dispatched to the French ambassador at St. Petersburg instructing him to ascertain from the Czar how far the latter would go, under the secret military convention of 1894, toward supporting his ally in the west.

By June 26, the French attitude had somewhat stiffened, due in part to word from Russia that the Czar was urging Wilhelm to climb off his high-horse. French officials at a reception that evening at the British Embassy in Paris took heart also when Clemenceau bellowed to any guest who would give him ear—preferably those in the proximity of Prince von Radolin, the German ambassador—that "We won't give way any farther. . . . If Germany wants war, well, we'll fight!"

At last, on July 8, the two countries arrived at a compromise. France agreed to maintain the independence of the Sultan of Morocco and to commercial freedom in his States. For her part Germany admitted the "special interests of France in Morocco" and undertook "not to attempt anything which conflicts with the rights she has derived from her treaties." With that concession from Germany, the Rouvier Government agreed to the despised meeting—the abortive Conference of Algeciras (Spain), which was the genesis of another, and far more serious, threat of war.

iii

Algeciras was the conference demanded by Germany over the Moroccan question, but that meeting had no more to do with the Moors than the Brussels Conference of 1890, or the Berlin Conference of 1885, were concerned with the rights of the natives elsewhere in Africa.

The conference opened January 16, 1906, in the little town, and the "General Act of the International Conference at Algeciras," to give its formal title, was signed by the delegates on April 7. So far as Germany was concerned, her purpose was to break up France's European alliances by provoking quarrels at the meeting. In this von Bülow failed where the far more astute Bismarck, a genius at that game, might have succeeded, or partly succeeded.

The actual negotiations, at which the Sultan cast a baleful eye, need not be detailed. The Act eventually signed, consisting of 123 articles, provided for recognition of the independence of the Sultan, guarantees of the indivisibility of his territory (important in light of the 1911 crisis), and free trade for the Powers. The Sultan consented to organize a police force of 2,500 Moors for service in the eight ports, officered by sixty French and Spaniards, and commanded by an inspector-general of Swiss nationality. To improve— i. e., control—the Empire's finances, a State Bank of Morocco was established, eleven parts of the capital subscribed by the nations participating at Algeciras, and two by France (Paris taking the share of the United States, which through

Henry White, ambassador at Rome, declined any part in the monetary project). German intransigence at the conference lost her the friendship of all the nations represented, save Austria. If Germans had expected territorial acquisitions in Morocco, they were sadly misled, and evidently in anticipation of criticism over the paucity of the Reich's achievements, von Bülow declared in the Reichstag, April 5, just before the conference closed, that:—

"We do not have, like Spain, a Mauritanian post of several centuries, and we have not, like France, a common frontier of several hundred kilometers with Morocco; we have no historic rights acquired by all sorts of sacrifices as have these two civilizing nations." The contrast to his tone of a few months before is severe. But to the Chancellor, at least, Germany had won a moral victory at Algeciras. "We wished to show that the German Empire does not allow itself to be treated as a negligible quantity. . . . The decisions of the Algeciras Conference provided a bell we could ring at any time should France show any similar tendencies again."

Even the Reichstag felt that the Chancellor's belief that Germany would "not be treated as a negligible quantity" was little in return for all the diplomatic blustering and saber-rattling. From the military standpoint, however, the army replacements which had accompanied the saber-rattling in 1905 proved a valuable investment in the early months of the World War.

The only satisfaction for Germany was a vindictive one. The Kaiser and von Bülow could congratulate and console themselves, if there was any satisfaction therein, that the French deals with Italy and Britain for a free hand in Morocco were now worthless, so far as Paris was concerned, while France was pledged nevertheless to keep out of Egypt.

But France soon forgot about Algeciras.

iv

Algeciras proved abortive because, (1) the European signatories were, for the most part, indifferent to contributing the necessary men and money to a Moroccan police force and international banking system, (2) the Sultan was not interested in recruiting a police force for the protection of European lives and investments in the ports, to the detriment of the rest of his Empire and, consequently, endangering his own position, (3) German firms began an underground munitions trade with Morocco, although this was specifically prohibited by the Act and, (4) increasing banditry, led by Raisuli and others, and fed in part by the smuggled munitions, led to rebellions against both the Sultan and Europeans. At various times before the 1911 crisis, French, British, Spaniards and Italians were massacred at Casablanca, Tangier and elsewhere in the Empire. Despite the pledges in the Act, Clemenceau, who had become premier in 1907, was urging intervention after repeated Moorish raids over the Algerian frontier; by intervention he meant, of course, to take a page from the British colonial practice—establishment of a protectorate.

After 1907, events moved rapidly toward a major concussion. Clemenceau sent Éugene Regnault to Morocco—characteristically, the special representative at Algeciras of French investors in Morocco. The Sultan Abdul Aziz, fearing the growing power of his brother, Mouley Hafid, and realizing that his only salvation lay with France, agreed to Regnault's demands for the immediate conscription of a police force, to payment of indemnity for massacred French citizens, and to the suppression of the munitions-smuggling —if that were possible. While Abdul Aziz was nodding in frightened consent to all the demands of Clemenceau's emissary, Mouley Hafid at Fez proclaimed himself Sultan

TURRET DIPLOMACY

of the Shereefian Empire and metaphorically thumbed his nose at his brother and the French—who had only the smallest force in Morocco. Clemenceau's answer was to order that Abdul be restored to power and kept there, and in March 1908 a force of 3,000 men was shipped to north Africa.

French and Germans in Morocco now came into open conflict. On the one hand, the Wilhelmstrasse overwhelmed the Quai-d'Orsay with demands for reparations, claiming that the French punitive measures directed against Mouley Hafid prevented the Germans from obtaining docking facilities, contracts with the local authorities, and that French troops had attacked German subjects. On the other hand, German engineers and other technicians were openly supporting Mouley at Fez, and on their advice he sent a delegation to Berlin to seek aid against the French. At Fez, incidentally, the usurper created wild enthusiasm by demolishing grand-pianos, bathtubs, miniature railways and captive-balloons, "presents" which Abdul had received from Europeans. Abdul was later defeated by his brother, and late in 1908 the Powers were forced to recognize Mouley.

France had picked the wrong horse, and Germany the right one, but the clumsy violation by the Reich of the Algeciras agreement, guaranteeing the sovereignty of the Sultan Abdul, did not increase the prestige of the Wilhelmstrasse, even in Germany. The *Frankfurter Zeitung* (September 3, 1908) stated that "we would prefer to assume that the action of the German Government represents another of those sudden impulses of German policy, which make a terrific noise but afterwards vanish, leaving nothing behind. But this unfortunately is harm enough." *

* The "action" referred to was the Berlin Government's immediate dispatch, after the defeat of Abdul, of its consular agent,

Nevertheless, Mouley Hafid was friendly to Germany and, because of her support of his brother, unfriendly to France. For all of that, the year 1908 was a fateful one for Germany: it saw ratification of the Triple Entente, which had certainly been fostered in some measure by German maneuvers in Morocco.

Relations between the two Powers were sufficiently strained once again that it is cause for astonishment war did not break out in September when the French seized three German deserters from the Foreign Legion, who were making their escape under the protection of an employe of the German consulate at Casablanca. The Wilhelmstrasse demanded their release and an immediate apology. Clemenceau laughed; he would not be browbeaten. Troop movements were again reported, this time on both frontiers. The incident blew over, and is significant only in that it led Wilhelm to give a celebrated interview to the London *Daily Telegraph*, in an effort to win British sympathy. In this he said that, for fear of offending British sensibilities in 1899, he had declined to give an audience at Berlin to Kruger's Boer delegates, "although German public opinion [then] was bitterly hostile to Great Britain [and that] the German people [at the capital] would have crowned them with flowers. . . . Far from Germany joining in any concerted action to put pressure upon England and bring about her downfall, Germany would always keep aloof from politics that would bring her into complication with a sea-power like England. Englishmen who now insult me by doubting my word should know what were my actions in the hour of their adversity." The interview is in a class, among mirthful State papers, with the same monarch's letter of pained sur-

---

at Casablanca, to Fez to greet Mouley Hafid, tantamount to extending him diplomatic recognition without first consulting the Powers.

prise to Victoria in 1899. . . . Eventually the Permanent Court of Arbitration at The Hague settled the Foreign Legion dispute in a decision upholding the arrest of the German deserters. *Le Temps* in Paris referred to "the controversy which, however trivial was its origin, had almost set Europe on fire."

France and Germany in 1909 (February 9) signed an accord, ratifying the sense of the Algeciras Act as between themselves, and providing for equal economic rights, although the Imperial Government recognized "the particular political interests of France" and pledged itself "not to impede these interests." The practical effect of this separate agreement, which was drafted within the framework of the Algeciras Act and consequently did not change the effect of that convention, was to lessen the tension between Paris and Berlin, and to give the former additional commercial guarantees in the event, now seen as probable, that Algeciras was to be scrapped by the action of one or several of the Powers.

But it was the calm before the storm.

v

The destruction of his brother's grand-pianos and bathtubs had won for Mouley Hafid only a short-lived popularity. Early in 1911 he called upon the French to help him against rivals, and to fulfill the military provisions of the Algeciras convention by sending a column to his relief at Fez. The French were not concerned over the attitude of most of the Powers, which they judged would be friendly, but Germany was sounded out with care. Reinforcements were sent out under Marshal Lyautey, ostensibly to protect European lives, and the German Government meanwhile was asked its attitude. The Wilhelmstrasse replied, as regarded the

Fez column, "We do not say no, we do not say yes. You know the German opinion regarding Morocco. You tell us: 'If we go to Fez it will only be temporarily to reëstablish the authority of the Sultan and to prevent anarchy.' But once at Fez, will you be able to withdraw?"

The question was reasonable, although the reference to "German opinion" was camouflage. The French might relieve the pressure on Mouley Hafid, but Europeans would still remain at Fez, their investments would still be there, and both would need continued protection. Even with Fez relieved, no one could guarantee there would be peace forever. And implicitly, there was more to the German inquiry: would the French, once having invested Fez, politically and militarily, consider it *expedient* to withdraw? There are a number of reasons to believe that the French recognized that the immediate necessity of the expedition would furnish an ideal pretext later for the proclamation of a protectorate.

On May 21 the French had arrived beneath the walls of Fez. German newspapers renewed their warnings. The Crown Prince, meeting the French ambassador at an aviation demonstration, congratulated him in a cryptic sentence.

"Well, my dear Ambassador, here you are at Fez. Accept my compliments! Morocco is a fine bit of territory. We won't speak of it any more now, but *you fix it up with us and it will be all right.*" On June 20, with the district cleared of the Sultan's besiegers, the order was given by Lyautey for the march back to the coast, although it did not go into effect immediately.

On June 23, Joseph Caillaux formed a new government of eminent nobodies, at least in the vital posts of war and foreign affairs.

For Germany it was a propitious moment to reassert herself over Morocco. Four days later, on June 27, a low-lying

TURRET DIPLOMACY

gray hull appeared off the harbor of Agadir, an obscure port on the Atlantic side, about 300 miles southwest of Tangier. It was the German gunboat *Panther*.

The *Panther* has long since been scrapped, but the menace of her six guns fore and aft, any one of which could have razed the miserable port in three minutes, lent force to the German argument. That argument was four-fold, and by means of it, supported by the threat of the *Panther*, Germany wrested from France a territory of about 144,000 square miles, nearly the size of California.

On June 28 Prince Radolin left the German Embassy in the rue de l'Université, and walked the few yards to the French Foreign Office to see M. Caillaux's foreign minister —whose appointment was bitterly criticized, incidentally, by *Le Matin*, which referred to M. de Selves, a former prefect of the Seine Department, as an official "who during fifteen years has been unable to clean, pave or light the capital [and] as a recompense is put at the head of foreign affairs of his country." The German envoy swung his stick and hummed a merry tune.

After informing the French Government that the *Panther* was at Agadir, the Prince fired this diplomatic salvo:

1. Earlier in the year (1911), a French cruiser had put in at Agadir, ostensibly to make a courtesy call upon the local pasha: a violation of Algeciras, in the view of the Wilhelmstrasse, which recalled the "indivisibility of the Sultan's territory," and, through Radolin, pointed out that Agadir was a closed port, i. e., barred to European commerce. In other words, the French naval visit was, in German eyes, the obvious prelude to a protectorate.

2. Despite the 1909 agreement covering economic equality in Morocco, France had consistently made difficulties for German firms interested in contracts for public-works.

3. German businessmen in Morocco, because of French obstructionism and the uncertainty of police protection, had appealed to the Government to defend their lives.

4. Germany had just learned of five secret articles in the Anglo-French agreement of seven years before (1904), which were indisputable evidence of France's (and Britain's) bad faith toward Germany and the other Powers. The most damning of these were two stipulating that while neither Britain nor France foresaw any political changes in the political status, respectively, of Egypt and Morocco, *should* changes be deemed advisable each party would continue to recognize the other's freedom of action in the two countries where each had "special interests." In other words, both had envisaged protectorates seven years before.

The concussion of this legal blast upon the gentleman who, it was said, for fifteen years had been unable to keep Paris clean and lighted, was violent. He turned helplessly to Caillaux and the premier turned to Jules Cambon, the ambassador in Berlin. The outcome of that envoy's interview on July 15 with Wilhelmstrasse officials was that Germany demanded, in return for withdrawal of the *Panther* and dismissal of her indictment of French violations of Algeciras, the cession of all the French Congo from the Atlantic to the Sangha River.

Clearly this had been in the mind of the Crown Prince several weeks before when he had told Cambon, ". . . you fix it up with us, and it will be all right."

The German foreign minister was blunt to Cambon. "You have purchased your liberty in Morocco from Spain, England and even Italy," he said, "and you have thrust us aside. You should have negotiated with us before going to Fez."

Both in France and England this demand aroused public fury. In the former the growing sentiment for war—if it must come, *en finir tout de suite*—was fanned unwittingly by the Countess de Brazza, widow of the explorer, who appealed to the Republic not to cede to the Reich any part of the territory for which her husband had given his life. In London, Lloyd George, Chancellor of the Exchequer, took up the cudgels for France. But Caillaux was reluctant to accept the British suggestion that France and England each send a warship to Agadir and send the *Panther* off—or, if her commander refused to be dismissed, blow him out of the water together with the Moorish chiefs aboard.

Inevitably, German and French mobilization again took place on the frontiers, on this occasion openly—there seemed no need for secrecy, but chiefly haste, if war was a certainty (the generals were three years ahead of their governments). So close were hostilities that, reacting to rumors of a moratorium, stocks in Berlin on September 10 ("Sinister Saturday") began falling sharply.

On November 4 a treaty was signed. So far as Morocco was concerned, Germany granted France complete freedom of action and recognized the right of the Third Republic to jurisdiction over the foreign relations of the Sultan. Moreover, "in the event of the French Government deeming it necessary to assume the protectorate of Morocco, the Imperial Government would place no obstacle in the way." Once again commercial liberty was conceded by Paris.

France ceded about one-half of her Congo territory. Despite anti-German sentiment in France and England, the governments of both nations realized that the moment had not arrived for the final and, so it was believed by many, unavoidable explosion, although the fuse had been smouldering for six years.

The final convention was satisfactory to neither parliament. There is no evidence on which to base any estimate of the satisfaction felt by the Moors or, in the French Congo given to the Empire, of the Bantus and other tribes. In

France and Germany both, when the agreement was presented for ratification the ministerial chiefs were compelled to equivocate.

To the Reichstag, von Bethman-Hollweg, the Chancellor, pleaded:

"I believe that by thus multiplying the [commercial] regulations, we have rendered a good service to the German economic interests in Morocco. Prior to Fez and to Agadir, Morocco was nominally independent, but in fact already in the power of France. What is the real position? We have given nothing in Morocco which we had not already given, and we have gained a substantial increase in our Empire abroad."

The Crown Prince laughed and the Conservatives took the cue. . . . Germany may have won a jungle territory overseas, which was the Chancellor's private assignment from Wilhelm, but the Reich in the process had alienated England, and lost any opportunity of seizing a port on the Atlantic.

In France the parliamentary reaction was equally derisive. Caillaux's later trial for treason was due in great part to his speech before the Chamber of Deputies, in which he claimed that the paramount factor was peace with Germany. The Senate put Foreign Minister de Selves on the stand, that poor gentleman who failed to illuminate Paris, and he collapsed when Clemenceau—then becoming God, judge and jury in France—demanded to know whether Caillaux had had private transactions with Germany. The bewildered lamplighter declined to reply, resigned, and Caillaux left the ministry two days later. The *Journal des Débats* dismissed the passing of Caillaux (since returned very influentially to the French political circus) as the result of "occult negotiations [which] would have resulted in the dismemberment of the French African Empire without

Note locations of Tangier and Agadir on northwest coast, and Fashoda in southern Sudan.

visible compensation, a rupture with Spain, the ruin of our influence in the Levant, a falling-out with England. . . . For France this fall [of the ministry] is the end of a nightmare."

vi

Battalions of the Royal Prussian Guard were withdrawn from Alsace-Lorraine eastward over the Rhine, and the *Landwehr* military control ended. At Agadir the *Panther* sent its power-launch ashore with the flea-bitten sheiks that its officers and crew had endured for 154 days. West of the Vosges the French turned their backs on Germany. . . . The next year the Moors began their long and futile struggle against the French protectorate.

XIV

"Specialist Assistance"
[1908-30]

BRITAIN'S record in Africa is not one of unmixed altruism, the reader may have inferred, but she was not the chief European culprit on the Dark Continent. That is a verdict which has been made too easily, and too often. Although France's holdings in Africa are larger territorially than those of England, the latter's confiscations are more valuable economically and strategically, and were more spectacularly achieved than those of the other Powers; it follows—erroneously—that her exploitation of the natives was on a vaster and crueler scale. But if the London Government closed its eyes, or conveniently looked the other way, when it heard revolting reports of the *corvée* in Egypt, of the degradation of natives by the gin of British agents, official and civil, and of other abuses, it was not the only European ministry which condoned outrages. Civilization was administered the Negro in forced doses, and the effects of rum, serfdom and mutilation were necessary phases of a treatment which disciplined his soul. Morally, no one of the European Powers has a blacker record in Africa than another. . . . In the Berlin Act they all pledged themselves "to insure the preservation of the native populations and [to] the improvement of their moral and material conditions of existence." The pledges are there—if made with fingers crossed.

Here will be considered briefly the treatment of African natives by Belgium—more correctly by Leopold II—France, Germany and the United States.

ii

Leopold's investment in the Congo Free State was such that, as the record shows, he did not propose to concern himself with much save financial return. After 1891, when the enormous wealth of his domain overseas in ivory and rubber could not be disputed, he moved quickly to tighten his control and get back his investment. The year before, in return for a loan from the Brussels Government, he had been forced to agree to permit Belgium to annex the State within ten years. It behooved the "businessman King" to get his compensation in a hurry.

In a secret decree of 1891, all "vacant lands" were declared the property of the Free State (i. e., Leopold's), and in these the Congo Government awarded itself a monopoly in the collection of ivory and rubber. Other decrees within the next two years, drafted in the Palace at Brussels, limited the rights of the white traders, forced natives to sell only to agents of the Free State—a violation of the Berlin Act—and bound them not to move from their homes without a pass. The natives, moreover, lost all title to lands which were not "effectively occupied" by them—that is, they might own their settlements only and such plots as they cultivated. In 1896, by virtue of another secret decree (of which the Powers did not learn officially until 1902), there was established a "Crown Domain," the exclusive property of the King, consisting of a territory of approximately 115,000 square miles, lying between the Ruki and Kasai rivers; the profits from exploitation of this domain went directly into the King's privy purse. The worst of the outrages—slavery, mutilation and murder—occurred within this "state within a state."

Leopold's monopolistic practices brought him inevitably the enmity of British, French, German, Dutch and American traders. It is impossible to gauge at this date how concerned they were, if at all, with Leopold's treatment of the natives, but many among them professed to be deeply shocked by the outrages, and took pains to see that their home governments learned of the abuses. In relaying the data and evidence to European Powers and the United States, the missionaries were of invaluable aid to the traders, for their reportorial indictments were vivid in detail, in tone they were plausibly affronted and shocked, and the majority of them had no other interest in the native than teaching him the Bible and urging him to wear a few clothes on Sunday.

By 1901, protests against the inhuman treatment of the native in the Free State were mounting in Belgium, France, Germany, England and the United States, and Congo "reform associations" sprang up in these and other countries. The international campaign against Leopold obtained its greatest impetus from Britain where parliamentarians and home missionaries added their exclamations of horror and incredulity to those of various chambers of commerce and export organizations whose eyebrow-raising might be thought slightly specious.

Whether or not it explains some of the vehemence of British statesmen over the Belgian atrocities is anyone's guess, but Sir Edward Grey, Lord Lansdowne and other influential Englishmen, in and out of Downing Street, had material reasons for wanting to check Leopold. Under the Berlin Act, the British had no consular jurisdiction in the Free State, which placed their traders under great handicap. Lord Monkswell, former Under-Secretary for War, demanded in the *Fortnightly Review* (in 1907) that Britain obtain consular jurisdiction by summoning a "conference of all the Powers and [by endeavoring] to get the navigation of the Congo placed under the control of an international commission. *Let us insist on our trade rights,* and attack the monstrous claim put forward by King Leopold to a monopoly of the lands and the products of the Congo." That peer's reference to British trade rights rather invalidates his passion elsewhere in the article for a more humane treatment of the native. Sir Harry Johnston, who as Special Commissioner in the East African Protectorate showed no fanatical interest in the welfare of the natives—and who has been cited earlier in this account as the chief apologist for the British seizure of the Orange diamond-fields—decided suddenly that, in the absence of British civilizing influences, the Belgian Congo might become the crater of a human volcano that could desolate the entire African Continent by "an eruption against which, except so far as the actual coastline is concerned, the resources of men and money which Europe can put into the field will be powerless."

A more spiritual tone was adopted by Lord Lansdowne, Foreign Secretary in 1900-06, who before the House of Lords became exercised over the "bondage under the most barbarous and inhuman conditions . . . maintained for mercenary motives of the most selfish character." Sir Edward Grey, Lansdowne's successor at the Foreign Office, told the House of Commons in 1908 that the Congo Free State (*alias* Leopold, for annexation by Belgium was delayed until late that year, although the option permitted preëmption in 1901) "has morally forfeited every right to international recognition." In Washington Mr. Elihu Root was equally condemnatory.

In 1903 Britain had forced Leopold, by the threat of summoning a Congo conference among the Powers (just as Germany threatened France with a Moroccan conference) to appoint an inquiry commission, after the House of Commons had requested the Government to consult with the Berlin Act signatories "by virtue of which the Congo Free State exists, in order that measures may be adopted to abate the evils prevalent in that State." Leopold's Congo commission, which remained in Africa from October 5, 1904, to February 21, 1905, in its findings sustained most of the charges which had been brought: the most vicious had been made by Roger Casement,* the British consul at Boma, Free State capital, and involved murder of natives by Belgian or native police, mutilation of men, women and children, forced labor to a degree resulting repeatedly in death from exhaustion, forced military service, seizure of women and children as hostages when family-heads failed to produce their rubber quota, and the demolition of entire villages to make room for plantations which required clearings. Casement, later knighted, estimated that Leopold's practices were costing the lives of 100,000 yearly in the Free State—other estimates went as high as four hundred a day.

Reforms were forced upon Leopold not only by the action of the British Parliament, his own legislature (in which it was charged in July 1903 that "this work of 'civilization' is an enormous and continual butchery") and the United States Senate (which in 1906 had adopted a motion upholding President Roosevelt's efforts to improve native conditions in the Congo), but chiefly by the cumulative effect of an avalanche of pamphlets which all but buried him at Brussels.† They appeared in English, French, German, Swedish, Turkish—and even Flemish. The most prolific anti-Leopold

* The Irish patriot, hanged by the British for treason on August 3, 1916.

† Defenders of Leopold II, notably Count Louis de Lichtervelde in *Leopold of the Belgians*, charge that the British Government White Paper of 1907, on abuses in the Congo Free State, was "clearly aimed to provoke foreign intervention."

society was the Congo Reform Association, with headquarters at London and branches throughout the Occident, and with which was associated the British and Foreign Anti-Slavery Society. Next most articulate were, naturally, the missionary societies on both sides of the Atlantic.*

The sequel was that Leopold signed several decrees by which forced labor was limited to forty hours weekly (soon thereafter found insufficient by the natives, if they were to escape mutilation by the police, which followed when their rubber quotas were below par), and military conscription of the Congolese was "restricted." That is not to say, of course, that it was abolished. The improvement in conditions was not marked, and harrowing tales of the natives' plight continued to reach European ears. Leopold was unruffled. When a missionary bishop protested on one occasion against

* Typical of British pamphlets, some of them containing graphic illustrations of mutilation of children, are "Abuses in the Congo Free State," "Evidence Laid Before the Congo Commission of Inquiry," "What is Taking Place *Now* in King Leopold's 'Crown Domain,'" "Britain's Duty: An Appeal to the Nation," "Red Rubber," "The Christian Church and the Congo Question," etc., etc. In the United States there was published, for example, "Evidence in the Congo Case," "The Treatment of Women and Children in the Congo State," "The Duty of the U. S. Government to Promote International Action for Relief of Conditions in the Congo State," "Congo Misrule Today," and Mark Twain's caustic "King Leopold's Soliloquy" (1905). The French and German equivalents are, for the greater part, sensationalized and general. Leopold had his own propaganda organization to combat the campaign against him—the Fédération pour la Défense des Intérêts Belges à l'Étranger—and it published its *ripostes* in French, English and German. In the English version some of them were "Are They All Liars?" "The Congo Free State and African Civilization," "The Story of a Belgian 'Crime'"; etc. A number of them was published by the Consul-General of the Congo Free State at Baltimore, James Augustus Napoleon Talleyrand Whitley, an American, writer on international law, who after General Sanford's death (1891) became Leopold's chief spokesman in the United States.

the abuses of the Free State administration, the King responded philosophically, "without doubt, Monsignor, that is sad, very sad, but one cannot accomplish a great work without doing some evil. You build a Cathedral: during its construction there inevitably occur many regrettable incidents. There will be injustices, accidents, disputes, sometimes violent fights. Insults and blasphemies will be heard, but in the end the monument is completed to the glory of God and the salvation of souls. . . . It goes the same way in the Congo." *

He was rarely without an answer, King Leopold II of the Belgians.

The oppobrium which indirectly fell on the Brussels Government led to realization, by everyone save Leopold, that a reform must occur. Despite the option which he had given Belgium in return for the 1890 loan, and which could have been exercised in 1901, the monarch demurred, particularly over ceding the Crown Domain—where the rubber and ivory yield was richest, and the atrocities less publicized. "To the author assuredly belongs the reward of his labors," he protested to his Senate. At last, for fifty million francs, and the assumption by the Government of Leopold's obligations, the King gave Belgium the Congo.

On November 15, 1908, the Belgium Government took over the Congo Free State as a colony. Thirteen months later Leopold was dead. "Popularity! Popularity!" he told the abbé at the end, "I had it and it left me. . . . It is made of light froth, it is not even foam. There remains nothing of it."

iii

The fabulous wealth of the Congo must be counted as one of the reasons for the publicity given the atrocities in

* Lichtervelde, *op. cit.*

the Free State, whether or not it is true that Britain sought deliberately to provoke foreign intervention. Leopold's strangle-hold upon the Congo had been effective. Europeans believed that forced labor was the only way in which the wealth of the continent could be extracted—which was true enough; that there was no moral extenuation for stealing the wealth was one of those questions which only Liberals and kindred crackpots at large evoked, and they could be answered by the hoary casuistry that, as compensation for that wealth, Africa was reaping the benefits of white civilization.

Thus it is only in extent and degree that other Powers were not equally guilty as Leopold. Certainly they were equally callous, equally concerned with finding riches overnight, equally indifferent to the welfare of the native. All of them used forced labor, all of them condoned murder, described sometimes as "extreme disciplinary measures"; they all taxed the black, filled him with rum, bribed him with playthings, flogged him, and took his wife and children as hostages.

De Brazza was withdrawn from the French Congo (French Equatorial Africa) in 1897 because he was disliked by traders. Four years later, learning that the colonial administrator who succeeded him was taking his cue from the Belgians on the other side of the river, he reminded the Government that "France has assumed a duty toward the native tribes of French Congolese, who for twenty-seven years have given her their assistance in the work of expansion. These people have rescued from us the soul of their future liberties. We must not sacrifice them in the vain hope of immediate results, by thoughtless acts of coercion at variance with the generous ideas that our Flag symbolizes. We should be committing a great mistake . . . by compelling the natives to work in the form of forced labor or military service." *

De Brazza was dismissed; he was considered honest, which was his weak point, and the Minister for Colonies remarked upon his failure to achieve the results of Leopold's pioneers to the south. Monopolies were granted to forty-two "companies," and the tribes enslaved to bring out the ivory, rubber, copper and gum. Finally, Paris realized that between the maladministration and atrocities in the Congo Free State, and those in the French Congo, there was not much to choose. A Governor-General was sent out in 1908 to end the abuses—chief of which was the handing over of tens of thousands of natives to the concessionaires—after de Brazza had been sent back to make a report to Paris. He was shocked by the depopulation of the country since 1897. He died, trying to explain it, enroute home.

But British, French and Belgians had no monopoly on savagery, in the art of which many a European gave the African native pointers. In German South-West Africa, the administration was particularly paternalistic. Here the copper mines were rich in the extreme, and lands were appropriated without so much as a bottle of rum or a Tyrolese hat, for which it appears the Hottentots had a passion as deep-seated as that of the Congolese for jack-in-the-boxes and gin. In 1904 the Hereros rebelled against the theft of their lands, compulsory labor, and assaults upon their women, and signified their discontent by murdering several Germans and their families. General Lothar von Trotha was dispatched to Africa. His diplomacy and military astuteness were illustrated by the proclamation he issued, late

* *Le Temps*, November 17, 1901.

in 1904, when he had nearly 10,000 troops in the field against the Hereros:

"I, the Great General of the German soldiers, send this letter to the Herero nation. The Hereros are no longer German citizens. They have murdered and robbed, they have cut off the ears and noses, and other members, of wounded soldiers, and they are now too cowardly to fight. Whosoever brings one of the chieftains as a prisoner to one of my stations shall receive 1,000 Marks, and for Samuel Maherero (their leader) I will pay 5,000 Marks.

"The Herero Nation must now leave the country. If the people do it not, I will compel them with the big tube. Within the German frontier every Herero, with or without a rifle, with or without cattle, will be *shot*.

"I will not take over any more women and children, but I will either drive them back or *have them fired on*.

"The Great General of the Mighty Emperor,
"Von Trotha."

Bülow ordered the repeal of this proclamation, as terrible as it was fatuous. Before the close of the two-year Herero War, the German "big tube" had killed 30,000—women and their children had been driven eastward into the Kalahari Desert where they died in droves. The total loss of native lives between 1904 and 1908 in German South-West Africa is estimated by German historians at 100,000. Other writers place them a good deal higher. Whatever the casualties, the colony became a liability to the Wilhelmstrasse. The cost of firing the "big tube" and other military activities to the Imperial Treasury was $115,000,000, with the consequence that labor became so scarce that the colony collapsed. But the expenditure of that enormous sum bore out, at least, the contention of the editor of the *Deutsche Südwestafrikanische Zeitung*, of Lüderitz, who had warned in 1904 that "the country must be inhabited by white colonists. Therefore, *the natives must disappear*, or rather put them-

"SPECIALIST ASSISTANCE" 277

selves at the disposal of the whites." . . . A blunt statement, and a surpassingly accurate one.

iv

Since October 1935, when the ultimate fate of Ethiopia was evident, it has been conventional to refer to Liberia as the last of free Africa. Liberia is self-governing, and its finances are in the paternal hands of the Firestone Tire & Rubber Co., of Akron, Ohio, acting through the National City Bank of New York.

A glance at the map is necessary to understand the rather peculiar status of Liberia, and to foretell its evident future. The Negro Republic of Liberia, a miserable 140,000 square miles, lies in west Africa, extending along the coast of northern Guinea, uncomfortably situated between the British colony of Sierre Leone on the northwest, and the (French) Ivory Coast on the southeast. London and Paris, in consequence, have always shown a jealous interest in Liberian affairs, particularly before the League of Nations. In and out of the League, the United States Government has been a major factor in the development of that republic for more than a century.

The first modern-day settlement at Monrovia—now the capital—was established in 1822 on the insistence of the American Colonization Society, whose members sought a dumping-ground for freed Negroes. Twenty-five years later the missionary society was thoroughly bored, or its members were, for lack of results. The black stepchild was a nuisance. A republic was proclaimed in 1847, and by 1862 had been recognized by nearly all the Powers. Theoretically, Liberia stood on its own feet.

Afro-Americans who governed did not mix well with the indigenous people. They did not encourage trade with the British, French, German and Dutch traders, and on the coast that meant the loss of the white man's toys and refreshments. In 1871, British agents offered the Monrovia Government a loan of £100,000, and it was accepted. The natives were sufficiently astute to fear the consequences, and they deposed their President (E. J. Roye) who approved it. The next Government, however, had tasted the delights of foreign loans—and Liberia's two million Negroes are still in pawn.

Another loan, to repay the first, was obtained in London, in 1907, "to institute reforms." A British customs-inspector was appointed as treasury watch-dog. When Washington recognized these overtures as the prelude to a protectorate, it sent an unofficial mission to Monrovia. In its report the mission criticized British and French meddling. Its members urged that the United States float a loan enabling Liberia to discharge its indebtedness to Europe. The Powers were not receptive to this proposed solution, and in 1911 the German Government went so far as to send the *Panther* —of Agadir fame—into the harbor of Monrovia, her guns trained on the Executive Mansion. The next year an international loan of $1,700,000 was raised (by the sale of forty-year bonds), the European Powers appointed bookkeepers to the Liberian customs organization (revenue of which was collateral for the bonds), and an American appointed adviser to the Government. . . . The 1907 loan was repaid, and a larger loan saddled upon the Negro Republic.

Enter Harvey S. Firestone, of Akron, Ohio, president of the corporation bearing his name, and in the last decade leader of the campaign against British export restrictions on crude rubber. Mr. Firestone is also a philanthropist. From the Monrovian Government he obtained a ninety-nine-year lease on 1,000,000 acres, in return for which the Firestone Plantation Company was to build harbor-works at Monrovia. The harbor project proved impractical, but the Firestone interests have built a hospital, subsidized public sanitation, and medical researches by Harvard and Yale universities, established a trade-school for natives, radio facilities, and built roads. In 1933 the company informed the Liberia Committee of the League of Nations that their total investment was more than $8,000,000 and that ten million rubber-trees had been planted.

In exchange for the concession, the Firestone interests consented to lend the Government $5,000,000, of which it would advance $2,500,000 immediately, at seven per cent interest, through its Finance Corporation of America. The Liberian Government charged before the League that it had accepted the loan on condition it was not to be issued by Firestone. Inevitably, ninety per cent of the loan went to discharge past indebtedness of the Republic. When the League of Nations, at the request of Monrovia, investigated charges of forced labor, it found among its papers a complaint from the Secretary of State that the country "did not desire a loan [in 1926], either for financial or economic rehabilitation, or any other existing necessity," but that its "reluctant acceptance" was forced on Liberia by the Firestone interests.*

The League committee of inquiry did not establish that the Monrovian Government used forced labor, save for road-construction. The difference between enforced labor, and that which is paid ten cents a month, is academic. It responded to the Liberian plea for League assistance with, among other recommendations, a proposal that the na-

* For a pro-Firestone view of the controversy before the League, see *Liberia Rediscovered*, by James C. Young, New York 1934. A less partial and more comprehensive work is *Liberia in World Politics*, by Nnamdi Azikiwe, London 1934. "Utter disregard of international law by certain European Powers," he writes, "has made Liberian independence a fiction."

tive district commissioners be supplanted by Americans or Europeans, because officials had been known to collect the wages of natives at the Firestone plantations. . . . The Government declined the League's "Plan of Assistance," with a bewildered no. The financial concessions of Akron were insufficient, and seemed to make no sense.

Liberia turned to a Danish syndicate from which 18,000,-000 crowns were obtained in return for a road-building concession. In comment upon this move, Gabriel L. Denis, the Liberian Finance Minister in 1932, told newspapermen in London that "in the past the United States has been a powerful ally, but the steady uniformity of counsel given by the American State Department and the Firestone Company, and the threat of United States' non-cooperation in securing a reduction in the Firestone terms [eventually reduced from seven to five per cent] if Liberia does not accept her suggestion of an [American] adviser with full power, suggest forcibly that in present conditions real [economic] safety is only to be found in numbers, i. e., among the members of the League of Nations."

The misery of Liberia today originated in its resort to loans abroad. However much you denounce the Firestone loan now, at the time it was manna. "The Liberian politicians were delighted by the prospect of some more ready money after the lean years. Big times were had with the first receipts. Pompous officials bounded over the rocky streets in expensive automobiles, and the din from cabarets vied with the rattle and rumble down in the native quarter. But the celebration was short-lived. The service of the loan weighed heavily and the customs revenues grew smaller." *

The debt service has been such that hut-taxes and other imposts have been decreed, despite repeated protests by the natives. They also protested against the forced road-

* George S. Schuyler in "The American Mercury," July 1933.

"SPECIALIST ASSISTANCE"   281

labor, and the occasional preventive measures taken by the Government to keep men from working for the Firestone Plantations—where the maximum native employment reached 20,000. But officials argued that public safety demanded forced labor on the roads, and that accordingly the Firestone Plantations could not hire all the natives wanting work. A Government witness testified to the League Commission that "if we did not control the enlistment of men for work with Firestone, so many would go to the Plantations that none would remain to carry on the Government's requirements."

Whatever censure is deserved by American and European interests for the present state of affairs in Liberia, one thing is certain: the days of the Republic are numbered. Nothing so clearly signifies the approaching end of "independent" Liberia, the hands of its Government tied by financial obligations, than the closing paragraph of the report (1930) of the League's Inquiry Commission (composed of an American, an Englishman, and a Liberian), which read:

"The Commission cannot too strongly express its conviction that, as regards most officials, mere advice to greater efficiency and honesty will not be sufficient. The tolerance given to gross dishonesty in office, the general ignorance of the interior and its people, the lack of means of education in the provinces and its total absence in the hinterland, except where a few missionaries are installed; the powerful influence of family connections between the executive officers of the Government, few of whom have ever left the country; and the general insularity of outlook, *render futile any hope of improvement in the present conditions without the introduction of outside, specialist assistance.*" *

* The Commission's report may be found in *League of Nations Publications*, vi, B.6, 1930. It provoked Henry L. Stimson, then United States Secretary of State, to declare it "a shocking indict-

V

The phrase cannot be improved. Britain bestowed "outside specialist assistance" upon Egypt, France upon Morocco, and it is that peculiar aid also that Mussolini is now lending Ethiopia.

---

ment of the Liberian Government's policy of suppression of natives, permitted, if not actually indulged in, by nearly all the high officials of Liberia. . . . International public opinion will no longer tolerate those twin scourges of slavery and forced labor." Mr. Firestone, complimenting Secretary Stimson, wrote (January 12, 1931) to "express my appreciation of the firm stand which our Government is taking in demanding that Liberia take effective measures to abolish enforced labor. . . . As you know [this] has seriously interfered with our obtaining free labor."

XV

Marianne in Morocco
[1912–27]

AT the colonial ministries in Paris and Madrid, the foreign inquirer is told with unblushing conviction, and not the remotest trace of humor, that if the natives of French and Spanish Morocco were once the enemies of those European governments, today they are grateful in the extreme for the white man's protection. If you point with polite skepticism to the annual eruptions, and refer with mild irony to the "pacification" campaigns which these successive rebellions provoke each year, you are plainly regarded as an individual of no breeding, with a disgusting ignorance of the historical facts of life.

Frenchmen and Spaniards who are not professionally employed to extenuate their governments' rôles in Morocco argue, with more display of intelligence, that the conquest of the Empire was made necessary by the fact of its geographical situation, on one side flanking a major trade-route of the world, the Mediterranean—as Egypt, for example, is so oriented as to command the shortest route between East and West. That is to say, if that reasoning is pursued, the theft of Morocco was made necessary either by, (1) a haphazard act of God in creating the world as it is, or, (2) the chemical-geological factors which governed the cooling-off of this planet and which (unhappily for the Moors and Arabs) left a certain rich and strategic area in northwest

Africa jutting into the eastern Atlantic and the western Mediterranean. . . . Possibly the Hamitics, Zulus, Bantus and other African races have found philosophical consolation in this perversity of Nature or, if one prefers, carelessness of God.

Occasionally in the two capitals the less dishonest argument will be heard that the depredations of the Barbary pirates against the commerce of the civilized world, and of the interior tribes against Europeans, compelled the reluctant intervention of the white man, but that is putting the cart before the horse. The simple and evident truth that Morocco was confiscated for her copper, iron, lead, silver, gold, petroleum and the richness of her soil, is seldom heard.

ii

In 1912, after France had bought off Germany, the Paris Government undertook the conquest of Morocco in earnest. To compensate the French for relieving the Berber siege of Fez, the helpless Mouley Hafid attached his name to a treaty (March 30) granting a protectorate. French officers began training the native police force for which the Algeciras Agreement had provided six years before. The native forces expressed their gratitude for this instruction, and their appreciation of the Sultan's spinelessness, by beheading those of the St. Cyr alumnæ then at Fez. (Shouts of rage in France and expressions of bewildered astonishment.) Louis Hubert Lyautey was hurried there as Resident-General. Mouley Hafid was as useless to the French as he was regarded despicable by most of his subjects, and a brother, Mouley Yussef, supplanted him. The same year General Charles Mangin was sent to Marrakesh where the natives, in further manifestation of their sentiments toward France, had gleefully jailed every French infidel. With

French troops in control of both Fez and Marrakesh, much of western Morocco was lost to the natives by the end of 1912.

It remained, however, to induce the natives to pay taxes to their new masters. The Moorish disinterest in French imposts seemed a singularly ungrateful manifestation to Paris. But the Sultan's authority had vanished and chieftains were joyously raiding one another. The measures eventually adopted to collect these taxes came to be grouped under a delightful euphemism—"pacification." France and Spain have been pacifying their respective protectorates in north Africa for more than a generation, and at last this noble pursuit is showing a return to the treasuries of Madrid and Paris. In justice it should be added that the returns on this investment in men and money went not exclusively into the coffers of the two capitals, but also into roads, schools, hospitals, and efforts at sanitation in the towns.

General Lyautey reprieved a number of Moors who had been condemned to death for the Fez massacres, and generally quieted the hostile native settlement by the exercise of considerable intelligence—immediately, for example, he rescinded the huge indemnity which the French had saddled on the Sultan for the uprising. But outside the limits of the two capitals—Marrakesh and Fez—looting continued; the tribes in the desert and the mountainous regions suffered from no scarcity of modern rifles, and the munitions-smuggling by Europeans kept them amply supplied with lead.

The French did much to consolidate their new position in the country by ruling that all government would be in the name of the Sultan, and not in that of Paris. This was to prove an empty concession, but it meant a good deal to Moorish pride. When and as tribes capitulated, they swore allegiance to the Sultan—not to the European chief of state, as was the British, German and Italian practice. However academic a distinction, this was nevertheless a marked innovation in colonial procedure, as it avoided religious conflict, and did not change the puppet-status of the Sultan. The French were, moreover, authors of another piece of colonial reform: in the organization of a Moroccan army, Moors and *poilus* served without color distinction, living and eating together in garrison and in the field, again in contrast to British, German and Italian custom.

On the outbreak of the World War, General Lyautey was forced to send back to France thirty-seven battalions and a large part of his *matériel*. But he promptly vetoed the recommendation of the Paris Government that he withdraw the forces of all his inland garrisons and posts to the coast. It was due chiefly to his military astuteness, diplomacy in dealing with chieftains, and courage that, although raiding Rifi tribes were in German pay during the World War (receiving tens of thousands of modern rifles from Berlin), Morocco was retained by France. When the hostilities in Europe were over, Paris determined to extend the Protectorate south and westward, and it was then that the final conquest began.

The Franco-Spanish frontier had been delimited by treaty in November 1912. The northern coastal and desert zone went to Spain, which agreed to rule also in the name of the Sultan—acting, of course, through a Spanish High Commissioner—and consented also to the French condition that all foreign affairs in the Spanish Zone should be under the jurisdiction of their Resident-General. The frontier was an imaginary line running roughly east to west, some two hundred miles in length, from the Algerian western frontier point at the Mediterranean to a point a few miles south of Laraiche on the Atlantic Coast; the average depth inland was sixty miles. It was within this zone that the Germans conducted their native campaigns against the French during the World War.

Before reviewing the final subjugation of Morocco, it is well at this juncture to consider the Spanish activities up to the eve of the Franco-Spanish collaboration.

iii

In secret negotiations during 1901–04 between the chancelleries of Paris and Madrid, agreement in principle was reached covering the eventual partition by the two Powers of Morocco. The Spanish Government, however, remained hesitant, fearing German objections, until the signing of the Franco-British Treaty in 1904, in which London agreed to stay out of Morocco, it will be recalled, in return for freedom of action in Egypt. Delcassé assured the Madrid Government that the Agreement with London also stipulated that Spain's "zone of influence" was to be respected—which was true. Incidentally, priests were eager to extend the influence of the Church to north Africa, while the army wanted to redeem its prestige after the defeat by the United States of the Spanish garrisons in Cuba and the Philippines. Thus, early in the century, Franco-Spanish collaboration in Morocco was initiated. . . . Until fairly recently, Spain's Moroccan adventure was a succession of sanguinary reverses leading finally to a catastrophe to which Adowa was, in comparison, a mere skirmish.

At first, because of public apathy over further colonial adventure, the Government was content with consolidating her territory around Ceuta, on the Strait of Gibraltar, and Melilla to the east. But when in the latter vicinity iron ore was discovered in practical quantities, in 1909, the Spanish mine-owners persuaded Madrid that troops should be sent south to expand the Government's protectorate. The

Spaniards were severely beaten the same year by Rifi tribes, and 20,000 men had to be sent from the Peninsula before Melilla was again secure. At home the Government fell when the opposition charged that the considerable loss of lives was attributable to the greed of the mine-owners who had bribed officials to undertake the military expedition.

For the next several years, Spain was content to forget about her protectorate. During the World War the Germans were active along the coast of Spanish Morocco, fomenting attacks on the French by the Rifi, and as a neutral there was not much the Madrid Government could or would do in prevention. Such minor advances as the Spaniards made were not opposed by the natives, who were more interested in receiving German gold to harass the French. But after the Armistice, General Berenguer, the Spanish High Commissioner, launched a campaign to rid the Zone of Raisuli and his Jibala followers, and advancing southwestward he surrounded Tazrut, the chieftain's headquarters. Spanish discipline was hopeless, essential supplies non-existent, and leadership incompetent. By July 22, 1921, the Rif was lost to Spain, together with at least 16,000 Spanish troops. Abdel Krim with his brother and some 2,500 Rifi had pushed the surviving troops back to Melilla and were bombarding that town with captured artillery.* Seventy thousand fresh troops were hurried to the relief of Melilla. The subsequent findings of a commission of inquiry, which found that army stores had been rifled, that officers stole from their men and fled at the Rifi approach, constitute a record of human cowardice and corruption difficult to exceed. It is dismal reading.†

* The extent of the Spanish loss of life was sedulously kept secret by the Madrid Government until recent years.
† Report of General Picasso, President of the Commission of Inquiry, to the Special Parliamentary Council, 1923.

Spain had not been more successful in the East. In 1924 Abdel Krim's power was such that Sheshuan, south of Tetuan, was hurriedly evacuated by the Spanish, but the haste of the retreat did not prevent thousands of Spanish casualties at the hands of the pursuing Rifi. That withdrawal so cheered Abdel Krim that he decided to turn southward and expel the French, who for two years had steadily encroached upon his territory. In April 1925 his tribes overran the French frontier posts and came within twenty miles of Fez.

In correspondence with intermediaries seeking peace, Abdel Krim declared he had no quarrel with the French, so long as they remained on the south bank of the Wergha River, that the Rif was neither French nor Spanish territory, for he certainly had not been a party to the 1912 frontier treaty, and that although European governments pretended to desire order in Morocco, he had already established order in the area the French were now attempting to invade.

Paris hurried troops from both Algeria and France. The French Protectorate administration at Rabat had good reason to dispatch alarming telegrams to the War Ministry at home. When reports of the precariousness of the French position, and the mounting toll of casualties, began to reach Paris, the public and political outcry was so violent that Premier Paul Painlevé flew to Morocco to inspect the front, and was followed by Marshal Henri Pétain, the defender of Verdun. The latter assumed supreme command August 22, 1925, after conferring at Madrid with General Primo de Rivera, President of the Spanish Directorate, over details of a joint campaign against Abdel Krim. In October, Painlevé reported to the Chamber of Deputies that the French campaign against the Rifi in eight months had cost 2,176 lives (of which 632 were French), and that 8,287 men had been wounded. The financial cost was $43,500,000, and the end not yet in sight.

But in May the following year, after France and Spain had recruited an additional 40,000 native troops, Abdel Krim surrendered unconditionally. He could not withstand forever airplanes, tanks and gas, and was exiled to Madagascar. France and Spain now were free to reopen their respective "pacification" campaigns.

iv

The year after Abdel Krim's capitulation (1927), Mouley Yussef died, and his third son, Sidi Mohammed, was proclaimed Sultan. His actual authority does not extend beyond religious matters. The French Resident-General at Rabat has the effective administration of the 200,000 square miles, as well as peace-time control over the conscript army. The Spanish Zone of 13,125 miles is ruled—on behalf of the Sultan—by the High Commissioner at Tetuan. In 1923 the Tangier Zone was internationalized and its administration entrusted to a Committee of Control on which are represented France, Britain, Spain and Italy. The Islamized Berbers and Arabs must conduct official business in French, in that Protectorate, and in Spanish in the Zone belonging to Madrid.

Thus, the decline and fall of the Moorish Empire. The present Sultan has salvaged something from the wreckage, however: each year, on his annual visit to Paris, the French Government pays for his suite at the Hotel de Crillon. . . . If it has nothing more spectacular to do, the band of the Garde Républicaine consents to play the *Marseillaise* in the Place de la Concorde, outside his windows. When this signal honor is bestowed, Sidi Mohammed is invariably some place else in Paris.

XVI

Field-Day for Diplomats
[1919]

EUROPEAN elder statesmen are fond of claiming in their memoirs that their partition of Africa, in the period 1884–1912, without recourse to war was the greatest achievement in the history of diplomacy. They want to believe that despite the friction caused by commercial rivalries in Africa, they succeeded by negotiation in preventing Europe from bursting into flames.

This may be dismissed as pure fantasy, since it is so remote from the truth. British, French and German trade competition in Africa during 1900–12 was one of the prime factors which led to the explosion of 1914. But even if there were any truth in that traditional claim by a coterie of gentlemen most of whom are now dead, the Versailles Treaty made Africa the almost inevitable cause of another world conflict. It is one of those ironies of diplomacy that statesmen participating in a peace conference assiduously prepared the path along which the world is tottering to suicide. This was achieved by a variety of clauses in that memorable document, least of which were the gratuitous humiliations heaped upon the Central Powers.

Here will be considered those articles which relate to Africa. There are none grimmer in their import nor any in which war is more implicit. Like the rest of that document, they sprang from the virtuous doctrine that to the victors belong the spoils. That homily may be applicable to a street brawl, but it is singularly fallacious when applied to disputes between nations.

ii

Germany's African colonies covered an area of 1,030,150 square miles (German East Africa, South-West Africa, the Cameroons and Togoland), a total five times the size of the pre-war Reich and about one-third that of the United States. There were about 18,000 Germans in the colonies, and some 12,500,000 natives. By the outbreak of hostilities in 1914, the colonial administrators had built railroads over a distance of 2,610 miles. Substantial public works included harbor facilities, roads, bridges, telephones, telegraphs and wireless stations. The late George Louis Beer, chief of the colonial division of the American delegation to the Peace Conference, who prepared a survey for use at Versailles, wrote in 1919 that the German "public buildings in the chief ports—such as Lome, Duala, Swakopmund, Dar-es-Salaam and Tanga—were of an exceptionally solid and imposing character. These cities were distinguished by order and cleanliness and, insofar as mere outward appearance was concerned, they generally compared more than favorably with similar ports in the British and French colonies." *

The original German delegation to the Conference refused to sign the treaty offered by the Allies. Its head, Count Brockdorff-Rantzau, tossed it on the floor of the Trianon. He was particularly infuriated, after the post-Armistice food blockade of six months, by the proposed seizure of the colonies. "We know," he said, "the power of the hatred that we encounter here!" A second delegation eventually signed the treaty, June 28, 1919—virtually at the point of a gun.

* G. L. Beer, *African Questions at the Paris Peace Conference*, New York 1923.

Article 119 of that document served notice on the Reich delegates that "Germany renounces in favor of the Principal Allied and Associated Powers all her rights and titles over her overseas possessions."

The area of 1,030,150 square miles was carved up as follows:

To Britain, as a mandated area: German East Africa (today Tanganyika Territory), one fourth of Togoland, a smaller slice of the Cameroons; German South-West Africa was awarded under mandate to the Union of South Africa.

To France: the remainder of Togoland and the Cameroons (part the area which France gave Germany in 1911 as a bribe to stay permanently out of Morocco), under mandate.

To Belgium and Portugal: strips of German East Africa.

To Italy (of the German colonies): nothing.

The mandates were another of the irrealizable dreams of Woodrow Wilson. Writing of them a decade later, Colonel E. M. House, who had served as the United States' representative at Versailles before the President's arrival, declared that "the mandate principle gave an excuse and a method for taking over the German colonies by the several countries interested." Lloyd George's change of heart was evidenced so recently, and his *apologia* pronounced with such calculated regard for dramatic effect, that its sincerity is not self-evident. Honest or otherwise, however, his opinion is that the mandate theory has failed in practice, and that a reallocation of African territory among the Powers is essential, if war is to be averted. That revelation is scarcely scriptural, but it is an interesting admission from the statesman who, with Clemenceau, led the raid on Germany's colonies. Speaking in the House of Commons (February 5, 1936), he declared:

"I don't believe you will have peace in the world until you reconsider the mandates, and I feel an obligation on me, as one of those who represented the British Empire in making the treaty of Versailles, to say this:

"There is Belgium, with a population of seven or eight millions, who has the best piece of German East Africa. She has also the whole Congo. Portugal, with a small population, has a million square miles [in Africa]. . . . Each of these countries has great tropical territories, and here you have Germany with none and Italy with practically none.

"This time we should come to realities. If we don't, realities will come to us, and they will come in a very grim form."

But with or without the mandates, the German colonies would have gone to the Allies. To have returned the territories to the natives was a quixotic idea not worthy of the white man.

Before the signature of the treaty, two of the delegations protested vehemently against this redistribution. As was reasonable enough under the circumstances, the German howls were the loudest and longest. They had asked at Versailles for the retention of their colonies in Africa, on the ground that the balance of power must be preserved on the Black Continent: otherwise, the nations which received the lion's share would not only dominate Africa but, of greater danger to civilization, would be empowered to unite and conquer Europe by conscripting black armies for service abroad. This prescient argument, generally overlooked today, was rejected on "moral grounds" by the Allies (i. e., in this instance, Britain and France), in the "Covering Letter of the Reply to the German Observations." As an example of a diplomatic holier-than-thou rebuttal, it is perfect of its kind.

"The Allies and Associated Powers," it read, "are satisfied that the native inhabitants of the German [African] colonies are strongly opposed to being brought again under Germany's sway, and the records of German rule, the traditions of the German Government and the use to which these colonies were put as bases from which to prey upon the commerce of the world, make it impossible for the Allied and Associated Powers to return them to Germany, or to entrust to her the responsibility for the training and education of their inhabitants."

The other protest was, of course, from Italy which complained of fraud and deception by Britain and France. Although allied to Germany and Austria by the Triple Alliance, Italy had remained neutral in 1914. As an inducement to abandon the Alliance, and join the Allies, Britain and France signed with Italy the Pact of London (April 26, 1915). Here it was stipulated unequivocally that "in the event of an extension of the French and British colonial possessions in Africa at the expense of Germany, France and Great Britain recognize to Italy in principle the right to demand for herself certain compensations, in the form of an extension of her possessions in Eritrea, Somaliland [French and British], Libya, and the colonial districts bordering on French and British colonies."

That being agreed, twenty-seven days later Italy declared war on Austria.

At Versailles, her demands were over-ridden. The Italian delegates wanted Libya extended east into Egypt, an avenue into the Sudan, and the territory south to Lake Tchad (in French Equatorial Africa), and thence west to the frontiers of Nigeria. She wanted British and French Somaliland, enough of Kenya Colony to command Ethiopia's southern frontier, and finally a substantial slice of Asia Minor. The request for British and French Somaliland was countered by pious references to the Treaty of 1906, suddenly become sacred, among Britain, France and Italy, which guaranteed the *status-quo* of Ethiopia: the French and British delegates argued that should they cede their Somaliland holdings to Italy, Addis Ababa would have reason to anticipate a violation of the 1906 Convention—in any event, the Negus might very well feel injured. . . . The other demands were laughed away, at least for the present.*

iii

In the midst of the bickering over the territorial division of the spoils, it occurred to some humorist at Versailles that the Conference had altogether lost sight of the 140,000,000 inhabitants of Africa, who might be suspected of having a casual interest in the proceedings. Accordingly a Pan-African Congress was opened in the French capital, and for three days (February 19–21, 1919) much oratory was expended, after the florid style established at the Berlin and Brussels conferences of the century past. This pantomime was organized by M. Diagne, a deputy for Senegal. The actors resolved that:—

"The Negroes of the world demand that henceforth the natives of Africa . . . be governed by the following principles wherever such are not already applied:

"The Allied and Associated Powers should establish a code of international protection for the natives; a permanent secretariat within the League of Nations should be set up especially for the execution of all political, social and economic measures for the welfare of the natives; land and natural resources to be reserved and protected for the na-

* In agreements subsequently reached with Britain and France, Italy obtained the extension of Libya southward to its present line, a path into the Sudan, an adjustment of the Egyptian frontier on the east, some 60,000 square miles of Kenya Colony to add to Italian Somaliland (where the frontier is the immediate cause of the dispute with Ethiopia), and commercial and fiscal equality with the French in Tunisia.

tives; concessions to be controlled by the State and to be only temporary, not to be permitted to exploit the natives or to exhaust natural resources; some part of the proceeds to be devoted to the moral and material advancement of the aborigines; slavery and corporal punishment to be abolished; forced labor to be permitted only as punishment for crime; an official regulation of labor to be promulgated; all Negro children to be instructed both in their native tongue and in the language of the Tutelary Power; professional education also to be given them . . . ; the African natives shall be admitted to share in the conduct of public affairs in progressive proportion to their intellectual development, in virtue of the principle that governments exist for peoples, and not peoples for governments." *

Everyone felt virtuous, and everyone forgot the conventions overnight. But it had a lofty ring, the Pan-African Congress.†

iv

Germany's losses in Africa were not only colonies. In the fantastic bill of reparations was included indemnity for loss of French lives and property in the Cameroons, during the fighting; the 1911 treaty relating to the Congo was revoked;

* At St. Germain-en-Laye, outside Paris, delegates representing the United States, the British Empire, France, Belgium, Italy, Japan and Portugal signed a "Convention Relating to the Liquor Traffic in Africa," purportedly to prohibit the exportation of spirits anywhere in Africa "with the exception of Algeria, Tunis, Morocco, Libya and the Union of South Africa"—a very considerable part of the Black Continent. The Convention, signed September 10, 1919, and another restricting the exportation of arms and ammunition to Africa, signed the same day, were so qualified by special "exceptions" that they proved as ineffective as the Berlin and Brussels acts which they were intended to bolster.

† Subsequent Pan-African congresses at London and Brussels, in 1921, at London and Lisbon in 1923, and at New York in 1927, were scarcely more effective.

the right of the Reich to representation on the customs-board of Liberia was rescinded, together with the exterritoriality which German subjects had enjoyed with other Europeans in Egypt and Morocco (i. e., the right of trial by non-native, international tribunals); German public and private property in Morocco was confiscated by France without payment, Reich shares in the State Bank of Morocco were liquidated against the reparations' account, her Suez privileges of free navigation and participation in the Sanitary, Maritime and Quarantine Board of Egypt were canceled, and German property in Egypt was transferred to the Egyptian Government, also without payment therefor. The Versailles clauses authorizing the seizure of German property and revocation of former treaty rights were included in the peace treaties made with Austria, Hungary and Turkey; the latter nation, parenthetically, lost its annual tribute from Egypt of £692,350.* The sick men of Versailles made a clean sweep, not forgetting regulations to embarrass German missionaries in Africa, whose property was seized in the mandated colonies and who, at the will of the mandatory country, may be expelled.

Germany has no colonies in Africa, and Italy has demonstrated that she will wrest her share by more direct means than sterile negotiations in Paris, London or Geneva. Over

* The British assumed liability for Turkish loans issued with the Egyptian tribute as collateral. When Turkey declared war (December 18, 1914), Britain rather unnecessarily declared a protectorate over Egypt—unnecessary, because she had been in effective control since the Alexandria bombardment of 1882. The Egyptian Protectorate was terminated March 16, 1922, and Sultan Fuad became King. He signed the new Constitution April 19, 1923, which far from giving Egypt a greater degree of autonomous government, proved restrictive in the extreme, and manifestations against the Constitution and British domination are unceasing, notably among Cairo university students.

Italy, the Reich has one legal and moral advantage, that her former colonies are still administered in the name of the League of Nations, whereas Ethiopia is a sovereign State. Mussolini's penetration is, in consequence, a violation of international covenants, and no pleading, however ingenious, can construe it as anything else. But illegal or otherwise, the odds must be on the Duce. A mandate is merely an exalted synonym for the "effective occupation" of the Berlin Act. Neither the League, on which Germany has turned her back, nor the mandatories themselves will ever return the former colonies of the Reich—peacefully. The only method by which Germany can seek to regain territory in Africa is by direct action—in Europe.

Since Versailles, the severest restrictions and penalties placed upon Germany by the *élite* of the world's statesmen have been nullified by their own absurdity or impracticality. Reparations are buried, together with the articles restricting German military, naval and aërial armaments. But the Reich is still without colonies.

So far as Africa is concerned, and with it the peace of Europe, the genius of the men who framed the Versailles treaty is at last revealed in its full magnificence. An unwitting appraisal of the sublime wisdom of that document was made in an address (January 16, 1936) by Dr. Joseph Paul Goebbels, the Nazi Minister of Public Enlightenment, before a mass-meeting at Berlin. He warned that:—

"The time is coming when we must demand colonies. It cannot go on like this. There are countries which have more colonies than they know what to do with. What others possess, we also must possess. . . . And the Italian people also must live."

XVII

Roma Rediviva
[1934-36]

THE Italian invasion of Ethiopia is the concluding phase of the rape of Africa, although one may say that Liberia, insignificant territorially, is at least technically self-governing. How many months will pass before the conquest of Haile Selassie's constitutional monarchy is complete, and the nation split among Britain, France and Italy, is a military and diplomatic question, not to be confused with moral considerations. Since late in 1934 there have been no substantial reasons to doubt the eventual fate of Ethiopia; and when the conflict between Rome and Addis Ababa today is regarded against the background of the theft of the remainder of Africa in the last sixty years, skepticism over future alignments in east Africa is ludicrous. For all the ostensible weight of public opinion, the solemn deliberations of the League of Nations since August 1935, and even if one weighs the military difficulties encountered by the Italians since October of the same year, it should still be apparent that Ethiopia will not fare otherwise than Morocco or Egypt or the Congo or South Africa.

What is commonly lost sight of in the current discussions of sanctions, or such irrelevancies as the moral aspects of the present dispute, is that the Powers of Europe in sixty years have never left room for uncertainty over their attitude or action when gold or diamonds or other wealth was

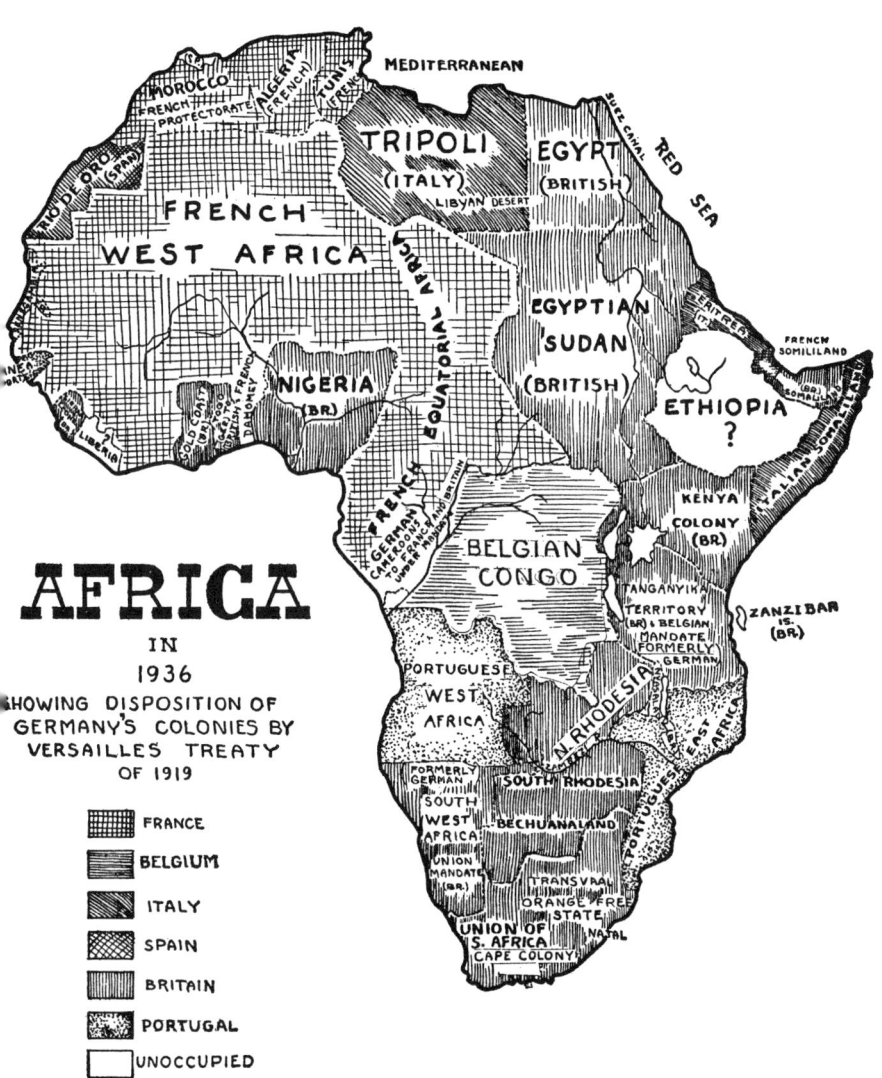

discovered in Africa. The sole question that has ever arisen is which among them would reach that wealth first. There is not the slightest reason, whatever rhetorical stops are pulled at Geneva, to believe that Ethiopia will share a fate any different from the rest of Africa. Conquest may be by military occupation, by forced economic concessions, or by mortgage to foreign money-lenders, but by whatever means that conquest is inevitable and imminent.

It may be well to summarize the recent diplomatic history of the present Italo-Ethiopian War.

The 1906 treaty among Britain, France and Italy, guaranteeing the *status-quo* of Ethiopia, did not extend to the Government at Addis Ababa the right to call upon any of the three Powers for aid should one of them turn aggressor. In its attitude to the rights of the native, that treaty was typical —they were ignored. By its terms the three Powers agreed to respect among themselves the frontier of Ethiopia: if reasons arose subsequently that made it appear expedient to revise the frontier, the Powers needed only to agree among themselves. Ethiopia was not a party to the convention.

In September 1923 Ethiopia became a member of the League of Nations. This brought her, more theoretically than in practical fact, under the protection of the Covenant of the League of Nations, with its provisions for arbitration of international disputes, sanctions and other punitive measures against an aggressor nation. Her election to Geneva, however, did not affect in any way the validity of the 1906 treaty among Paris, London and Rome, and indeed Article 21 of the Covenant specifically upholds such "regional understandings" as the aforementioned instrument. Accordingly, Italy, France and Britain may partition Ethiopia in any way and at any time they wish, without technical violation of their respective pledges at Geneva.

They must, however, agree as to the distribution of the spoils. In the present instance, neither France nor Britain, with interests themselves in East Africa, will consent to giving Mussolini all of Ethiopia, but a division among them would be distinctly something else.

The present conflict did not burst suddenly upon the world in October 1935. It could have been foreseen at Versailles in 1919, but it became a certainty in 1928 when Ethiopia refused entry to Italian engineers who were to build a road from Assab (Eritrea) to Dessye (Ethiopia). The Addis Ababa Government had consented to this undertaking, and was itself to construct a road from Dessye to the capital—which, by the way, would have proved a godsend to the Italians today. But European and other advisers of the King of Kings recognized in time the import of a series of Italian military reinforcements in Eritrea, and although early in the year Italy and Ethiopia had signed a "treaty of arbitration, amity and perpetual friendship," it was plain that Italy was preparing an invasion. (By Article II of this treaty, the two Powers undertook "not to engage under any pretext in action calculated to endanger or prejudice the independence of the other.") Relations were not improved, on the other hand, by the consistent repudiation by Addis Ababa of commercial agreements with Italy, and repeated delays by Ethiopia in settling by negotiation the frontier in the southeast bordering on Italian Somaliland.

ii

Relations between the two countries were so strained in 1934 that it became common talk in Europe that Mussolini had determined upon a "preventive invasion" of Ethiopia to forestall an attack on Eritrea. An "incident" was required to furnish the pretext. Late in the year it was conveniently supplied when a force of Italian colonial troops encountered at Ualual, in the southeastern province of Ogaden, members of a joint Anglo-Ethiopian boundary commission. The Ethiopians, who claimed to be within their own territory, ignored the Italian command to withdraw. In the clash that followed, about thirty-five of the Italian force were killed, and 107 Ethiopians.

At Addis Ababa the Italian minister demanded reparations. The Ethiopian Government, while willing "in principle" to pay for any substantiated damages, countered this demand by invoking the 1928 pledge of "arbitration, amity and perpetual friendship." At Rome the Duce rejected arbitration in language that left no reason to doubt that his Government welcomed the Ualual incident. Thereupon Haile Selassie invoked Article XI of the League Covenant (January 4, 1935), protesting meanwhile against the dispatch by Italy of troops to east Africa. The Italian explanation of the reinforcements was that they were a precautionary move in the interest of civilization.

In upholding civilization, the Italians inevitably clashed again with Ethiopian patrols. In February the first Italian mobilization order was issued, affecting two army divisions. In Ethiopia the *riposte* to this was the massing of natives along the disputed frontier in Italian Somaliland.

The Italian premier in March declared that he was prepared to arbitrate under the 1928 treaty, thus removing the controversy from League consideration under Article XV of the Covenant. As a corollary of this pacific gesture, mobilization in Italy continued on an increasing scale. In May the Emperor appointed an American, P. B. Potter, and a Frenchman, A. de la Pradelle, as his delegates to a conciliation commission whose deliberations were fruitless. At London there were by this time demands in the House of Commons that the Suez Canal be closed to Italy in the event of hostilities, followed in Rome by the first of a series of anti-British demonstrations. The following month Haile Selassie protested to Geneva that France was blocking shipments of arms to Ethiopia (via Djibouti), implying that Pierre Laval, the French premier and foreign minister, had reached a secret agreement at Rome whereby Paris would tacitly uphold Italy in Ethiopia, in exchange for guarantees of aid against Germany.

By July, the first of Ethiopian protests were arriving at Geneva demanding immediate convocation of the Council as the only step by which war could be averted. That body met at the end of the month. The session was adjourned to September when Italy warned that the imposition of sanctions would mean war—in Europe. In a masterly report which left the controversy as far from solution as ever, the arbitration commission declared that neither Italy nor Ethiopia was to blame for the Ualual incident, which had long since faded into insignificance. The issue now was solely whether the League Council could stop Italy. The Council again withheld action, appointing a five-Power commission (Britain, France, Poland, Spain and Turkey) to give additional study to the dispute.

At this stage, there were echoes of the French and German diplomatic strategy against Britain in the 'nineties. A *ballon-d'essai* was released by the Italian delegation at Geneva: if the descendants of Cæsar were to be excluded by the League from Ethiopia, Italy would demand Britain's exclusion from Egypt—the old threat. The September meeting of the League Assembly sedulously avoided discussion of the controversy, save for a few generalizations by Sir Samuel Hoare, the British Foreign Secretary, and M. Laval on the virtues of collective action. By late September the dispute had grown from a purely Italo-Ethiopian quarrel to a European crisis that was a good deal more than merely a "war scare." Britain began to order cruisers, destroyers, submarines and mine-sweepers to Gibraltar and the eastern Mediterranean. Rome responded by sending troops to the Egyptian-Libyan frontier.

On September 18 the five-Power commission recommended an international administration for Ethiopia by experts to be appointed by the League Council and approved by the Emperor; it also proposed the grant by France and Britain of Somaliland outlets for Ethiopia, and the recognition by those powers of Italy's "special economic interests" in the Empire. Four days later, Mussolini rejected the compromise plan.

The military invasion began early the next month.

With manifest reluctance, the Council fixed November 18 as the date for imposition of economic sanctions against Italy. The sanctions' deadline was put forward to December 12 after Italy warned that a ban on oil would be construed as an unfriendly act. The inherent weakness of the League machinery in adopting sanctions was disclosed by another advance in the date to January 20, 1936. On that day, supineness again intervened and it was resolved to give still more study to the practicality of a ban on oil. At that meeting, moreover, there was an eloquent silence on sanctions affecting coal, pig-iron and steel.

Before the close of the year, a Hoare-Laval proposal to obtain peace at the price of a gift to Italy of all of Tigre Province then occupied, the lowland regions from Adigrat to Makale, all of Ogaden and part of Harar Province, was howled down with not a little mirth at Geneva, Paris and London. The baldness of the proposal, after Britain and France at Geneva had prayed for sanctions against Italy, provoked laughter even among statesmen. . . . By universal acclaim, it was awarded the palm as the year's most flawless example of diplomatic buffoonery. Shortly after this performance, Sir Samuel Hoare retired from the Cabinet, and in this he was soon followed by his colleague in Paris.

The threat to the peace of Europe as a result of the war in Africa had become so real at the outset of 1936 that five Powers, Britain, France, Turkey, Greece and Yugo-Slavia, agreed to a united front should Italy attack any one of them, and they had, in addition, the implicit support of the Little Entente (Czechoslovakia, Yugo-Slavia and Roumania).

iii

The drift to war over Africa is unmistakable. That cheering outlook is the result of sixty years of duplicity and chicanery practised by the chancelleries of Europe. If a continent has been stolen from 140,000,000 natives, it is assuaging to remember that the fraud was committed in the holy cause of civilization; and that in compensation the African is tasting the transcendent delights of chain-gangs, taxes, military conscription, missionaries, flogging, gin, rum, jack-in-the-boxes and other boons of Occidental invention.

Bibliographical Note

THE major sources consulted by the writer in this account of European diplomacy, relating to Africa, have been indicated by footnotes. A comprehensive bibliography of source material on the political history of that continent might be restricted to ten volumes, but it is doubtful. The student or other reader, however, who may want more extended treatment should consult, in the main, *Die Grosse Politik der europaischen Kabinette (1871–1914)*, Berlin 1922–26, the *Documenti Diplomatici*, Rome 1897, the *Documents diplomatiques français*, Paris 1929, the *British and Foreign State Papers*, of the Foreign Office, and the *British Parliamentary Papers*. These include or cite the pertinent blue-, yellow- and green-books, white-papers, *et cetera*. The *Official Journal* of the League of Nations is also valuable for post-War developments, particularly on the question of the mandated territories.

The standard work on African territorial treaties is the *Map of Africa by Treaty*, by Sir Edward Hertslet, which takes the reader to 1908. Memoirs, studies and histories of the foreign policies of the Powers, have been indicated in the text or in footnotes, together with relevant newspaper files.

Index

Abdel Krim, 288-290
Abdul Aziz, Sultan of Morocco, fears brother, Mouley Hafid, 256
Abyssinia, *see* Ethiopia
Acqua, King (Cameroons), letter to Queen Victoria, 79
Addis Ababa (Ethiopia), 128, 181; Count Antonelli at, 182; French agents at, 186; Russian expedition arrives at, 189
Aden, Gulf of, 124, 129
Adowa, Battle of, 129, 175, 180; significance of, 192; Italian occupation of, 193; description of, by General Baratieri, 195; Italian advance preceding, 197; casualties of, reaction in Europe, 197
Africa, political map of (1876-1877), 25, 26; "Monroe Doctrine" in, 76; prospect of war in Europe over, 80; "legal partition" of, 92; results of Berlin Conference on, 96; European raids in, 107; European "zones of influence" in, 108; population of, 122; partition of by chancelleries, 184; "public law" of, 205; war in, threatened, 206; commercial rivalries in, 291
African International Association, *see* Association Internationale du Congo
Agadir (Morocco), *Panther* appears off harbor, 261; history of "Agadir Madent," 261-266
Albert (Lake), 162, 203
Alexander (the Great), 16

Alexander VI (Pope), endorses Portuguese claims in Africa, 20
Alexandria, -to-Cairo railraod, breakwater of, 48; anti-foreign agitation in, Anglo-French fleet arrives at, 54; rioting suppressed by gendarmerie, Europeans killed at, 55; Britain sends additional gunboats to, 56; bombardment of, casualties at, 57; 203; foreign investments at, 210
Alfonso XII (of Spain), suppresses Second Carlist War, 22
Algeciras (Spain), Conference of, 254-255; failure of, 256; German violation of, 257
Algeria, 13; French regard Tunisia from, 24; early French action in, 70-71; 175; raids from Morocco, 256
Algiers, German gunboats at, 221
Alsace-Lorraine, Bismarck's concern over, 86; 228, 266
Alula, Ras, 131
Alvensleben, Count, joins bloc at Brussels Conference, 157
America, *see* United States
American Revolution, 228
Ampthill, Lord, warns Bismarck, 75
Anderson, Sir Percy, to Berlin Conference, 90; quoted on Anglo-German treaty (1890), 137
Anglo-Congolese Treaty (1894), French and German campaign against, 203; Article III of, 205
Anglo-Egyptian Sudan, *see* Sudan

311

INDEX

Anglo-French Agreement (1904), genesis of Entente Cordiale, 243; conditions of, dealing with Madagascar, Newfoundland, Siam, New Hebrides, 244; 287

Anglo-French Treaty (1890), 136-137; French concede Upper Niger, 138

Anglo-German Treaty (1890), 137, 162

Anglo-Portuguese Treaty (1884), denounced, 94

Anglo-Portuguese Treaty (1891), 141-142, 171

Angra Pequena, arrival of Lüderitz at, 75; Cape Colony plans seizure of, German sovereignty recognized, 76

Antanànarìvo (Madagascar), bombardment of, 175

Antonelli, Count Pietro, at Addis Ababa, 182; signs treaty with Menelik II, 183; charges French gift of rifles to Menelik II, 184; 192

Arabi Pasha, nationalist Egyptian leader, 50; dismissed by Tewfik Pasha, returns in next cabinet, 54; raises Alexandria earthworks, 56; charged with plot to seize Suez Canal, 58; defeated at Tel-el-Kabir by Wolseley, banished to Ceylon, 58; — forces conscripted by Khedive, 110

Asmara (Eritrea), demanded by Menelik II, 193

Assab (Eritrea), seized by Italy, 73

Assal (Lake), 184

Association Internationale du Congo (Brussels, 1882), 36, 38; France, Germany, recognize sovereignty of, 84; recognition by other Powers, 85; area obtained at Berlin Conference, 97-98; Leopold II asks sovereignty over, 104; liquidation of, 105; cost of to Leopold, 106

Atherstone, Dr. W. G., 42

Austria-Hungary, financial interest in Egypt, 47; at Berlin Conference, 85; at Brussels Conference, 152; friendly to Italian protectorate over Ethiopia, 186; at Algeciras Conference, 255

Baden-Powell, Sir Robert, recruits troops, 238

Bagida (Togoland), German flag raised at, 79

Bahr-el-Ghazal (river), 216

Baker, General Valentine, attempt to relieve Sudan garrisons, escapes death, 113

Baldissera, General, negotiates peace with Menelik II, 199

Émile Banning, adviser to Leopold II, 30; appointed delegate to Berlin Conference, 90; 96

Bantu (tribes), 42, 161

Baratieri, General Oreste, ultimatum to Menelik II, 193; demands reinforcements, 194; account of Adowa battle, 195; battle-orders of, 196-197; courtmartial of, 199

Barbarigo, Italian warship, sent to Zanzibar, 129

Bargash ibn Said, Italian negotiations with, 129-130; German ultimatum to, 136

Baring, Major Evelyn, *see* Lord Cromer

Barkly, Sir Henry, 43

Barrère, M., 250

Basutoland, British seizure of, 42

Bayard, Thomas (U. S. Secretary of State), receives report on Stanley, 68

Bechuanaland, British penetration into, 122; Cecil Rhodes quoted on, British protectorate declared, 123; natives sold as slaves, 124; conscript labor in, 145; seizure recalled, 164; German threat to, 205; British troops recruited in, 238

Beernaert, Auguste, confers with Leopold II, 139

Belgium, Parliament authorizes Leopold II to issue loan, 139; loan to Leopold II, 141; takes over Congo Free State, 273

INDEX 313

Berlin, interest of, in Stanley, 16; reaction of, to Stanley's discovery, 30; stockmarket collapse (1911), 263

Berlin Conference (1884-1885), 77, 82; proposed by Portugal, rôle of Bismarck at, 86; formal aims of, 87; delegates to, 87-91; opening of, 92; Britain and Germany checked at, 95; General Act of, 98-100; ratifications of, 102; closing addresses at, 103-104; 142

Bethman-Hollweg, Chancellor von, addresses Reichstag (1911), 264

Bismarck, Prince Otto von, reparations' demand of France, 13; wants markets overseas, 16; hesitates over colonies, 17-18; quoted on Leopold II, 36; criticizes Anglo-French policy in Egypt, 53; Lüderitz expedition forces hand, 75; replies to Granville, 76; ignores British protests over Cameroons, 78; attitude toward Berlin Conference, 86; Stanley's opinion of, 96; quoted on Leopold II, 103; suppresses Livonius report, 133

Blignières, M. de, represents France in Egypt, 49; unpopularity of, 50; nervous over Arab demonstrations, 55

Bloemfontein, Anglo-Boer conference at, deadlock of, 238

Boadicea, British gunboat, 76

Boer War, *see* South African War

Boers, natural wealth of, 40; capitulation of, to British (1806), 41; retreat north of Orange River, 42; rebellious sentiment of (1893), 166; distrust of British, in Transvaal, 226; anti-, pro- pamphlets, 236-237

Bolton, J., to Berlin Conference, 90

Boma (Belgian Congo), Stanley at, 18; departs from, 20; 96; kingdom of, 105

Brand, Jan Henrik, asks diamondfield arbitration, 43

Brazil, loss of, by Portugal, 22

Brazza, Countess de, appeals to French public, 263

Brazza, Pierre de, idolized by French, 60; ascends Ogowé river, 61; return to Paris, interview with Leopold II, rebuffs Belgian monarch, 62; claims in Congo Basin, 63; leaves for Lisbon, 64; diverted to Middle Congo, reaches Gabun, establishes Franceville, 65; meets Makoko, establishes French Congo protectorate, 66; relations with Stanley, 67-69; report to Delcassé (1894), 207; urges haste, 208; quoted on French Congo abuses, 274; dismissed from post, death of, 275

Brazzaville, French concession south of, 95

Britain, *see* Great Britain

British African Exploration Committee, 17

British East Africa Company, asks Stanley to negotiate treaties in lake regions, 126; lobby of, 163

British East India Company, activities in Somaliland, 124-125

British India Steam Navigation Company, *see* British East Africa Company

British South Africa Company, concessions from Lobengula, 142; invades Matabeleland, 167; obtains military reinforcements, 168; "unofficial war" of, 172; interest in gold-fields, 225

British United African Company, territory wrested from France by, 46; interests in Niger Basin, 64; buys French interests, 65; receives charter (1890), 138

Brockdorff-Rantzau, Count, refuses to sign Versailles Treaty, 292

Broglie, Duc de, Bonapartist premier, 13

Brussels Conference (1890) liquor traffic recognized at, 101; background of, 142-143; proceedings, 144-159; nations invited to, 146-

314　INDEX

147; tariff discussions at, 153, 155, 159; "General Act" of, 153-154
Bülow, Prince Bernhard von, adviser to Wilhelm II, 243; telegram to Wilhelm II, 246; gives Kaiser *carte-blanche*, 247; address before Reichstag, 255; orders repeal of Herero proclamation, 276
Bülow, Princess von, quoted on Delcassé's dismissal, 251
Burgers, M. (Transvaal President), protests British annexation, 44
Busch, Dr. Moritz, at Berlin Conference, 92-93
Butler, Sir William, discourages *uitlander* petition, 236

Caillaux, Joseph, forms ministry, 260; secret transactions with Germany charged, resigns, 264
Cairo, weary of international interference, 50; anti-foreign agitation in, 54; British financial hegemony at, 115; 123; foreign investments at, 210
Caisse de la Dette (Egyptian), 117; French and Russian obtain injunction restraining, 210
Cam, Diogo, Portuguese explorer, 95
Cambon, Jules, ambassador, 262
Cameron, Verney, at Brussels, 36
Cameroons, acquired by Germany, British missionaries in, 77; warship *Möwe* arrives at, Dr. Nachtigal active in, native chiefs paid in rum, 78; Meade quoted on, 93; British concessions in, 137
Cape Colony (South Africa), population of, emigration to, 41; abuses of British in, 41; officials of, distrust British governor, 45; informs London will seize Angra Pequena, 76; seeks Bechuanaland compromise, 123; 241
Cape-to-Cairo railroad, 203
Capetown (South Africa), seized by British (1795), returned to Holland, 40; diamond-prospectors sail for, 42; 123, slave-mart at, 124

Caprivi, General von, demands Helgoland of Britain, 137
"Caprivi Strip," 137
Carnavon, Earl of, Colonial Secretary, 15; as apologist, 40; approves Boer diamond compensation, 43; authorizes Transvaal annexation, 43
Carnot, François, President, 203, 204
Carola, German warship, sent to Angra Pequena, 76
Carrière Fils et Cie, 199
Casablanca, massacres at, 256; German deserters from Foreign Legion, 258
Casement, Roger, report on Congo atrocities, 271
Cecil, Lord Robert, Kitchener's aide-de-camp, 217
Ceechi, Captain Antonio, sent to Zanzibar, 129; seeks concessions, 130
Chamberlain, Joseph, Cape-to-Cairo plans, 203; imperialism of, 227; *uitlander* petition welcomed, 236; dispatch of, 237; victory of, in South African War, 241
Chambrun, General de, quoted on de Brazza, 62, 68
Chefneux, M., Italian protests over entry of, 185
Chimay, Prince de, quoted on Brussels Conference, 150
Christoforis, Colonel de, commands Saati expedition, 131
Churchill, Winston, quoted on Battle of Omdurman, 211; quoted on Fashoda, 220
Churchill, Lord Randolf, overtures to Sultan of Turkey, 109
Clare-Ford, Sir Francis, 190
Chérisey, Count René de, 247
Clemenceau, Georges, finance minister, 187; readiness of, to fight Germany, 253; urges intervention in Morocco (1907); orders restoration of Abdul Aziz, 257; leads fight against Caillaux, 264

INDEX 315

Cleveland (Grover) Administration, attitude to Berlin Act, 102

Clochette, Captain, Nile mission of, 208

Colby, Sir George, death of, 45

Colville, Sir Edwin Henry, leads expedition from Uganda, 207

Comité d'Études du Haut Congo, organization of, 34; object of, 34; underlying purpose of, 36; predecessor of, 37; Hollanders withdraw from, liquidation of, 38, 39; scrapped, 105

Commons, House of, Gladstone address to (1882), 51

Comoro Islands, Peters proposes seizing, 135

Compèigne, Marquis Louis de, 36

Congo "reform associations," 269, 271-272

Congo (river), Stanley's description of, 16, 18, 20, 23; compared to Mississippi, 29; Stanley's dispatch on, 31; future trade of, 33; discovery by Diogo Cam, cited, 95; navigation treaty of, 98

Congo Free State, birth of, 105; income of (1887), 139; conscript labor in, 145; native abuses in, 268 et seq.

Congo (French), one-half ceded to Germany, 263

Conrad, Admiral Charles, commands French fleet at Alexandria, 56; abandons British, steams to Port Saïd, 57

Consolidated Gold Mines of South Africa, shares in, held by Rhodes, 225

Constantinople, Powers invited to conference at, 54; failure of conference, 56; French intervention at (1884), 109

Corti, Count Luigi, 129

Courcel, Baron Alphonse de, to Berlin Conference, 91; Stanley quoted on, 97; views on Berlin Conference, 104; protests speech by Sir Edward Grey, 206; pronounces

French neutrality in Anglo-German Boer dispute, 233; opinion of Wilhelm II, 248; advised by King Edward, 251

Crabitès, Pierre, 48

Crampel, Paul, murder of, 175

Crispi, Francesco, ministry of, 128; notifies Powers of Uccialli Treaty (1896), 179; political future imperiled, 182; seeks aid in east Africa, 188; turns to allies, 189; in political retreat, 194; telegram to General Baratieri, 195; attacks on, 199

Cromer (Sir Evelyn Baring), Lord, represents Britain in Egypt, 49; unpopularity of, 50; nervous over Arab demonstrations, 55; confers with Northbrook, 115; view on Egyptian finances, 117; quoted on London Convention, 118; "Modern Egypt" quoted, 209; appeals Caisse de la Dette injunction, 210; quoted on British loan, 211; quoted on cost of Sudan campaign, 213; address at Omdurman, 215

Crowe, Sir Eyre Evans, to Berlin Conference, 90

Dahomey, French annexation of, 176

Daily Chronicle (London), 212

Daily Telegraph (London), Stanley's dispatches in, 29; first dispatch of Stanley to, 31; quotes Stanley on Congo trade, 33; interview with Wilhelm II, 258

Daily News (London), retains Stanley, 126

Dal, gunboat at Fashoda, 219

Dartnell, Colonel J. G., report on crime in Natal, 165; report on liquor-traffic, 166

Decken, Baron von der, explorations of, 132

De Kaap Valley (Transvaal), gold discovered in, 225

Delagoa Bay (Mozambique), 233, 239

Delcassé, Théophile, receives report from de Brazza, 207; Fashoda con-

316 INDEX

troversy with Salisbury, 221-222; concedes Sudan, 222; obtains ratification of Anglo-French Agreement, 245; back stiffened by Kaiser's address, 248; attacks on, 250; adamant against conference with Germany, ousted, 251

Deloncle, Jean-Louis, 185

Denis, Gabriel, L., quoted on Firestone interests in Liberia, 280

Depretis, S., Premier (of Italy), fears French ambitions in Tunisia, 24; suspects French support of Menelik, 129; defeat of, 130

Derby, Lord, reminder to Granville, 115

Dessye (Ethiopia), 303

Deutsche Lüdwestafrikanische Zeitung (Lüderitz), quoted on natives in German South-West Africa, 276

Devonshire, Duke of, quoted on Transvaal Boers, 241-242

Dey-Hussein (of Turkish Directory), 70

Djibouti (Somaliland), British concede to France, 73, 125

Diamonds, in Africa, first discovered, shown at Paris Exhibition (1867), 42; Transvaal, Orange claims to, rejected, 43

Disraeli, Benjamin, buys Suez-Canal shares for Britain, 15; preoccupied with Russo-Turkish War, 30

Djibouti (French Somaliland), guns shipped to Menelik II from, 194; rifles consigned to, 199; Marchand's retreat to, 222

Doelwyk, Dutch freighter, seized, 199

Dogali, battle of, 130-131

Dongola (Sudan province), conquest of, 209

Donnersmarck, Prince Henckel von, sent to Paris, 250

Doumer, Paul, quoted on Egypt, 244

Downing Street, (*see* also Great Britain) attitude toward Powers (1877), 30; attitude on Congo discovery, 33; seeks depose Ismail Pasha, 39; rejects Orange appeal in diamond controversy, 43; attitude toward Berlin Conference, 86; appoints delegation to Berlin Conference, 90; denounces Anglo-Portuguese treaty, 94; recognizes wealth of Egypt, 119; Cape-to-Cairo view, 123; value of Somaliland to, 125; pressure of at Brussels Conference, 152; acts in Uganda missionary dispute, 163; considers Sudan reconquest, 187; realizes diplomatic blunder, 190; Cape-to-Cairo project, 203; frandulent Cairo dispatch, 209; ignores Continental bankers, 210

Dreyfus Case, charge of British implication in, 202; effect on French public, 250

Dudley, Earl of, 42

Dufferin, Lord, mission to Cairo, 58; visit to Hanotaux, 204

Duveyrier, Henri, at Brussels, 36

Eckstein & Company, interest in gold-fields, 225

Edward VII, King, on Kaiser's telegram to Kruger, 231; 241; goes to Paris (1905), advises French government, 251

Egypt, British invasion of compared South Africa, 47; interest of bankers in, Bank of, owned by British, 48; debt of (1880), Dual Control of, bondholders of, 49; nationalist movement begins in, 50; British occupation of completed (1882), 58; ordered to abandon Sudan, 113; British efforts to stabilize government of, indebtedness mounts, 115; Caisse de la Dette of, 117; Mixed Tribunals of, 118; London Convention relating to, 118-119; British avert Powers' intervention in, 119; officials of warned by Granville, economic reforms in, forced labor reduced, 120; improved conditions in (1890), 121; conscript labor in, 145; question of British legality in, 206; loan to

INDEX 317

from Britain, 210-211; lost Sudan territory recovered, 213; corvée in, 267

El Obeid (Sudan), Mahdist army at (1883), Hicks' army destroyed near, 111; reports of massacre at, 112

El Teb, General Baker ambushed at, 113

Emin Pasha (Eduard Schnitzer), plight arouses British, isolated by Mahdi's victories, 126; rescue by Stanley, 127; 162

Emmanuel, King (of Portugal), claims to Africa, in 1500, 20

England, see Great Britain

État Indépendant du Congo, see Congo Free State

Ethiopia (Abyssinia), 27; clamors for munitions, 28; Italian penetrations into, 109; treaty of with Italy (1889), 132; French agents active in, 184; Italo-British disposition of, by secret treaty (1894), 190; League of Nations' deliberations over, 300-306

Étienne, Eugéne, quoted, 203; spokesman for Hanotaux, 205

Etna, Italian gunboat, 199

Euan-Smith, Sir Charles, sent to Fez, 172; demands respect of British flag, 173; failure of mission, 174, 244

Eugènie, Empress, 148

Europe, war threatened in (1895), 204; danger of Fashoda incident to, 215; Anglo-German war-threat (1896), 233; fears of war in, over Moroccan dispute, 252 et seq., peace of threatened, over Africa, 307

Farman, Judge E. E., defends Ismail Pasha, 48

Fashoda, French reversal after, 207; "incident" minimized, 215; meeting of Kitchener and Marchand at, 219-220; German gunboats at Algiers, 221; snub to Kaiser of, 243; checkmate of French at, 244

Ferry, Jules, supports de Brazza, 63

Fez, Americans and British at, 173; French checkmate of British at, 244; enthusiasm over Kaiser's visit to Tangier, 246; French expedition to relieve Mouley Hafid, 260

Figaro, Le (Paris), 13

Firestone, Harvey S., 278, 282

Firestone Tire & Rubber Co., in Liberia, 27, 277

Fleet Street, disbelieves El Obeid reports, 112

Foureau-Lamy, M., 175

France, effect upon of Prussian War, 13; Senate dissolved (1877), 13; Egypt as vassal of, 47; control of Egypt, with Britain, 49; refuses Turkish intervention in Egypt, 53; sends fleet to Alexandria, 54; orders Admiral Conrad not to bombard Alexandria, 57; colonial empire of, 59; proposes exploration of Niger Basin, 64; sends gunboat to Cameroons, 79; signs preëmption treaty with Congo Association, 84; area obtained at Berlin, 96; oppose British over Egypt (1884), 115; attacks Northbrook's financial plan for Egypt, 118; demands concessions in Congo Free State, 139-140; objections to slave-traffic restrictions, 152; concessions to, at Brussels Conference, 153; ratification of Brussels Act delayed, 154; emblem of, 161; annexation of Madagascar (1896), 175; public indignation over Crampel death, 175; annexation of Dahomey, 176; intrigues against Italy in Ethiopia, 184; writers of, on Triple Alliance, 188; expects concessions from Ethiopia, 202; interest in Nile, 202; diplomatic campaign against Britain (1893), 202; desire for territory north of Lake Victoria, 203; reminds Leopold of preëmption rights in Congo, 203; "colonial technique" of, 204; Sir Edward Grey attacks, 204-205; position vis-à-vis Sudan, 207; prepares Nile expedition led by Marchand, 208; rivalry with Britain at Fashoda, 219; controversy with Britain, 221-222; fleet races through Gibraltar, 222; obtains unoccupied north Africa west of Nile, in deal with Britain, 222; given free hand in Morocco, 245; Kaiser's Tangier speech addressed to, 247; fears loss of prestige in Morocco, 248-249; reported ultimatum to Morocco, 249; public nervousness over false ultimatum reports, 250; frontier scouts watch for German mobilization, 253; agreement with Germany on Morocco, 253; 3,000 troops sent to Morocco, 257; arrests three German deserters from Foreign Legion, 258; troop movements on frontier, 258; Germany's position made known after Agadis incident, 262; open mobilization of, 263; conquest of Morocco, 283-290; announces Moroccan protectorate, 284

Franco-Belgium Agreement (1884), articles of, 84

Franco-British Convention (1888), 187

Franco-Italian Agreement (1904), Italian concessions in Tripoli, 244

Frankfurter Zeitung, criticizes German policy, 257

Frederic, John, treaty with Lüderitz, 75

Frelinghuysen, Frederick T., signs act recognizing Congo sovereignty, 82; nominates General Sanford to Berlin Conference, 87; attitude to Berlin Act, 102

French Equatorial Africa, origin of, 175

French West Africa, 176

Freycinet, Charles Louis de, Egyptian policy of, defeated in Chamber of Deputies, 53-54; fears complications with Belgium, 64

Gabun, 59-60
Gallaland, 187
Gambetta, Leon, negotiates with Lord Granville over Egyptian crisis, 52; supports de Brazza, 63
Gaulois Le (Paris), quoted on Donnersmarck-Rouvier Conference, 250
Gené, General Carlo, orders advance beyond Massawa, 131
"General Act of the Berlin Conference," articles of, 98-100
Gentil, Émile, 175
Geographical Congress (Brussels, 1876), opens, 36; Leopold II quoted on, 37; compared to Berlin Conference, 85; 105, 106
Gericke, Baron de Herwjnen, 150
Germain, Captain, at Fashoda, 219, 221
German African Society (of Berlin), 17
German-Congolese Treaty (1884), 205
German East Africa, 74; ruse in establishment of, 133-134; protectorate proclaimed, 135; insurrection in (1888), 136
German East Africa Company, 17; flag raised in, 134; area of, 134; receives concessions from Peters, 135; pays tribute to Zanzibar sultan, 136
German Society for Scientific Exploration of Equatorial Africa, 17
German Southwest Africa, 74; abuse of natives in, 275-277
Germany, birth of African policy of, 31; financial interest in Egypt, 47; growth of Pan-Germanic sentiment in, 73-74; export-trade in spirits, 74; chambers of commerce urge colonies, 74; trade war with Britain, 79; recognizes Congo sovereignty, 84; annexations in Pacific, 94; Versailles action on colonies

INDEX

of, 98; action in east central Africa, 109; trade of with east coast, 133; objections to liquor-traffic restrictions at Brussels Conference, 154, 157; slogans of, 161; British and French criticism of, 178; warns Italy in east African dispute, 189; fears encirclement of German East Africa, 202; joins France against Britain, 205; interest of in Anglo-Boer tension, 230; threat of war with Britain (1896), 233; plans of War Office to aid Boers, 233; announces Kaiser to visit Morocco, 243; newspapers discuss Morocco, 246; seeks dismissal of Delcassé, 249; reported prepared to invade France, 250; troop concentrations in Baden, 250; nears ultimatum to France, 252; agreement with France on Morocco, 253; munitions' trade with Morocco, 256; supports Mouley Hafid in Morocco, 257; troop movements reported on frontier, 258; sounded by France on attitude to Fez expedition, 260; decides force Moroccan issue with French, 260; wrests 144,000 sq. mi. from France after "Agadir Incident," 261; open mobilization of (1911), 263; activities in Morocco (1914-18), 286; Versailles Treaty clauses affecting colonies of, 291-296; African colonies of, 292

Gibraltar, Britain closes approach to (1935), 29; cited by Lord Rosebery, 245; 287

Gladstone, W. E., 15; address to House of Commons on Egypt, 51; prophecy of (1877), 84; criticism of Northbrook, 118; foresees native revolt, 164; critical of Rhodes and Jameson, 168

Goebbels, Dr. Joseph Paul, quoted on German need of colonies, 299

Gold, discovered in Transvaal, 225

Gold Coast (British), becomes Crown Colony, area of, 46; 204

Goldie, Sir George, 64

Gordon, General Charles George, sent to Sudan, 113; death of, 114; compared to Northbrook, 118; avenge of, 213

Goshen, Boer protectorate over, 122

Grant, James A., at Brussels, 36

Granville, Lord (Foreign Secretary), negotiations of, with Gambetta, 52; quoted on dislike of French in Egypt, 56; explains Alexandria bombardment to French, 58; warns Bismarck not to violate British zone, 75-76; protests Nachtigal's activities in Cameroons, 78; disclaims responsibility for Sudan massacre, 112-113; warns Egyptian officials, 120

Graziani, General Rodolfo, 128

Great Britain (see also Downing Street) 1877, a breathing-spell, 15; masses warships in Mediterranean (1935), 29; cotton spinners of, 33; seeks depose Ismail Pasha, 39; foresees intervention in Egypt, Sudan and Transvaal, 40; encourages Cape Colony immigration, annexes Natal, 41; grants autonomy to Boer republics, 42; rejects Orange diamond appeal, 43; public aroused over death of Sir George Colby, Government dispatches troops to Capetown, 45; regrants Transvaal autonomy, 46; slave-trade of, 46; goods traded for Sierra Leone, 47; controls Egypt with France, 49; sends fleet to Alexandria, 54; increases fleet, 56; fears complications over Alexandria bombardment, 58; ultimatum to Portugal (1890), 71-72; outmaneuvered by Germany, 75; recognizes German sovereignty over Angra Pequena, 76; trade war with Germany, 79; appoints delegates to Berlin Conference, 90; expulsion from Sudan, seizure of Bechuanaland, 109; precarious situation of, in Egypt, 110; fear expressed for Sudan garrisons, 112;

320 INDEX

inability to withdraw from Sudan, orders Egypt to abandon, 113; maintains army in Egypt, 115; reacts to French hostility over Egypt, 119; sees violation of Transvaal Convention in Goshen and Stellaland, 122; Cape-to-Cairo ambitions, 123; blocks Italy in Somaliland, 128; agrees to French freedom in Madagascar, 137; concessions demanded of French (1890), 138; checks Portugal in South Africa (1891), proclaims Nyasaland protectorate, 142; measures against slave-traffic, 144; House of Commons resolution on slave-trade, 146; draft proposal at Brussels Conference (1890), 156; sends Captain Lugard to Uganda, 162; declares Uganda protectorate, 163-164; sends troops to Mashonaland, 168; competes with France in Morocco (1892), 174; explanation to Germany on Adowa, 200; backs down on Anglo-Congolese Treaty, 206; Sudan reconquest decided, 209; maintains Egypt must defray Sudan campaign costs, extends loan to Cairo government, 210-211; demands reward for Sudan reconquest, 213; rivalry with French at Fashoda, 219; controversy with French, 221-222; agitation over German emperor's telegram to Kruger, text of, 230; blocks German plan to aid Boers, 233; sends flying-column to Transvaal, 234; expeditionary force to South Africa discussed, 238-239; reply of, to Transvaal ultimatum, 239; cost of South African War, 240-241

Great Trek (Boer), 41
Greene, Conyngham, receives Boer ultimatum, 225, 239
Greindl, Baron, 32
Grey, Sir Edward, speech in House of Commons (1895), 204; apology for speech, 206-207; quoted on South African War, 242; seeks to check Leopold II, 269, 270

Hague, The (Permanent Court of Arbitration), upholds France in Foreign Legion controversy, 259
Haile Selassie, 181, 300, 305
Hamburg, Kaiser's yacht, 245
Hamburger Nachrichten, quoted on German policy, 251-252
Hamitics, 161
Harar (Ethiopia), customs-house at, 181; Franco-British Convention affecting Harar, 187
Harrington, Bishop of, murder of, 162
Hanotaux, Gabriel, reminder to Britain, 187; distrust of England, 200; urges colonial expansion, 202; favors Nile expedition, obtains credits, 204
Helgoland, 137, 162
Herero (tribes), expulsion of, 276
Hertslet, Sir Edward, to Berlin Conference, 90
Hewett, E. H., loser in race with Nachtigal, 79
Hicks, Colonel William, at Cairo, 110; destruction of army, death of, 111
Hicks-Beach, Sir Michael, threat against France, 222; quoted on South African War, 242
Hitler, Adolf, 92
Hoare, Sir Samuel, 305; resignation of, 307
Hohenlohe, Chancellor, 189
Holland, *see* Netherlands
Hottentot (tribes), murders of German colonists, 177
Humboldt, Alexander von, 16

Ifni (Spanish), 23
India, 40
International African Conference (Brussels, 1876) 19, 36; establishment of, 37; Britain withdraws from, 40
Ismail Pasha, Khedive of Egypt, sells

INDEX

Suez Canal shares to Britain, 15; apologizes to Italians, 24; idiosyncracies of, deposed, 47; charges against, defense of, 48; successor to, 49; 110
Italian Geographical Society, Somali expedition of, 24
Italo-Ethiopian Treaty (1896), terms of, 200
Italo-Ethiopian War, diplomatic background of, 302-307
Italy, colonial situation of (1877), 23; action of, in Libya, 28; masses warships in Mediterranean (1935), 29; political concern in Egypt, 47; joins Triple Alliance, 72; seizes Assab (Eritrea), Massawa, 73; ambitions of, at Berlin Conference, 86; Somaliland and Ethopian penetrations of, 109; desire of to connect Eritrea and Somaliland (1885), 129; notifies Powers of Somaliland protectorate, 130; parliamentary action after Dogali massacre, 132; signs treaty with Menelik II (1889), 132; slogans of, 161; controversy with Menelik II, 179-186; loan to Menelik II, 181; sends Count Antonelli to Addis Ababa, 182; charges French conspiracies in Ethiopia, 183; declares protectorate over Ethiopia, 186; expels Mahdists from Kassala, 186; absence of enthusiasm over Triple Alliance, 188; certain of war, 190; disorders in, over Adowa, 199; agreement (1904) with France over Tripoli, 244; reports French ultimatum to Morocco, 249; protests Versailles distribution of German colonies, 294-295

Jackson, Colonel H. W., at Fashoda, 219; admiration of Marchand, 220; gives Marchand ammunition, 222
Jameson, Dr. Leander Starr, Mashonaland administrator, 168; quoted on Lubengula, 169; Transvaal raid of, 169, 229; *Manchester Guardian* quoted on, 229; ends Anglo-Boer reconciliation hopes, 234
Joalland-Meynier, M., 175
Johannesburg (Transvaal), prospectors descent on, 225; Transvaal flag tore at, 229
John (Negus Johannes), 131; death of, 179
Johnston, Sir Henry H., quoted in diamond controversy, 43; quoted on German arrival at Zanzibar, 133; quoted on Congo Free State, 270
Journal des Débats, quoted on Caillaux, 264
Jub (river), 178
Jusserand, Jules, confers with President Roosevelt over Franco-German dispute, 252: reports to Quai-d'Orsay, 252

Kabinda, West Africa, Stanley's dispatch from, 31; Portuguese enclave at, 95
Kaffraria, annexation of, by British, 42
Kalabu Falls, loss of Stanley's men at, 16
Karolyi, Count, 51
Kassala, Mahdists expelled from, 186; British gratitude for capture of, 188; 190
Kasson, Ambassador John A., at Berlin Conference, 87; signs Berlin Act, 102
Katonda (tribal god), 162
Keate, R. W., rejects Transvaal diamond claims, 42
Keith, A. B., quoted on Leopold II, 105-106
Kenya Colony (and Protectorate), origin of, 126
Khalifa, The ("True Prophet"), British determination to destroy authority of, 209; army of, massacred, 212; death of, 213; Kitchener letter on, 217
Khartum, garrison of, attempts to re-

322 INDEX

lieve Gordon, 113; seige of, death of Gordon at, 114; capitulation of, 187; recaptured by Kitchener, 213

Kimberley, Lord, Colonial Secretary, annexes diamond fields, 43; French protest to, 206; apology of, 207

Kirk, Sir John, suspects German arrivals at Zanzibar, 133; pressure on sultan of Zanzibar, 147

Kipling, Rudyard, imperialist songs, 15; "pore benighted heathen" of, 160

Kitchener, General Herbert, considered for Sudan reconquest, 187; confers with Major San Miniatelli, 188; Sudan expeditionary force of, 211; attacked for cruelty, 212-213; hears of Marchand party, 216; note to French leader, 217; protests French flag at Fashoda, 219; raises Egyptian flag outside Fashoda, 219-220

Kotze, Sir John, removal from office of, 235

Kraaipan (Transvaal), South African War begins at, 240

Kruger, Paul (Transvaal), quoted on Goshen and Stellaland, 122; South African Republic of, 225; franchise restrictions of, 226; appeal of Transvaal National Union to, reply, 229; sends emissary to Berlin, 230; response of to Wilhelm II, 231; restrictions against foreigners, 234-235

Krupp Works, 250

Kuhlmann, Herr von, advice to French consul, 246

Lagos (British), wrested from French, 46

Lambermont, Baron August, to Berlin Conference, 91, 96; elected President of Brussels Conference, 148

Lancaster, U. S. flagship, at Alexandria, 56; U. S. Cairo consul and staff board, 57

Landwehr, control ended, 266

Lansdowne, Lord, 269, 270

La Roncière, Baron de, at Brussels, 36

Launy, Count de, addresses Berlin Conference, 103; returns empty-handed, 129

Laval, Pierre, compared to de Freycinet, 54; proposal to League of Nations, 305

Lavigerie, Cardinal Charles, 146

League of Nations, investigates Liberia, 27; Assembly of, on African partition, 28; compromise recommended in Italo-Ethiopian controversy (1935), 52; investigation of forced labor in Liberia, 279-281; mandates of, 293-294; deliberations in Italo-Ethiopian dispute, 300-306; Covenant of, 304

Leo XIII (Pope), 146

Leonard, James, 229

Leopold II (of the Belgians), plans African Empire, 18, 19; visits Algeria, Tunisia and Egypt, 30; talk with Émile Banning, 30; sends envoys to Marseilles, 31; follows Stanley's movements, 33; invites Powers to Geographical Congress, elected President of, 36; bestows decorations, 37; obtains control of Congo Committee, 39; fears over Germany and Portugal, 81; policy at Berlin Conference, threatens sabotage of Congo project, 94; concession to Powers at Berlin Conference, 95; obtains good-will of France and Portugal, 96; letter to Lambermont, 97; asks sovereignty over Congo State, granted, 104; notifies Powers of Free State creation, 105; economies of, 106; exchequer exhausted, 138; authorized by Parliament to issue loan, 139; indicates willingness to make Belgium heir to Congo, 140; invites Powers to slave-traffic conference, 146; ignores claims of Schweinfurth on Welle river, 177;

INDEX 323

lease of Congo strip to Britain, 203; permits native abuses in Congo Free State, 270-273; limits forced labor, 272; sells Congo Free State to Belgium, death of, 273

Lesseps, Comte Ferdinand de, undertakes Suez Canal, 47; cited by Doumer, 244

Lewin, Evans, quoted on German East Africa, 134

Leyds, Dr., interviews Wilhelm II, 230

Liberia, population of, 27; H. L. Stimson quoted on, 27; activities of Firestone Tire and Rubber Co., 277-282

Lichtervelde, Count Louis de, quoted on Leopold II, 95, 96

Liotard, Victor, sent to Ubanghi, 208

Liquor Traffic, evaded at Berlin Conference, Stanley quoted on, 101; 108; Barolong chief protests liquor distribution (1886), 124; discussed at Brussels Conference, 149, 153-159; report of Colonel Dartnell on, 166; convention of St. Germain-en-Laye, 297

Lisbon, Wilhelm II at, 245

Livoñius, Vice-Admiral, quoted on Zanzibar annexation, 133

Lloyd George, David, attacks on Salisbury government, 242; supports France in Agadir dispute, 263; quoted on mandates, 293-294

Loango (French Congo), arrival of Marchand at, 215

Loch, Sir Henry, succeeds Rhodes, 168

Loma (Togoland), German flag raised at, 79

H.M.S. London, withdrawn from slave patrol, 144

London Convention, stipulations of, 118-119; 225, 227, 234, 235

Louis Napoleon, death of, 45

Lubengula, agreement with British South Africa Company, 142; denounces agreement, 167; correspondence with Victoria, 168-169; deposed, 169

Lüderitz, Franz, west coast settlement, 75, 77; supported by warship *Carola*, 76

Ludwig, Emil, quoted on Karl Peters, 135

Lugard, Captain F. D., sent to Uganda, 162

Lugh (Ethiopia), Italian station at, 178

Luiz (King), of Portugal, seeks revenue, 22; abolishes slavery in African colonies, 22; flees palace, 22

Lux, A. E., at Brussels, 36

Lyautey, General Louis Hubert, leads column to Fez, 259; orders withdrawal from Fez, 260; to Morocco as Resident-General, 284

Mackenzie, Dr. John, seeks Bechuanaland compromise, 123; quoted on Bechuanaland, 124

Mackinnon, Sir William, raises fund for Emin Pasha relief, 126

MacMahon, Marshal Maurice de, pleads to army, 13; service in Algeria, 29

Madagascar, Peters proposes seizing, 135; snubbed by Bismarck, 136; French annexation of, 175; cited in Anglo-French Agreement, 244

"Mad Mullah" (in British Somaliland), 125

Madrid, aversion to colonies (1877), 22

Mafeking, in Matabeleland War, 170

Magdeburger Zeitung, threatens invasion of France, 247

Mahdi (the), leadership of, 111; victories of (1883), 113

Makale (Ethiopia), Italian defeat at (1895), 193

Makoko, negotiations with de Brazza, 66; 68; cited at Berlin Conference, 95

Makonnen, Ras, Ethiopian envoy to Rome, 181

324 INDEX

Malet, Sir Edward, reports on Egypt, 51; returns to England, recommends provocation against foreign control in Egypt, 55; leads delegation to Berlin Conference, 90; policy at Berlin, 94; quoted on Congo State, 104

Manchester Guardian, quoted on Jameson Raid, 229-230

Mandates (League of Nations), E. M. House quoted on, 293; Lloyd George quoted, 293-294

Mangasha, Ras, 193

Mangin, General Charles, 284

Mangungo, German treaty with cited, 134

Marchand, Captain Jean, Nile mission, 208; departure from Marseilles, 215; privations of, 215-216; reply to Kitchener, 218; departs for Cairo, 220; retreats to Djibouti, 222; cited by Wilhelm II, 223

Marschall, Baron Adolf von, advises Crispi, 188; threatens Britain, 205-206

Mashonaland, mineral survey of, 142; seizure recalled, 164; becomes part of Rhodesia, 170

Mashonas, 167

Massawa (Eritrea), seized by Italy, 73; expedition to of Count Salimbeni, 131

Matabeleland, mineral survey of, 142; war of —, 167-170; Cambridge pamphlet on, 170

Meade, Robert, to Berlin Conference, 90; interview with Dr. Moritz Busch, 92; reports to Granville, 94

Menelik II (of Ethiopia), 128; attitude of Depretis toward, 129; treaty with Italy (1889), 132; denounces Uccialli Treaty, 179-182; Italy's gift of rifles to, 180; signs treaty with Italy (1891), terms of, 182-183; death reported, 190; estimations of, 192; politico-military strategy of, 193; cheered by Italian Socialists, 199

Milner, Sir Alfred, receives Chamberlain reply to petition of *Uitlanders*, 236; urges intervention in Transvaal, 238

Missionaries, in Africa,

— (British), 39, lobby of, 40; apprehensive over Boer Trek, 41; activities in Cameroons, 77; task of John Mackenzie in Bechuanaland, 123; in Somaliland, 124; Church Missionary Society, 161; dispute with Catholics, 163; activities in Natal, 166

— (French) quarrels with British Protestants in Uganda, 162; receive indemnity from Britain, 163

— (German) in Africa, 74; Versailles Treaty clauses dealing with, 298

Mizon, Louis, mission to Addis Ababa, 208

Mogadiscu (Italian Somaliland), 130

Mohamed Ahmed, *see* Mahdi

Monkswell, Lord, 269

Monroe Doctrine, Britain unwritten version, 76; cited by Hanotaux, 207

Monrovia (Liberia), 277, 278

Montiel, Colonel Louis, Nile expedition of, 204; diverted to Ivory Coast, 206-207

Montsion, Barolong chief, 124

Moors, *see* Morocco

Morgan, Senator John T., suspicions of General Sanford, 81; 103

Morning Post (London), quoted on Wilhelm's telegram to Kruger, 231

Morocco, Algerian chiefs flee to, 71; early British interest in, 172; sultan receptive to German influence, 249; German munitions trade with, 256; 3,000 French troops arrive at, 257; French and German nationals in conflict, 257; French conquest of, 283-290; German agents active in, 286, 288; cast of subjugation of, 290; Sidi Mohammed proclaimed sultan, 290

Morton, Levi Parson, presides at

INDEX 325

Stanley banquet, 68; thanks de Brazza, 69

Mouley Hafid, proclaims self sultan, 256-257; Powers recognize, 257; friendly to Germany, 258; asks French aid, 259; signs protectorate treaty with France, 284

Mouley Hassan, Sultan (of Morocco), government of, 172-174

Möwe, German warship, takes Dr. Nachtigal to Cameroons, 78

Mussolini, Benito, on surplus population, 16; urges immigration to Libya, 41; specious argument of (1935), 52; quoted, 145, 160, 189, 306

Nachtigal, Gustav, Sudan travels of, 31; at Brussels, 36; sent to west coast on "scientific" mission, 77; negotiates treaties, 78; beats E. H. Hewett, British consul, in Cameroons race, proceeds to Togoland, 79

Napoleon III, Algerian policy, 71; 148

Natal, Boer march toward, British annexation of, 41; extenuation of seizure of, 42; invaded by Transvaalers (1880), 45; seizure recalled, 164; autonomy proposed for, 165; native education in, autonomy granted (1893), 166; 241

National Bank of Italy, 181; Menelik II refuses payments from, 182; fraud charges made against, 186

National City Bank of New York, 277

Natives (African), abuse of by Europeans, 98; military conscription of, 100; "currency" used among, 102; cited at Berlin Conference, 104; — in Congo Free State estimated, 105; murders of by Italians, 132; German treatment of, 136; Leopold's disregard of, 140; dog-tax on, 165; education of (in Natal), 166; casualties among in Matabeleland war, 169; wages in Nyasaland, 172; execution of women —, 177; European exploitation of, 267-282

Negri, Christoforo, at Brussels, 36

Nembana (Naimbana), 47

Netherlands, The, subscription of, to Congo Committee, 34; 43; slave-trade of, 46; objections to liquor-traffic restrictions at Brussels Conference, export-trade of in gin, 154, 157

Newfoundland, provisions for in Anglo-French Agreement, 244

New Hebrides, provisions for in Anglo-French Agreement (1904), 244

New York Herald, Stanley's dispatches in, 29

Niari-Kuilu river, ceded to France, 95

Nicholas II (Czar), decoration of Menelik, 200; letter from Wilhelm II, 232; asked to support France, 253

Nicholson (U. S.), Admiral James W., commands warships at Alexandria (1882), 56; withdraws seaward, 57

Niger (river and basin), 64; navigation treaty of, 99; French raids on, 109; 177; French threat to, 205

Nigeria (British), size of, 46, 65

Nile, French interest in, 202; French expeditions to, 207; de Brazza quoted on, Liotard mission to, 208; headwaters of, 209; Britain obtains control of, 222

Northbrook, Lord, mission to Egypt, 115; quoted on mission, 116; authorizes revenue diversion, 117; financial proposals of, 118

Nova Scotia, British expulsion of French from, 41

Nyasaland, British protectorate over, 142; Portuguese claims to, 171

Ogowé river, French settlement on, 65

Omdurman (Sudan), chained army sent to, 110; Winston Churchill

326 INDEX

quoted on Battle of —, 211; casualties at, 212
Oppenheims (bankers), 48
Orange Free State (and territory), Boer march to, 41; autonomy granted, claims diamondiferous region, 42; compensation for diamond-field seizure, 43; seizure recalled, 164; Bloemfontein conference in, 238; joins Transvaal against Britain, 239; incorporation with Union of South Africa, 241
Orange River, Boers retreat north of, 42; diamonds found on banks of, 42
Orange River Colony, 241
Order of Leopold, 148
Order of the African Star, 148

Painlevé, Paul, flies to Morocco, 289
Paléologue, Maurice, quoted on visit of Wilhelm II to Tangier, 246-247; quoted on Kaiser, 248; quoted on Rouvier, 253
Pan-African Congress, 296-297
Panther, German gunboat, at Agadir, 261; leaves Agadir, 266; at Monrovia harbor, 278
Paris Exhibition (1867), Orange River diamond exhibited at, 42
Paschen, Commodore Karl, 136
Paul, Count Hatzfeldt, to Berlin Conference, 91
Pavia, 199
Persia, invited to Brussels Conference, 147
Pétain, Marshal Henri, commands Moroccan campaign, 289
Peters, Dr. Karl, heads German Zanzibar expedition, 133; negotiates in East Africa, 134; gives treaty concessions to German East Africa Company, 135; permits execution women, trial of, 177
Petit Journal, Le (Paris), on Dreyfus scandal, 202
Petti, Baron, 189
Pheil, Count Joachim, 133
Pinto, Major Serpa, expedition of, 71

Pirmez, Theodore, delegate to Berlin Conference, 90
Porto Seguro (Togoland), German flag raised at, 79
Portugal, African claims in 1877, 20; discovery of Sierra Leone by, 47; expedition of, to central Africa, 71; proposes Berlin Conference, 86; British sympathy for, at Berlin, 94; area obtained at Berlin, 95; in east central Africa, 109; treaties with Britain, 1885-91, 141; claims area between Angola and Mozambique, 142; grants Zambezi region to Britain, 142; passive to slave-traffic, 146; seeks redress at Brussels Conference, 149-150; deposes Zulu chiefs, 178; refuses Germany troop transit in Mozambique, 233
Potter, P. B., 304
Powers (European), *see* under individual nations
Pradelle, A. de la, 304
Pretoria (Transvaal), Sir Garnet Wolseley at, 45; Convention of, 46; Volksraad at, 227; government of, 228

Quai d'Orsay (*see also* France), learns of Bismarck's criticism of Britain, 53; secret funds of, 59; interests in Ethiopia, 184

Rabat (Morocco), 289
Radolin, Prince von, at Paris reception, 253; informs Quai-d'Orsay German position over Agadir, 261-262
Raisuli, leads revolt against Sultan in Morocco, and Europeans, 256
Rawlinson, Sir Henry, at Brussels, 36
Red Sea, 124, 128, 181, 199
Regnault, Éugéne, represents French investors in Morocco, 256
Retief, Pieter, quoted on Great Trek, establishes Boer republic, 41
Reuters (news agency), 209
Rhodes, Cecil, in Cape Colony oppositions, 123; deputy commissioner of Bechuanaland, 142; activity in

INDEX 327

Matabeleland, removed by Gladstone, 168; plans Cape-to-Cairo railroad, 202; shares in gold-fields, 225

Rhodes (island), 161

Rhodesia (north and south), named after Matabeleland war, 169; claims of British South Africa Company, 171; British troops recruited in, 238

Rif, *see* Morocco

Rio de Oro, Spain sends warships to, protectorate proclaimed, 109

Rimski-Korsakov, Petrovich, to Brussels Conference, 148

Ripon, Lord, 164; Sir Henry Loch reports to, 169; appoints Nyasaland high commissioner, 171

Robinson, Sir Hercules, supports Rhodes on Bechuanaland, 123; warns Jameson's supporters, 234

Rohlfs, Dr. Gerhard, 133

Rohlfs, Frederick, at Brussels, 36

Roosevelt, President Theodore, intervenes in Franco-German dispute, summons Jusserand, 252

Roscher, Wilhelm, quoted on German colonial doctrine, 17

Root, Elihu, 270

Rosebery, Lord, 164; proposes Natal autonomy, 165; address to Liberal League, 245

Rothschilds (bankers), 48

Rouvier, Maurice, ministry of, 250; votes against Delcassé, 251; agrees to conference with Germany, 254

Rubattino Steamship Co., 73

Rubber (*see also* Fisk Tire & Rubber Co.), 106

Rudolf (Lake), 162

Russia, support of French at Constantinople, 109; invited to Brussels Conference, 147; **perversity** of, 188

Russo-Turkish War, 30, 72

Saar, The, 228

St. Germain-en-Laye, convention of, 297

Salimbeni, Count, expedition of, 131

Salisbury, Lord, Foreign Secretary, 14; quoted on Egypt, 51, 52; rejoices over French timidity in Egypt, 54; deals with French over Tunisia, 72; instructions to Moroccan envoy, 172; charges French bribed sultan of Morocco, 173; cables order of Sudan invasion to Lord Cromer, 208; controversy with Delcassé over Fashoda; quoted on Boer War, 227; quoted on war against Germany, 233; reply to Transvaal ultimatum, 239; victory of, in South African War, 241

Sanford Exploring Expedition for Trade, 147

San Miniatelli, Major, 188

Sanford, Gen. H. S., meets Stanley, 32; comment on, by Ludwig Bauer, 32; encounters Stanley at Paris, 34; pursues de Brazza for Leopold II, 62; engaged to win U. S. recognition of Congo sovereignty, 81; represents U. S. at Berlin Conference, 87; attitude toward Stanley, 89; — and Frelinghuysen, 102; attends Brussels Conference, 147; joins bloc at Brussels Conference, 157; proposal at Brussels, 158; death of, 272.

Saturday Review (London), quoted on Wilhelm's telegram to Kruger, 231

Savoy, House of, 181

Schweinfurth, Georg, at Brussels, 36; claims along Welle river, 177

Schnitzer, Eduard, *see* Emin Pasha

Scott-Moncrieff, Sir Colin, reduces forced labor in Egypt, 120

Selassie, *see* Haile Selassie

Selborne, Earl of, quoted on Transvaal Boers, 242

Selves, M. de, receives German ambassador, 261; testifies before Senate, 264

Senegambia, 59

INDEX

Senoussi, orders execution of Crampel, 175
Seymour, Vice Admiral Sir Beauchamp, commands Alexandria fleet, delivers ultimatum to Arabi Pasha, 56; bombards Alexandria, 57
Shepstone, Sir Theophilus, annexes Transvaal, 43; favors Natal self-government, 165
Shiré (river), French agents dominate region, 175
Siam, provisions for in Anglo-French Agreement, 244
Sidi Mohammed, proclaimed sultan of Morocco, 290
Sierra Leone (British), discovery of by Portuguese, British purchase price of, 47; 277
Slave-traffic (Africa), in 17th, 18th centuries, 46; agitation by General Sanford over, 81; effect of Berlin Conference on, 99; — in Bechuanaland, 124; charge headquarters at Quilimane, 143; sentiment against in U. S., 144; Brussels Conference on, 144-159; House of Commons resolution on, 146; restrictions adopted at Brussels Conference, 153; supervisory-office established at Zanzibar, 159; Arabs and Mohammedan Yaos active in, 171-172; — as pretext for colonial expansion, 178
Society for Prevention of Sale of Alcohol to the Native Races, representatives at Brussels Conference, 149
Somaliland (British), British encroachment in north, 109; missionaries in, 124; protectorate declared, 125
Somaliland (French), concessions from British, 125
Somaliland (Italian), protectorate over, 109; area of, 128; expansion of blocked by Britain, 128; Italian protectorate over, murder of Italians in, 130; Italian massacre at Dogali, 131

South Africa, British record in, 40; invasion of compared to Egypt, 47
South African War (1899-1902), 46; "altruistic necessity" cited in, 224; genesis of, 224-240; hostilities open, duration of, casualties of, 240; peace treaty of, 241
Spain, zone of influence of (1877), 22; African territories (1877), 23; holdings of (1900), 23; hopes of, at Berlin Conference, 86; sends warships to Rio de Oro, 109; conquest of Morocco, 287-290
Stanley, Henry Morton, enroute down Congo (1877), 14-25; speculation in England over, 15; disappears from Zanzibar, 20; newspaper dispatches of, 29; rebuffs Leopold's envoys, 32; feted at London, 33; at Brussels, 34; quoted on Congo Committee, 34; contract with Leopold, 35; meets de Brazza at Isangila, 66; quarrels with French explorer, 67-69; speech on de Brazza, 69; represents U. S. at Berlin Conference, 87; recalled by Leopold II, 89; attitude at Berlin Conference, 95-96; opinion of Bismarck, 96; asked to rescue Emin Pasha, 126; meeting with Emin Pasha, return to Zanzibar, 127; decorated by Leopold II, 141; cited at Brussels Conference, 152; declines act in Uganda, 162
Stanley Pool, de Brazza and Stanley race to, 64
"Star of Africa" (diamond), 42
State Bank of Morocco, 254
Stellaland, Boer protectorate over, 122
Stewart, Sir Herbert, death of, 113
Steyn, M. T., seeks Anglo-Transvaal compromise, 238
Strauch, Col. M., directs Stanley, 35; orders seizure of Loango, 215; offers France Congo preëmption rights, 83-84; delegate to Berlin Conference, 90; 96, 105
Sudan (Anglo-Egyptian), British

INDEX 329

concern over, 39; Egyptian sovereignty over, 110; loss of British prestige in, 112; General Gordon sent to, 113; last to Egypt, 115; reconquest studied by Britain, 187; French threat to, 205; French legal attitude to, 207; nature of campaign, 210

Sudan Agreement (1899), text of, 214

Suez Canal, 44 percent. shares to Britain, 15; Italians pass, enroute to Somali coast, 24; Britain considers closing approach to (1935), 29; de Lesseps' construction of, 47; British and French stake in, harbor-works of, 48; French weigh investment in, 53; strategic value of, 119; British warships protect after Mahdist victories, 125

Suez, Isthmus of Panama, 54

Sweden, 1

Taillandier, Saint-René, interview with Sultan of Morocco, 249

Tanganyika (Lake), 203

Tanganyika Territory (*also see* German East Africa), 137

Tangier, British mission leaves, gunboats arrive at, 173; announcement of Kaiser's visit to, 243; German and French consuls at, 246; Wilhelm II welcomed, 247; massacres at, 256

Tattenbach, Count von, sent to interview sultan of Morocco, 249

Tchad (Lake), 175; region partitioned among Britain, France, Germany, 176

Temps, Le (Paris), quoted on Foreign Legion dispute, 259

Terrell, Edwin H., delegate to Brussels Conference, 147; address at Brussels Conference, 150

TeWater, Charles T., quoted on African partition, 28

Tewfik Pasha, succeeds father, character of, 49; dismisses Arabi Pasha, 54; flees Alexandria, 56; authority restored, 58; Hicks sent in support of, 110

Thomson, Joseph, expedition to Lake Tanganyika, 17

Tiedemann, Baron von, at Omdurman, 211

Tigre (province, Ethiopia), 193, 200

Timbuctoo, French occupation of, regional area, 177

Times, The (London), quoted on Gladstone, 15; on El Obeid massacre, 112; on Hicks, 113; quoted on Northbrook mission, 116; quoted on Brussels Conference, 148; criticizes Portugal, 149-150; publishes false Cairo dispatch, 209; death of correspondent of, 211

Tisdel, Thomas, quoted on Stanley, 68; sent to Congo, 103

Togoland, Nachtigal arrives in, 79; British Concessions in, 137

Transvaal, The, British threaten annexation of (1877), 15; Boer march toward, 41; autonomy granted, claims diamondiferous area, 42; finances of, annexation of, 44; reproclamation as republic (1880), invades Natal, 45; regranted autonomy, gold discovered in, 46; seizure recalled, 164; ultimatum in South African War, 225; discourages gold-prospecting, 226; Volksraad of, 227; language restrictions in, 228; National Union of, 229; Germans in, cited by Kaiser, 232; British flying-column sent to, 234; Aliens' Expulsion Act of, 234; ultimatum, conditions of, 239; 241

Triple Alliance, 72; Germany's colonial plans strengthened by, 80; French campaign against, 188; Baron Petti cites, 190

Triple Entente, ratifications of, 258

Tripoli, 188, 204

Trotha, General Lothar von, proclamation of, 276

Tsana (Lake), British interest in, 164; Italian threat to, 213
Tudhope, J., 229
Tunis, see Tunisia
Tunisia, Italy's fear of French in, 24; finances of, 24; Italian purchase of railroad in, French invasion of, 25-26; Italians in, 73; 86; Rome recalls French raid on, 129
Turkey, Egypt vassal of, 47; invited to Brussels Conference, 147; sovereignty over Sudan, 207
Twiss, Sir Travers, to Berlin Conference, 90

Uccialli Treaty, denounced by Menelik II, 179-182; Article XVII of, 179; Italian and Amharic texts of, 180; General Baratieri revives, 193
Uganda, tribal worship in, 162; Britain contemplates protectorate over, 162; protectorate proclaimed by Britain, 163-164; German threat to, 205; British expedition from, 207
Uitlanders (in South Africa), increase of in Transvaal, 225; activities, 226 *et seq.*
Umberto, King, letter to, from Menelik II, 180
Union of South Africa, proclaimed (1910), 241
United African Company, *see* British United African Company
United Kingdom, *see* Great Britain
United States, defense to State Department of Ismail Pasha, 48; Senate recognizes Congo sovereignty, text of resolution, 82; at Berlin Conference, 85; fails ratify Berlin Act, 102; sends Tisdel to Congo, 103; invited to Brussels Conference, sends delegates to, 147; Senate resolutions on Congo atrocities, 271; interest in Liberia, 277, 281, 282

Versailles Treaty, cited, 123, 137, 291; disposition of German colonies, 293
Victor Emmanuel II (of Italy), watches other Powers, 24
Victoria (Fort), Matabele attack on, 168
Victoria (Lake), 162, 203
Victoria Nile, 162
Victoria, Queen, 14; letter to from King Acqua, ignores Sudan chief's marriage offer, 79; upbraids Gladstone, 115; quoted on Egyptian finances, 116; Brussels Conference summoned in name of, 142; criticized by Lubengula, 167-168; correspondence with Lubengula, 168-169; reply to Menelik II, 179; subjects of, 227; quoted on Wilhelm II, 231; letter from Wilhelm II, 231-32; *Uitlanders* ask intervention of, 236; 243
Vincent, Sir Edgar, financial administration of (Egypt), 120
Vivian, Lord, efforts at Brussels Conference, 152

Waddington, W. H., 72
Walfisch Bay, British claims to, 76; 77
Warren, Sir Charles, ordered to annex Bechuanaland, 123
Welle (river), claims of George Schweinfurth, 177; Liotard at confluence of, 208
White, Henry, at Algeciras Conference, 254
Whitley, James A. N. T., in service of Leopold, 272
Whittaker, American filibuster in Matabeleland, 168
Wilhelm I, proclaims protectorate in east Africa, 135
Wilhelm II, of Germany, as Crown Prince, 17-18; early criticism of Bismarck, 31; drops Bismarck, 137; reply to Menelik, 179; dismay over Fashoda, 222-223; receives

INDEX 331

Transvaal state secretary, 230; telegram to Kruger after Jameson Raid, 230; letter to from Queen Victoria, 231; duplicity of, letter to Czar, 232; snubbed after Jameson Raid, 243; announcement of visit to Tangier, 245; misgivings over visit, 246; reception at Tangier, 247; speech to German Legation, 247; speaks on "free" Morocco, 248; jubilant over dismissal of Delcassé, makes von Bülow prince, 251; interview with London *Daily Telegraph,* 258

Wilhelm, Crown Prince, statement on Fez to French ambassador, 260; remark recalled, 262; derides Congo concession, 264

Wilhelmstrasse (*see also* Germany), out-maneuvers Britain, 75; complaint to Britain, 200; attitude toward Anglo-Congolese Treaty, 205; jubilant over position in Morocco, 249; sends Prince von Donnersmarck, 250; demands reparations of France, 257

Williams, Captain W. H., succeeds Captain Lugard, letter quoted, 163

Wingate, Sir Reginald, flying-column of, 213; at Fashoda, 219

Wissmann, Captain Hermann von, 133; obtains native troops from Britain, 136

Witwaters Rand (Transvaal), gold discovered in, 225

Woermann, Adolf, to Berlin Conference, 91

Woermann Steamship Line, liquor shipments, to Africa, 74-75; investments in Cameroons, 77; interests in Zanzibar, 133

Wolseley, General Sir Garnet, addresses Transvaalers, 45; heads Cairo expedition, defeats Arabi Pasha, 58; Dr. Moritz Busch, quoted on, 93

Wood, Sir Evelyn, appointed Sirdar, 120

Work, Ernest, quoted, 182

World War, 182, 193, 207, 243, 255, 287; 288

Wylde, Augustus B., quoted on Menelik II, 192

Zambezi (river), German access to, 137; tribal sentiment along, 165; British agents north of, 171

Zanzibar (island), Stanley disappears from, 20; return of Stanley to, 38; 127; Italian warship arrives at (1885), 129; British protectorate over, 129; mainland protectorate of, to Italy, 130; German consulate, 133; German gunboats arrive at, 136; sultan invited to Brussels Conference, 147; slave-traffic supervisory office at, 159

Zeila (Somaliland), Italian expedition to, 24; interest of British in, 125; offer of aid from, 200

Zululand, annexation of, to Natal, 167

Zulu War (1879), British casualties in, 45

Zulus, oppose Boer invasion, 41; Transvaalers refuse alignment with, 45; chiefs deposed by Portuguese, 178

WAYNESBURG COLLEGE LIBRARY
WAYNESBURG, PA.